T0366756

Key Issues

EMPIRE AND IMPERIALISM
The Debate of the 1870s

Key Issues

EMPIRE AND IMPERIALISM

The Debate of the 1870s

Edited and Introduced by
Peter Cain
Sheffield Hallam University

Series Editor
ANDREW PYLE
University of Bristol

ST. AUGUSTINE'S PRESS
SOUTH BEND, INDIANA

© Thoemmes Press 1999

Published by
St. Augustine's Press
South Bend, Indiana, USA

ISBN
Paper: 1 890318 24 8

Empire and Imperialism
Key Issues No. 20

Library of Congress Cataloging-in-Publication Data

Empire and imperialism : the debate of the 1870s / edited and
    introduced by Peter Cain.
        p.   cm — (Key Issues; no. 20)
    Includes bibliographical references.
    ISBN 1-890318-24-8
    1. Great Britain—Colonies—History—19th century
Sources. 2. Great Britain—Politics and government—
1837–1901 Sources.
    I. Cain, P. J., 1941–   . II. Series : Key Issues (Bristol,
England); no. 20.
    JV1017.E56   1999
    325'.32'094109034—dc21   99–38503
                                                          CIP

Printed in Great Britain by Antony Rowe Ltd, Chippenham.

CONTENTS

INTRODUCTION

The 1870s is in many ways a key decade in the evolution of British thinking about the nature, purpose and future of the overseas empire. It was in this decade that the rapidity of growth and the sheer size of Britain's major competitors began to impinge upon the consciousness of political and intellectual elites. The insecurity prompted by this was compounded by the prolonged and severe economic depression after 1873 which began to undermine confidence in free trade amongst agriculturalists and even manufacturers. Faith in Cobdenite nostrums about the inevitability of peaceful progress in an increasingly interdependent and harmonious world was severely dented. One reaction to the crisis was to reassert and reassess the importance of Britain's overseas empire. The idea of a union of Britain with its settler colonies captured the imagination of many and a renewed interest was taken in the fate of the dependent empire especially in India. Encouraged by Disraeli's flamboyant assertions of British power, empire enthusiasts engaged in a furious argument over the rights and wrongs of imperial policy and, in so doing, set a large part of the agenda for discussion of these issues for the next fifty or sixty years.[1]

When Gladstone's Liberal government came to power in 1868 it set in train a review of defence expenditure in the colonies of white settlement in North America, Australasia and South Africa. All expenditure deemed necessary to the protection of the empire as a whole was to remain the responsibility of the mother country but the colonies were expected to provide for their own internal defence. There was nothing

---

[1] The best introductions to the ideological debate remains R. Koebner and W. Schmidt, *Imperialism: the History of a Political Word* (Cambridge: Cambridge U. P., 1964), chap. V; and C. A. Bodelsen, *Studies in Mid-Victorian Imperialism* (London: Heinemann, 1960).

particularly novel about the policy; all administrations, whatever their political colour, had pursued a similar line on the
defence budget for twenty years, the leading argument being
that the colonies would never grow to maturity and justify the
award of 'responsible government', if they did not take charge
of their own internal expenditure. That Gladstone's handling of
the issue provoked an agonised debate was due partly to the
fact that he and his colleagues, the chief priests at the altar of
balanced budgets and financial rectitude, undoubtedly attacked
supposed colonial extravagance with unusual zeal: but it also
reflected changing perceptions about Britain's position in the
world and set off controversies which were features of British
political life for several generations.[2]

There is no doubt that the prevailing attitude to white colonial development at the beginning of the 1870s was deeply
influenced by the trauma of the American Revolution nearly a
century before. The secession of the thirteen colonies seemed
to provide convincing proof that colonial independence was
foreordained: the subsequent development of the newly-formed
United States of America as Britain's chief foreign market also
appeared to suggest that the consequences of separation in the
long run were economically benign. Some few radicals were
wholeheartedly separatist in sentiment, regarding colonies as
a costly burden whose defence might easily involve Britain in
war yet offering benefits only to those members of traditional
élites who enjoyed the jobs and patronage colonies generated.
The way in which Canada provided a point of tension with
the United States, threatening Britain with a war which would
have disastrous economic consequences, was proof enough for
radicals like Cobden that colonial possessions were a menace.[3]
Cobdenite radicals never dominated policy making and they
may even have been outnumbered by the true believers who
maintained a faith in the idea of a united white empire. Yet

[2] For an excellent introduction to this subject see C. C. Eldridge, *England's
Mission: the Imperial Idea in the Age of Gladstone and Disraeli 1868–1880*
(London: Macmillan, 1973), chaps. 1–5. For the broader context see P. J.
Cain and A. G. Hopkins, *British Imperialism: Innovation and Expansion,
1688–1914* (London: Longman, 1993), esp. chap. 8.

[3] See Cobden's letter to Colonel Cole, 20 March 1865, in J. Morley, *The Life
of Richard Cobden*, vol. II (London: Chapman and Hall, 1881), pp. 470–71.

most prominent statesmen and publicists, though not keen to force separation, felt that it must come eventually.[4] Offering the colonies political freedoms as soon as they proved stable enough to handle them was, paradoxically, thought to be a method of delaying the inevitable and of ensuring that, when separation came, it would be on as friendly terms as possible. Gladstone himself was of this opinion.[5] He believed that the physical separation of the colonies from the motherland and from each other made union impossible and that the relations between Britain and the white settlements should follow the model of ancient Greece whose émigrés had carried Greek culture far and wide and who were friendly towards, but politically distinct from, the parent. In that sense, as Gladstone recognised, the United States was Britain's greatest colony.

So, by 1870, 'responsible government' as it was known was far advanced in the most mature settlements in Canada, Australia and New Zealand. In his famous report of 1840 advocating responsible government, Lord Durham had argued that Britain should retain its hold over colonial tariff policy and assert its right to dispose of surplus lands: but, given the anxieties about the effects of keeping colonies in leading strings, these powers were soon abandoned and Britain found itself in the embarrassing position of being the world's leading advocate of free trade while giving to its colonies the power to tax the mother country's own trade. The more the colonies asserted their rights over their own destiny the greater grew the pressure in Britain to force them to accept the costs of internal policing.

The extract included here from Charles Dilke's *Greater Britain*[6] shows that the author, later a prominent Liberal statesman, veered towards the radical end of the spectrum of

[4] See the extended discussion in G. W. Martin, ' "Anti-Imperialism" in the mid-Nineteenth Century and the Nature of the British Empire' in R. Hyam and G. W. Martin (eds.), *Reappraisals in British Imperial History* (London: Macmillan, 1975), pp. 88–120.

[5] See extract from Gladstone's speech in the House of Commons, 26 April 1870, in G. Bennett, *The Concept of Empire: Burke to Attlee, 1774–1947* (London: A. & C. Black, 1962), pp. 252–5. The outstanding biography is H. C. G. Matthew, *Gladstone, 1809–74* (Oxford: Clarendon Press, 1986).

[6] The most useful biography of Dilke in this context remains S. Gwynn and G. M. Tuckwell, *Life of Sir Charles Dilke*, 2 vols. (London, 1917).

opinion on the future of colonies. Dilke's work is particularly noticeable for the fact that, like Gladstone, he thought of the United States as Britain's greatest colony because it was the most significant instance of the spread of British culture and free institutions. He expected the smaller white settlements to evolve in the same way, helping to create a great Anglo-Saxon federation with the United States as its economic epicentre which would dominate a free trade world in the twentieth century. By then, Britain would no longer be the world's chief centre of civilisation but it would be the venerable mother country of a global power – a true Greater Britain – and still responsible for the civilisation of large tracts of Africa and Asia. Dilke's panegyrics on pan-Saxonism suggest a Macaulay-like complacency about Britain's future development though it is clear that Dilke did not think that the island of Britain would retain the same eminence in the world in the twentieth century.

The reaction to Gladstone's policy between 1868–71 – led originally, as Eldridge has pointed out, mainly by groups in London who were often repudiated by the colonists they intended to serve[7] – is important because it reflected the beginnings of a sharp change of consciousness about Britain's future role in the world. It also provoked Disraeli into making his famous remarks, deploring the recent trend towards separatism, in his Crystal Palace speech of 1872. Disraeli was not simply playing politics: he had always been numbered amongst those who favoured some form of federation. Crystal Palace was, however, an indication that he now thought that the time had come to move the 'colonial question' up the political agenda.[8] But getting to the root of the disquiet felt towards Gladstone's supposed dismembering of the empire is not a simple matter as a close reading of the two articles from James Anthony Froude, the famous historian of the Reformation and

---

[7] Eldridge, *England's Mission*, pp. 98–101, 119.

[8] There is an extract from Disraeli's Crystal Palace speech in Bennett, *The Concept of Empire*, pp. 257–9. For Disraeli's earlier thinking on colonies, see S. R. Stembridge, 'Disraeli and the Millstones', *Journal of British Studies*, vol. 5 (1965), pp. 122–39. Although it is somewhat misleading on Disraeli's colonial views, by far the best biography remains that by R. Blake, *Disraeli* (London: Methuen, 1966).

of Elizabethan England, printed here indicate.[9] Some commentators on the rise of new imperial sentiment in the early 1870s point to the frightening military might exhibited by Prussia in its defeat of France and the rise of the new and threatening empire of Germany as the shock which spurred rethinking. This played its part in the wider debate no doubt: but Froude's first passionate attack on the arguments of Gladstone and Dilke was written before the Franco-Prussian war had broken out. Moreover, Froude was much more worried about the threat posed to Britain's future by the United States than he was about European military might; and his advocacy of union with the colonies also had deep domestic roots being founded on a profound dissatisfaction with the way British society was evolving. Froude's ideas on colonies and on imperial development are the most carefully thought out and best written of their time. Yet, unlike Dilke's work for example, they have rarely received close attention and their distinctive ideological basis has been ignored.

Underlying Dilke's Anglo-Saxonism was a deep respect for the liberal values of modernity and the market economy which underpinned them. And, since the United States was the country which most exemplified these values and where uninhibited capitalism had almost boundless prospects, it seemed natural to invest the Great Republic with his hopes for the future. Froude's vision could hardly have been more different. As a follower (later a biographer) of Carlyle and a friend of John Ruskin, he was dismayed by economic and political liberalism, the urban civilisation which it had spawned and the overthrow of traditional values based on land and aristocratic leadership.[10] Most of all, he was shocked by what he saw as a lack of communal purpose in modern Britain. In another essay written around the same time as those on the colonies reprinted here, Froude argued that the esteem in which Britain

[9] For background see W. H. Dunn, *James Antony Froude: a Biography*, 2 vols. (Oxford: Clarendon Press, 1961–3); J. P. Von Arx, *Progress and Pessimism: Religion, Politics and History in Late Nineteenth Century Britain* (Cambridge, Mass.: Harvard U. P., 1985), chap. 5; J. W. Burrow, *A Liberal Descent: Victorian Historians and the English Past* (Cambridge: Cambridge U.P., 1981), chaps. 9 & 10.

[10] When editor of *Fraser's Magazine* in the early 1860s, Froude had published, in the face of great public hostility, Ruskin's attacks on orthodox political economy later published as *Munera Pulveris*.

was held in the world was on the wane and he offered his own reasons why this was so.

> it is not our supposed unreadiness to fight which has lowered, and is still lowering, England's reputation. We have not allowed any occasion to pass by when our honour or our interest distinctly called us to arms – we are disesteemed because, as a nation, we no longer seem to live for any high or honourable purpose. Communities as well as private persons always set before themselves consciously or unconsciously some supreme aim towards which their energies are bent. Military power, extension of territory, political unity, dynastic aggrandizement, or the maintenance of some particular religious creed, have all been at various times the all-absorbing objects on which the minds of great nations have been bent; and as none of these has been entirely good, so none has been entirely discreditable. The noblest object, which all honour and few pursue, is the well-being of the people; the worst and meanest is that to which we in England are supposed to devote ourselves – the mere aggregation of enormous heaps of money, while we are careless what becomes of the 'hands', as we call them, by which all money is created.[11]

Like Carlyle and Ruskin, Froude's views could be broadly described as 'Tory paternalist': a rather despairing call to the traditional landed aristocracy to renew their strength and to reclaim the moral authority over the masses which, in their own scramble for wealth, they had ceded to urban capitalism. Indeed, like them, Froude thought of urban Britain as a hotbed of immorality, poverty and enervating luxury divorced from the true source of wealth and moral probity, the land. His views found a very faint echo in Disraeli's conceptions of modern Conservatism. In the Crystal Palace speech, Disraeli tried to rally the new working-class electorate created by the Reform Act of 1867 behind the defence of traditional institutions – Church, aristocracy and empire: as Prime Minister, he presided over a measure of social reform intended to mitigate the worst effects of unrestrained capitalism in urban areas. Yet Disraeli could hardly have implemented a Froudeian policy

[11] J. A. Froude, 'England's War', in *Short Studies on Great Subjects* (London: Longmans, Green, and Co., 1907), vol. III, pp. 285–6.

à l'outrance. His party's traditional rural constituency was in
decline: it now relied on urban voters to win elections and
Disraeli's call to paternalism could only be effective if it left
industrial capitalism essentially untrammelled. Indeed, Froude
himself believed that the landed classes of England were now
too effete to offer leadership and that England was condemned
to be, at best, an urban manufacturing country ruled by capitalist values; at worst, one in which tradition and the
constitution were overthrown by plebeian revolt.

Froude's essays also express, in a most vivid manner, the
conviction that the historic conditions under which Britain
could exercise world leadership were rapidly disappearing and
that it was only in conjunction with the British settlement
colonies that it could continue to exercise global mastery and
ensure global security. His position is summed up neatly in
'England's War' where he returned to the importance of the
'Colonial Question':

> which was infinitely more important to us than India...
> because the entire future of the English Empire depends upon
> us wisely availing ourselves of the opportunities which these
> dependencies offer to us. When we consider the increasing
> populousness of other nations, their imperial energy, and
> their vast political development: when we contrast the enor-
> mous area of territory which belongs to Russia, to the United
> States, or to Germany, with the puny dimensions of our own
> old island home, prejudice itself cannot hide from us that
> our place as a first-rate Power is gone amongst such rivals
> unless we can identify the Colonies with ourselves and mul-
> tiply the English soil by spreading the English race over
> them.[12]

This was a message which was to be endlessly repeated by
imperialists over the next seventy-five years.

It was the rise of the United States which worried Froude
most. Dilke saw America as an exemplar, Froude as the chief
carrier of a democratic civilisation he hated[13] and as a rival to
be feared. To become part of an Anglo-Saxon federation on

---

[12] *Ibid.,* pp. 276–7.

[13] Compare Ruskin's bitter diatribe against American democracy and capitalism in *Munera Pulveris* (London: Routledge/Thoemmes Press, 1994),
para. 124.

the lines advocated by Dilke would be a defeat for the ideal of Britain Froude cherished so strongly. Hence his bitter opposition to the prevailing *laissez-faire* conception that Britain could not, and should not, do anything to alter the fact that the chief destination of its emigrants was the United States. The upshot of this policy – which Froude thought typical of the lack of communal purpose in modern civilisation he so lamented – was that most emigrants were incorporated into a culture he despised and were thus helping to build up a civilisation which might one day destroy Britain's own. It is not surprising that his chief practical proposal was for a state-led policy which would give emigrants incentives to go to British lands. A larger British population would encourage British trade. Dilke pointed out how much greater was Britain's trade with the United States than with the colonies: Froude emphasised how much more trade per head was done with colonists than Americans and, therefore, how much more Britain would benefit from the growth of British territory.

Although he did not use the phrase, Froude anticipated J. R. Seeley's famous call in *The Expansion of England* (1883) for a Greater Britain founded on British political sovereignty rather than one headed by the United States as Dilke suggested. Indeed, Froude's aim was to give the British nation equality with the United States in the twentieth century: 'a second era of glory and power may be dawning upon us, to which our past history may be a faint and insignificant prelude'. But Froude's conception of Greater Britain was more backward-looking than Seeley's or Seeley's successors. Despairing of the dominance of land and of landed values in Britain itself, Froude hoped that a race of hardy British peasants would be created in the colonies who would 'reproduce the old English character and the old English strength over an area of a hundred Britains': the landed values which had made the island of Britain great in the past would be the foundation of greatness in Britain overseas. However, as Britain became more relentlessly urban in the late nineteenth and twentieth centuries and industry was challenged by foreign competition, the message of the supporters of imperial unity underwent transformation. Julius Vogel's contributions to the debate are interesting precisely because they show the direction in which that change was to occur.

Vogel, one-time Prime Minister of the fledgling colony of

New Zealand and later to be the colony's Agent-General in London,[14] had much in common with Froude. His conviction that unity with the colonies would prevent Britain from 'sinking into a small, money-loving state – a second Holland' is very Froudeian, as was his fear that an isolated Britain might suffer internal revolution. He also shared Froude's conviction that the same forces of steam and electricity which were making Russia and the United States possible were also giving Greater Britain a plausible future. But there are significant differences. Vogel, as a man of affairs, was much more inclined to offer concrete proposals for cementing imperial unity than were academics such as Froude or Seeley and his affinity here was with politicians like Forster and the founders of the Imperial Federation League in the 1880s.[15] More important, Vogel, writing when Britain was in the grip of deep depression and facing a new intensity of European competition and rising foreign tariffs, anticipated the future by emphasising the empire as a refuge from industrial competition. In doing so, he began to bridge the gap between Froude and groups such as the Fair Traders of the 1880s and the 'Constructive Imperialists' who formed the intellectual backbone of Joseph Chamberlain's Tariff Reform campaign after 1903.[16]

From Froude's perspective, industry was cosmopolitan and anti-colonial. But, during the 1870s, as competition increased, protected imperial markets began to appeal to vulnerable sectors of industry and Vogel's articles reflect this trend. He was also prescient in his alarm at foreign investment which, he argued, stimulated industrial exports initially but fostered manufacturing competition in the longer term: one reason he recommended firm measures of imperial unity was that they would stimulate investment in the colonies rather than in Europe or America. In taking this stance, Vogel was shifting

[14] For the life see R. Dalziel, *Julius Vogel* (Auckland: Oxford U. P., 1986) and the same author's article on Vogel in *The Dictionary of New Zealand Biography, 1769–1869* (Wellington: Allen and Unwin, 1990).

[15] W. E. Forster, *Our Colonial Empire: an Address* (Edinburgh, 1875). The best book on the movement for imperial federation is still J. E. Tyler, *The Struggle for Imperial Unity, 1868–95* (London: Longmans, Green, and Co., 1938).

[16] For Chamberlain see P. J. Cain, 'The Economic Philosophy of Constructive Imperialism', in C. Navari (ed.), *British Politics and the Spirit of the Age* (Keele: Keele U. P., 1996), pp. 41–65.

the focus of the argument about the economic value of colonies towards those later advocated by Joseph Chamberlain who, with another quarter of a century of relative industrial decline to ponder over, stressed the need for white colonial federation to ensure both industrial and agricultural strength in the face of the corrosive effects of free trade and foreign investment.

Vogel's articles also raised the delicate issue of colonial autonomy within a wider federal structure. He was frankly critical of the fact that Britain had allowed the colonies the freedom to impose tariffs and to dispose of their land without interference, as were a number of other distinguished advocates of federation.[17] Any agreement on unity would thus mean the loss of some colonial autonomy. Vogel, of course, thought that the benefits of federation to the colonies would vastly outweigh the costs but, in opposing Vogel, Lord Blachford, for many years a distinguished civil servant at the Colonial Office,[18] seized on this as a serious weakness in the pro-federation case. He, and Vogel's other opponent Robert Lowe, who had been Chancellor of the Exchequer in Gladstone's government of 1868–74,[19] both took it for granted, in the essays printed here, that unity was impossible between territories separated by thousands of miles of sea and that any attempt to impose it would simply drive the colonies to revolt. Although both agreed with Vogel that the combined populations of the white colonies would soon outnumber Britain's, they were convinced, as were many other liberals, that the political connection with the colonies was bound to fade eventually, though it could be preserved for longer by allowing maximum freedom to the colonies and thus, in Cobden's words, 'retaining them by their affections'.[20] Both Blachford and Lowe felt that attempts at union would simply highlight differences and promote disputes and the latter was sure that

---

[17] Such as the 3rd Earl Grey, who had been Colonial Secretary between 1846 and 1852. See his article, 'How Shall We Retain the Colonies?', *The Nineteenth Century*, vol. V (1879), pp. 935–54.

[18] The only book on Blachford appears to be G. E. Marindin (ed.), *Letters of Frederic, Lord Blachford* (London: James Murray, 1896).

[19] The modern biography is by J. Winter, *Robert Lowe* (Toronto: Toronto U. P., 1976).

[20] Quoted in Bennett, *Concept of Empire*, p. 169.

Britons themselves would object to colonials at Westminster. Nor could either of them see what interest the colonies would have in joining in a European war which, as part of a federated government, they would be bound to do: Blachford thought that the colonies might participate in one such war but that this would effectively end the connection.[21] Vogel, like all federationists, vigorously opposed this on the grounds that the interests of Britain and the colonies were globally intertwined and that any defeat for the mother country in Europe would also drastically reduce the independence of the colonies.[22]

Just as the debate over the future of Greater Britain took a new turn in the 1870s, so also a renewed interest was aroused in the destiny of Britain's dependent empire, especially India. Disraeli's striking innovations in policy in the late 1870s were the catalyst. His declaration, in 1876, that Queen Victoria would take the title 'Empress of India' proved the opening move in a policy which provoked a highly-charged discussion about the meaning of the word 'imperialism'. Hitherto it had been used to describe Rome under the emperors and it had also been applied, usually pejoratively, to Napoleon and his successors, especially Napoleon III after his coup in 1852. Indeed, in associating the word 'Imperial' with 'parvenu personages and with Asiatic modes of expressing reverence',[23] the *Spectator* was recognising their extended meaning; and its April 1876 article 'English Imperialism', printed in this collection, is one of the first clear recognitions of the new nuances in the use of the word. In 1878, Robert Lowe also extended its use in like manner in his article 'Imperialism' included here. In declaring that imperialism 'was the assertion of absolute force over others' and 'the apotheosis of violence' he referred to both French and Prussian examples. However, he also declared that the word was a 'new and most unacceptable addition to

---

[21] For similar arguments, aimed this time at Earl Grey, see Lord Norton, 'How Not to Retain the Colonies', *The Nineteenth Century*, vol. VI (1879), pp. 170–78.

[22] For a sympathetic response to Vogel and one which reviews the controversy, see G. Baden Powell, 'England and her Colonies', *Fraser's Magazine*, vol. 97 (1878), pp. 1–17. For the argument in relation to a specific colony, see the articles entitled 'The Future of the Canadian Dominion' by George Anderson and William Clarke in *Contemporary Review*, vol. 38 (1880), pp. 396–411, 805–26.

[23] *Spectator*, 18 March 1876, p. 360.

our vocabulary' and clearly saw it, in this guise at least, as a policy of making the preservation of the Indian empire Britain's chief priority and pursuing a militarist strategy to achieve this end.

Lowe's outburst was provoked not so much by the issue of the Queen's Indian title as by the new turn in Disraeli's policy in 1877–8.[24] The prime minister was convinced that Britain's global security would be undermined if the Turkish empire in Europe collapsed under Russian pressure. He not only threatened war against Russia but, in moving Indian troops to Suez, he advertised as dramatically as possible his view that the interests of the empire were at stake, that Britain's strength lay in its overseas possessions and that the whole resources of that empire should be used if necessary to defend it. In doing so, he set off a heated, sometimes bitter, argument as to whether British policy in future should, in Greg's words, be 'Imperial or Economic'.[25]

A measured attempt to define and defend an Imperial policy which also began to shift the definition of the word 'imperialism' was made by Lord Carnarvon in a speech, part of which is included in this book. Carnarvon, who was Colonial Secretary in Disraeli's government until 1878, confessed that 'Imperialism . . . is a newly-coined word to me'. He distinguished between a false imperialism (which he also associated with continental militarism) and a true. The latter included the pursuit of a 'united English-speaking community overseas' and the determination to bring the benefits of civilisation to the less developed and less privileged. Imperialism, in this sense, became the fulfilment of a destiny and a duty and was indissolubly connected with Britain's claim to a great place in the world.[26] This was a definition of imperialism which cast a long shadow but whether it captured the essence of the 'new imperialism' is doubtful. After all, Carnarvon felt obliged to

---

[24] For introductions to the historical background see Eldridge, *England's Mission*, chaps. 7–9; and the same author's *Disraeli and the Rise of a New Imperialism* (Cardiff: University of Wales Press, 1996).

[25] W. R. Greg, 'Foreign Policy of Great Britain – Imperial or Economic?', *The Nineteenth Century*, vol. IV (1878), pp. 393–407.

[26] For an approach which has similar implications, see J. Lubbock, 'On the Imperial Policy of Great Britain', *The Nineteenth Century*, vol. I (1877), pp. 37–49.

resign from the government in 1878 because he was uneasy about the nature of Disraeli's foreign policy. The author who best expressed the more aggressive spirit of imperialism in the late 1870s was Edward Dicey, editor of the *Observer* newspaper. In the pages of the new heavyweight journal, *The Nineteenth Century*, he defended Disraeli's Far Eastern policy as important to Britain's global security and to the defence of India arguing that, if necessary, Britain should occupy Egypt to shore up its position. Gladstone, who was violently opposed to Disraeli's foreign policy as recklessly immoral, repudiated Dicey's argument in detail.[27] In reply, Dicey defended himself by putting a more general case for an imperial policy. Gladstone responded in kind: and these two later articles are reprinted here as broadly representative of the arguments on both sides.

Dicey's support for Disraeli foreshadowed in a remarkable way many of the main contentions of the next two generations of imperialists. He recognised how much Britain's power and internal stability rested upon its global trading position and he believed the empire was vital not only as a market but because it provided the means for the defence of the global network of trade. Dicey felt that Britain's superior economic position in the world was due to the 'innate propensities of the race' and that 'a certain instinct of development inherent in our race' had made us builders of empire. This concern for secure imperial trade, the Darwinian sense of struggle and the feelings of race and destiny were all crucial components of the new imperial sentiment of the late nineteenth century. Dicey's article is also important for its frank recognition, missing from Carnarvon's contribution, that Britain ruled India and would, if necessary, conquer Egypt for its own selfish reasons rather than for the good of the natives. Empire had been acquired by immoral means: but immoral means could produce moral results since the natives were bound to benefit from exposure to British civilisation and to British justice which was the best in the world. Like most later supporters of imperial expansion, Dicey was convinced that British civilisation, including its cherished constitution and the freedoms which flowed from that,

---

[27] E. Dicey, 'Our Route to India', *The Nineteenth Century*, vol. I (1877), pp. 665–85: W. E. Gladstone, 'Aggression in Egypt and Freedom in the East', *The Nineteenth Century*, vol. II (1877), pp. 149–66.

depended upon British power which itself depended on empire and what was coming to be called 'imperialism'. He more than any other writer of the time captured in print the emerging idea 'of an Empire as a compact entity, ready for combat, commanded from one centre and relying on its collective military force'.[28]

Gladstone's response showed that he had something in common with the new imperialists in that he did not dispute the idea that the British were an expansive race with global responsibilities. Where he differed crucially from Dicey, and echoed in a more measured way the sentiments of Lowe, was in his insistence that the sources of British energies and cultural strength were in Britain itself. These energies depended crucially upon its liberal laws and constitution which created the stability that had made economic prosperity and global expansion possible. Gladstone was convinced that aggressive imperialism endangered this heritage. Disraelian policies meant heavy state expenditure, higher taxes, less investment and growth. Of even greater importance was that they indicated a dangerous lurch towards militarism which threatened liberal values and, therefore, the basis of Britain's greatness. He also asserted that such policies sapped the moral basis of Britain's position in the world which rested fundamentally on the fact that the nation had a mission to bring the blessings of liberty and freedom to those who had, often in regrettable circumstances, fallen under our control in the past. For Gladstone was convinced that, if this mission obliged Britain to accept ultimate separation from the white settlements, it also compelled Britain to bring the benefits of civilisation to India. Like Lowe, he believed that India was a source of military weakness even though India's forces were paid for locally because it increased Britain's vulnerability to attack. Yet he was also convinced that, since we had occupied India unjustly, we were honour bound to compensate for this by offering it the benefits of liberalism and the energies released by liberalism. For, as he argued, Britain's control over India had not come about because of 'a general inferiority of the Indian mind' or because India possessed 'a civilisation less matured by time'. It was rather the 'comparative force of manhood and faculties of

---

[28] Koebner and Schmidt, *Imperialism*, p. 133.

action' exhibited by Britons which had given them their exalted role in the world. Britain should never have occupied India but, having done so, could justify its continuing presence because of the moral benefits its rule brought to the Indians. Lowe had a less exalted sense of Britain's moral superiority but felt that Britain had assumed obligations in India it could not simply walk away from. Those who, following Cobden, claimed that the best thing Britain could do both for itself and for India was to leave the sub-continent forthwith were rare even on the progressive wing of politics.[29]

In another important article in this collection Frederic Seebohm, Liberal unionist banker and noted mediaeval historian, took the same line of reasoning further, pushing the continental associations of the word into the background. Placing India and other conquests at the centre of British policy *was* imperialism because it gave priority to the defence of an illiberal and undemocratic empire rather than to the pursuit of liberal policies in the metropolis. Seebohm was shrewd enough to recognise that Disraeli's policy was, to some extent, a 'mock Imperialism' based more upon bluff and appeals to sentiment than upon a serious commitment of resources to new policies.[30] No doubt this view was influenced by the disastrous failures of Disraeli's half-hearted 'forward' policy in Afghanistan and South Africa which helped to discredit his government and ensure its defeat at the general election in 1880. However, Seebohm was concerned that, if taken to extremes, the policy could destroy Britain by pushing it back into a form of militant authoritarianism, exhausting its resources, impoverishing its masses and forcing them into a helpless dependence on the state. Imperialism and socialism were thus inevitably bound together. Seebohm was particularly concerned by Disraeli's use of Indian troops because it invoked a comparison with the mercenary armies raised by Rome which led eventually to

---

[29] For the Cobdenite view see Cobden's letter to Ashworth, 16 October 1857, in Morley, *Life of Richard Cobden*, p. 207.

[30] In doing so, he anticipated the arguments of Joseph Schumpeter. See R. Swedberg (ed.), *J. A. Schumpeter: the Economics and Sociology of Capitalism* (New Jersey: Princeton U. P., 1991), pp. 146–9.

the latter's destruction.[31] While imperialism threatened Britain with poverty and social dissolution, liberalism would bring peace and plenty: Seebohm followed Dilke in asserting that the great overseas fruits of British liberalism were the settlement colonies, especially the United States, and that as a part of this free, spontaneously developing, English world the mother country had a prosperous and liberal future.

The 1870s also saw a revived interest in the question of India's economic importance to Britain. Gladstone was adamant that the possession of India was not crucial to Britain's economic well-being. He admitted that there was a flow of tribute[32] from India but declared that it was 'utterly insignificant: it is probably not near a hundredth part of the sheer annual profits of the nation, nor near a fourth part of the unforced gains of our commercial intercourse with that country'.[33] The clear implication of this was that Gladstone thought Britain's trade with India did not depend upon the latter's imperial status. In his article of 1877 printed here, Robert Lowe had a rather different perspective. The East India company had exacted tribute but, under Crown control after 1858, this had now disappeared. Instead, India was 'petted and subsidized' with cheap guaranteed loans. Although he believed that the military and the other members of the privileged minority were the main beneficiaries of empire, Lowe admitted that Britain's presence in India was crucial to its textile exports. However, he avoided the question of whether or not Britain's position in India depended on what is now known as 'free trade imperialism'.[34] In the long run, however, he thought that Britain, by bringing peace and good government to India, would raise against itself an intense local

---

[31] For an interesting counter argument see W. R. Greg, 'Employment of Our Asiatic Forces in European Wars', *Fortnightly Review*, vol. 23 ns (1878), pp. 835–49.

[32] Tribute is usually taken to consist of funds raised in India which were transferred to Britain. Exactly what constituted tribute, as opposed to payments made in the normal course of trading relations, was a matter of intense dispute.

[33] Gladstone, 'Aggression on Egypt and Freedom in the East', p. 153.

[34] For a discussion of this in a wider context see Cain and Hopkins, *British Imperialism*, chap. 10.

competition in manufactures which would erode the immediate advantages.[35]

The other side of the picture was painted less effectively: but George Chesney's article in this collection made some pertinent points against the radical position. He politely and systematically refuted the idea that India was a drain on our military manpower and, in true Disraelian fashion, reminded his readers that one of the great benefits of the Indian army was that it could be used as a general imperial force. As for trade, Chesney highlighted the significance of Indian imports as well as India's role as a market for manufactures though he did acknowledge that some Indian imports were undermining sections of British agriculture. He also ridiculed Lowe's claim that the gains from export trade were ephemeral because the Indians would soon become competitive. He claimed that Lowe's position implied that 'trade is of no value to a country if there is any danger of losing it' and that, in strict logic, Lowe was thus obliged to condemn as valueless Britain's trade with most of its partners.[36]

What can we make of this debate for our perspective of over one hundred years? Lowe was no doubt being characteristically hyperbolic when, in attacking Disraeli's Eastern policy in his article of 1878, he declared that the next election would be the most significant for six hundred years in determining Britain's future as a liberal state. However, even though many of Disraeli's critics were aware that his policy was often more show than substance, he did provide leadership for a movement in British politics which tried to shift the focus of interest and action to a new form of militant imperialism. This was a serious and disturbing challenge to the assumptions of Gladstone and the liberal élite. In more measured tones than Lowe, the veteran radical publicist and historian, Goldwin Smith, argued that Disraeli's policy was to form a new kind of conservatism based on an alliance between the aristocracy to whom 'the odour of feudal supremacy still clings' and the poorer sections of the urban population. The latter he

[35] For an even more thoroughgoing radical critique of Britain's position in India, see G. Allen, 'Why Keep India?', *Contemporary Review*, vol. 38 (1880), pp. 544–56.

[36] Another defence of Britain's position in India was provided by H. Taylor, 'The Future of India', *Contemporary Review*, vol. 39 (1881), pp. 464–77.

described as 'political Lazzeroni capable of being organised by wealth in opposition to the higher order of working men and middle class' who were the backbone of liberalism.[37] Smith saw the assertion of imperial power in India and the use of Indian troops in imperial conflicts as symptomatic of such a strategy and warned:

> England now stands where the paths divide, the one leading by industrial and commercial progress to increase of political liberty; the other, by career of conquest, to the political results in which such a career has never yet failed to end. At present the influences in favour of taking the path of conquest seem to preponderate, and the probability seems to be that the leadership of political progress, which has hitherto belonged to England, and has constituted a special interest of her history, will, in the near future, pass into other hands.[38]

Lowe's hyperbole and the ferocity of Gladstone's Midlothian campaign in the run-up to the election of 1880 make sense if seen in this context, however far-fetched Smith's fears may appear in hindsight.[39]

One of the chief elements underlying this shift in policy was a recognition, emerging in the early 1870s, that Britain's position in the world, both in economic and strategic terms, would be unsustainable in the twentieth century unless it was somehow able to unite itself firmly to its overseas possessions and use their strength to fight its battles. In claiming that this unity was impossible to achieve without wrecking the liberal state, most of those who supported Gladstone were also tacitly accepting that Britain's days as a great power were numbered. The best they could offer was that Britain should concentrate on eliminating the vestiges of privilege and thus make it easier to compete and prosper in the future. Some, like Dilke and Seebohm, saw a rosy future for a global Anglo-Saxonism in which Britain would play Greeks to America's Romans. They

---

[37] Goldwin Smith, 'The Greatness of England', *Contemporary Review*, vol. 34 (1878), pp. 7–8.

[38] *Ibid.*, p. 18.

[39] It may also be no coincidence that it was at this time that the sociologist Herbert Spencer published, in two articles in the *Contemporary Review*, vol. 40 (1881), his famous distinction between 'industrial' societies and 'militant' ones.

shared with Blachford and, to an even greater degree, Lowe the Cobdenite vision of an emerging world of peace, interdependence and prosperity. It would matter little in that world whether a nation was big or small because war would become obsolete. But not all anti-imperialists took the same rosy view of the future. Gladstone, for example, while happy to recognise that the United States would become the world's leading power in the twentieth century and sharing some of Dilke's and Lowe's pride in Britain's production of such a dynamic successor, still recognised that this transformation would subject Britain to fierce economic competition: one reason he gave for opposing Disraeli was that Britain was wasting its substance on war and defence when it should be preparing for the consequences of American hegemony by prudence in public expenditure.[40] Other free market liberals had an even less sanguine view of the future, foreseeing mass emigration and hardship as coal stocks ran out and the centre of economic gravity shifted across the Atlantic.[41] Underlying the division over imperialism there was a deeper consensus, one which acknowledged that the islands of Britain were not in themselves capable of sustaining the nation's position as a great power in the century ahead.

Peter Cain
Sheffield Hallam University, 1999

[40] W. E. Gladstone, 'Kin Beyond Sea', *North American Review*, vol. 127 (1878), p. 180.

[41] L. Courtney, 'The Migration of Centres of Industrial Energy', *Fortnightly Review*, vol. 24 ns (1878), pp. 801–20.

[FROM] GREATER BRITAIN*
Charles Dilke

Colonies.

When a Briton takes a survey of the colonies, he finds much matter for surprise in the one-sided nature of the partnership which exists between the mother and the daughter lands. No reason presents itself to him why our artisans and merchants should be taxed in aid of populations far more wealthy than our own, who have not, as we have, millions of paupers to support. We at present tax our humblest classes, we weaken our defences, we scatter our troops and fleets, and lay ourselves open to panics such as those of 1853 and 1859, in order to protect against imaginary dangers the Australian gold-digger and Canadian farmer. There is something ludicrous in the idea of taxing St. Giles's for the support of Melbourne, and making Dorsetshire agricultural labourers pay the cost of defending New Zealand colonists in Maori wars.

It is possible that the belief obtains in Britain among the least educated classes of the community that colonial expenses are rapidly decreasing, if they have not already wholly disappeared; but in fact they have for some years past been steadily and continuously growing in amount.

As long as we choose to keep up such *propugnacula* as Gibraltar, Malta, and Bermuda, we must pay roundly for them, as we also must for such costly luxuries as our Gold Coast settlements for the suppression of the slave-trade; but if we confine the term 'colonies' to English-speaking, white-inhabited, and self-governed lands, and exclude on the one hand garrisons such as Gibraltar, and on the other mere dependencies like the West Indies and Ceylon, we find that our true colonies in North America, Australia, Polynesia, and South Africa, involve us nominally in yearly charges of almost two millions sterling, and, really, in untold expenditure.

* 6th ed. (London: Macmillan & Co., 1872), pp. 393–9.

Canada is in all ways the most flagrant case. She draws from us some three millions annually for her defence, she makes no contribution towards the cost; she relies mainly on us to defend a frontier of 4000 miles, and she excludes our goods by prohibitive duties at her ports. In short, colonial expenses which, rightly or wrongly, our fathers bore (and that not ungrudgingly) when they enjoyed a monopoly of colonial trade, are borne by us in face of colonial prohibition. What the true cost to us of Canada may be is unfortunately an open question, and the loss by the weakening of our home forces we have no means of computing; but when we consider that, on a fair statement of the case, Canada would be debited with the cost of a large portion of the half-pay and recruiting services, of Horse Guards and War Office expenses, of arms, accoutrements, barracks, hospitals, and stores, and also with the gigantic expenses of two of our naval squadrons, we cannot but admit that we must pay at least three millions a year for the hatred that the Canadians profess to bear towards the United States. Whatever may be the case, however, with regard to Canada, less fault is to be found with the cost of the Australian colonies. If they bore a portion of the half-pay and recruiting expenses as well as the cost of the troops actually employed among them in time of peace, and also paid their share in the maintenance of the British navy, – a share to increase with the increase of their merchant shipping – there would be little to desire, unless, indeed, we should wish that, in exchange for a check upon imperial braggadocio and imperial waste, the Australias should also contribute towards the expenses of imperial wars.

No reason can be shown for our spending millions on the defence of Canada against the Americans or in aiding the New Zealand colonists against the Maories that will not apply to their aiding us in case of a European war with France, control being given to their representatives over our public action in questions of imperial concern. Without any such control over imperial action, the old American colonists were well content to do their share of fighting in imperial wars. In 1689, in 1702, and in 1744, Massachusetts attacked the French, and taking from them Nova Scotia and others of their new plantations, handed them over to Great Britain. Even when the tax time came, Massachusetts, while declaring that the English Parliament had no right to tax colonies, went on to say that the king could inform them of the exigencies of the public service, and that they were ready 'to provide for them if required'.

It is not likely, however, nowadays, that our colonists would, for any long stretch of time, engage to aid us in our purely European wars. Australia would scarcely feel herself deeply interested in the guarantee of Luxemburg, nor Canada in the affairs of Servia. The fact that we in Britain paid our share – or rather nearly the whole cost – of the Maori wars would be no argument to an Australian, but only an additional proof to him of our extraordinary folly. We have been educated into a habit of paying with complacency other people's bills – not so the Australian settler.

As far as Australia is concerned, our soldiers are not used as troops at all. The colonists like the show of the red-coats, and the military duties are made up partly of guard-of-honour work, and partly of the labours of police. The colonists well know that in time of war we should immediately withdraw our troops, and they trust wholly in their volunteers and the colonial marine.

So long as we choose to allow the system to continue, the colonists are well content to reap the benefit. When we at last decide that it shall cease, they will reluctantly consent. It is more than doubtful whether, if we were to insist to the utmost upon our rights as towards our Southern colonies, they would do more than grumble and consent to our demands; and there is no chance whatever of our asking for more than our simple due.

When you talk to an intelligent Australian, you can always see that he fears that separation would be made the excuse for the equipment of a great and costly Australian fleet – not more necessary then than now – and that, however he may talk, he would, rather than separate from England, at least do his duty by her.

The fear of conquest of the Australian colonies if we left them to themselves is on the face of it ridiculous. It is sufficient, perhaps, to say that the old American colonies, when they had but a million and a half of people, defended themselves successfully against the then all-powerful French, and that there is no instance of a self-protected English colony being conquered by the foreigner. The American colonies valued so highly their independence of the old country in the matter of defence that they petitioned the Crown to be allowed to fight for themselves, and called the British army by the plain name of 'grievance'.

As for our so-called defence of the colonies, in war-time we defend ourselves: we defend the colonies only during peace. In war-time they are ever left to shift for themselves, and they would undoubtedly be better fit to do so were they in the habit of maintaining their military establishments in time of peace. The present system weakens us and them – us, by taxes and by the withdrawal of our men and ships; the colonies, by preventing the development of that self-reliance which is requisite to form a nation's greatness. The successful encountering of difficulties is the marking feature of the national character of the English, and we can hardly expect a nation which has never encountered any, or which has been content to see them met by others, ever to become great. In short, as matters now stand, the colonies are a source of military weakness to us, and our 'protection' of them is a source of danger to the colonists. No doubt, there are still among us, men who would have wished to have seen America continue in union with England, on the principle on which the Russian conscripts are chained each to an old man – to keep her from going too fast – and who now consider it our duty to defend our colonies at whatever cost, on account of the 'prestige' which attaches to the somewhat precarious tenure of these great lands. With such men it is impossible for colonial reformers to argue: the standpoints are wholly different. To those, however, who admit the injustice of the present system to the taxpayers of the mother-country, but who fear that her merchants would suffer by its disturbance, inasmuch as, in their belief, action on our part would lead to a disruption of the tie, we may plead that, even should separation be the result, we should be none the worse off for its occurrence. The retention of colonies at almost any cost has been defended – so far as it has been supported by argument at all – on the ground that the connexion conduces to trade, to which argument it is sufficient to answer that no one has ever succeeded in showing what effect upon trade the connexion can have, and that as excellent examples to the contrary we have the fact that our trade with the Ionian Islands has increased since their annexation to the kingdom of Greece, and a much more striking fact than even this – namely, that while the trade with England of the Canadian Confederation is only four-elevenths of its total external trade, or little more than one-third, the English trade of the United States was in 1860 (before the war) nearly two-thirds of their total external trade, in 1861 more than two-thirds, and in 1866 (first year after the war) again four-sevenths of the total trade. Common institutions, common freedom, and common tongue have evidently far more to do with trade than union has; and for purposes of commerce and civilization, America is a truer colony of Britain than is Canada.

It would not be difficult, were it necessary, to multiply examples whereby to prove that trade with a country does not appear to be affected by union with or separation from it. Egypt (even when we carefully exclude from the returns Indian produce in transport) sends us nearly all such produce as she exports, notwithstanding that the French largely control the government, and that we have much less footing in the country than the Italians, and no more than the Austrians or Spanish. Our trade with Australia means that the Australians want something of us and that we need something of them, and that we exchange with them our produce as we do in a larger degree with the Americans, the Germans, and the French.

The trade argument being met, and it being remembered that our colonies are no more an outlet for our surplus population than they would be if the Great Mogul ruled over them, as is seen by the fact that of every twenty people who leave the United Kingdom, one goes to Canada, two to Australia, and sixteen to the United States, we come to the 'argument' which consists in the word 'prestige'. When examined, this cry seems to mean that, in the opinion of the utterer, extent of empire is power – a doctrine under which Brazil ought to be nineteen and a half times, and China twenty-six times as powerful as France. Perhaps the best answer to the doctrine is a simple contradiction: those who have read history with most care well know that at all times extent of empire has been weakness. England's real empire was small enough in 1650, yet it is rather doubtful whether her 'prestige' ever reached the height it did while the Cromwellian admirals swept the seas. The idea conveyed by the words 'mother of free nations' is every bit as good as that contained in the cry 'prestige', and the argument that, as the colonists are British subjects, we have no right to cast them adrift so long as they wish to continue citizens, is evidently no answer to those who merely urge that the colonists should pay their own policemen.

It may, perhaps, be contended that the possession of 'colonies' tends to preserve us from the curse of small island countries, the dwarfing of mind which would otherwise make us Guernsey a little magnified. If this be true, it is a powerful argument in favour of continuance in the present system. It is a question, however, whether our real preservation from the insularity we deprecate is not to be found in the possession of true colonies – of plantations such as America, in short – rather than in that of mere dependencies. That which raises us above the provincialism of citizenship of little England is our citizenship of the greater Saxondom which includes all that is best and wisest in the world.

From the foundation, separation would be harmless, does not of necessity follow the conclusion, separation is to be desired. This much only is clear – that we need not hesitate to demand that Australia should do her duty.

With the more enlightened thinkers of England, separation from the colonies has for many years been a favourite idea, but as regards the Australias it would hardly be advisable. If we allow that it is to the interest both of our race and of the world that the Australias should prosper, we have to ask whether they would do so in a higher degree if separated from the mother country than if they remained connected with her and with each other by a federation. It has often been said that, instead of the varying relations which now exist between Britain and America, we should have seen a perfect friendship had we but permitted the American colonies to go their way in peace; but the example does not hold in the case of Australia, which is by no means wishful to go at all.

Under separation we should, perhaps, find the colonies better emigration-fields for our surplus population than they are at present. Many of our emigrants who flock to the United States are attracted by the idea that they are going to become citizens of a new nation instead of dependents upon an old one. On the separation of Australia from England we might expect that a portion of these sentimentalists would be diverted from a colony necessarily jealous of us so long as we hold Canada, to one which from accordance of interests is likely to continue friendly or allied. This argument, however, would have no weight with those who desire the independence of Canada, and who look upon America as still our colony.

Separation, we may then conclude, though infinitely better

than a continuance of the existing one-sided tie, would, in a healthier state of our relations, not be to the interest of Britain, although it would perhaps be morally beneficial to Australia. Any relation, however, would be preferable to the existing one of mutual indifference and distrust. Recognising the fact that Australia has come of age, and calling on her, too, to recognise it, we should say to the Australian colonists: 'Our present system cannot continue; will you amend it, or separate?' The worst thing that can happen to us is that we should 'drift' blindly into separation.

After all, the strongest of the arguments in favour of separation is the somewhat paradoxical one that it would bring us a step nearer to the virtual confederation of the English race.

ENGLAND AND HER COLONIES*
James Anthony Froude

During the last quarter of a century, nearly four million British subjects – English, Irish, and Scots – have become citizens, more or less prosperous, of the United States of America. We have no present quarrel with the Americans; we trust most heartily that we may never be involved in any quarrel with them, but undoubtedly from the day that they became independent of us, they became our rivals. They constitute the one great Power whose interests and whose pretensions compete with our own, and in so far as the strength of nations depends on the number of thriving men and women composing them, the United States have been made stronger, the English empire weaker, to the extent of those millions and the children growing of them. The process is still continuing. Emigration remains the only practical remedy for the evils of Ireland. England and Scotland contain as many people as in the present condition of industry they can hold. The annual increase of the population has to be drafted off and disposed of elsewhere, and while the vast proportion of it continues to be directed on the shores of the Republic, those who leave us, leave us for the most part resenting the indifference with which their loss is regarded. They part from us as from a hard stepmother. They are exiles from a country which was the home of their birth; which they had no desire to leave, but which drives them from her at the alternative of starvation.

England at the same time possesses dependencies of her own, not less extensive than the United States, not less rich in natural resources, not less able to provide for these expatriated swarms, where they would remain attached to her Crown, where their well-being would be our well-being, their brains and arms our brains and arms, every acre which they could reclaim from the wilderness, so much added to English soil, and

* From *Fraser's Magazine*, vol. 81 (January 1870), pp. 1–16.

themselves and their families fresh additions to our national stability.

And yet we are told by politicians – by some directly in words, by almost all in the apathy with which they stand by and look on – that the direction of our emigration is of not the slightest consequence to us, that there is no single point in which an emigrant who settles on the Murray or the St. Lawrence, is of more value to us than one who prefers the Mississippi. In either case, if he does well for himself, he becomes a purchaser of English goods, and in this capacity alone is he of use to us. Our interest in him, so far as we acknowledge an interest, is that he should go wherever he can better himself most rapidly, and consume the largest quantity of English calico and hardware in his house-hold. It is even argued that our colonies are a burden to us, and that the sooner they are cut adrift from us the better. They are, or have been, demonstratively loyal. They are proud of their origin, conscious of the value to themselves of being part of a great empire, and willing and eager to find a home for every industrious family that we can spare. We answer impatiently that they are welcome to our people if our people choose to go to them, but whether they go to them or to America, whether the colonies themselves remain under our flag or proclaim their independence or attach themselves to some other power, is a matter which concerns themselves entirely, and to us of profound indifference.

Such an attitude of a Government towards its subjects is so strange, so unexampled in the history of mankind, that the meaning of it deserves study if only as a political curiosity. The United States have just spent six hundred millions of money, and half a million lives in preserving their national unity. The Russians when they find a pressure of population in Finland, load their ships of war with as many as desire to emigrate, and give them homes on the Amoor river. English subjects were once so precious in the eyes of our Government, that we did not allow them so much as a right to change their allegiance. When we look down the emigration tables we find only the Germans who are doing anything in the least resembling what we are doing, and the Germans cannot help themselves for they have no colonies; America is not a rival of Germany, and the strengthening of America threatens no interest of any German State. Had Prussia settlements in one hemisphere and France in another, do we suppose the Court of Berlin would see the peasants from the Elbe and the Oder denationalise themselves without an effort to reclaim them? No intelligent person will believe it. The Spaniards and French indeed parted with tens of thousands of their artisans to England during the wars of religion, but they did not part with them willingly, nor was the result of the experiment such as to tempt a repetition of it. It used to be considered that the first of all duties in an English citizen was his duty to his country. His country in return was bound to preserve and care for him. What change has passed over us, that allegiance can now be shifted at pleasure like a suit of clothes? Is it from some proud consciousness of superabundant strength? Are our arms so irresistible that we have no longer an enemy to fear? Is our prosperity so overflowing and the continuance of it so certain, that we can now let it flow from us elsewhere because we can contain no more? Our national arrogance will scarcely presume so far? Is it that the great Powers of the world have furled their battle flags? Is the parliament of man on the way to be constituted, and is the rivalry of empires to be confined for the future to competition in the arts of peace? Never at any period in the world's history was so large a share of the profits of industry expended upon armies and arms. Are our relations with the United States themselves at any rate in so blessed a condition? The Alabama claims are unsettled, and not in the way of settlement, and the tone of the Prime Minister was not encouraging when he last alluded in public to the state of his communications with Mr. Motley. Is it that the experience of the results of the emigration to America so far, has been so satisfactory as to convince us that we have no occasion to interfere with its direction? The Irish in Australia and New Zealand are as well-disposed towards us as the rest of the colonists. The Irish in America are our bitterest enemies. The Irish vote will be given unanimously for war with us if at any time any question between the two countries becomes critical, and their presence in America, and the influence which they are supposed to possess there, is the immediate cause of the present humour of Ireland itself. The millions who fled from the famine carried with them the belief that it was England that, in one shape or other, was the cause of their misery; that it was England which was driving them from their homes. The land was theirs and we had taken it from them, and therefore they were starving. It was their belief then. It is their belief now. Nine parts of it may be absurd, but one part is reasonable. We had superseded Irish law and Irish methods of management by English law and English methods of management. Landlords holding under our system had allowed the population to outgrow the legitimate resources of the country, because while the potato lasted, subdivision increased their rents without cost to themselves, and then when the change came, and the landlords' interests lay the other way, they said to their tenants, 'There is no room for you here; you are not wanted; you are an expense and a trouble to us; and you must go.' Their removal in itself was inevitable. In many instances, perhaps in most, the cost of the removal was paid for them, but they identified the system, under which they suffered with English tyranny, and they went away with hate in their hearts and curses on their lips. Those who went hated us because they were obliged to go. Those who stayed behind hate us because fathers have lost their sons, and sisters brothers, and friends have been parted from friends. And now we have Fenianism upon us saying openly we dare not put it down, for America will not allow us.

We did not make the potato famine. We could not fight with nature, or alter the irreversible relation between land and food. Civilisation brings with it always an overgrowth of people; for civilisation means the policeman, and the policeman means that the natural increase of population shall not be held in check by murder and fighting and robbery. In all ranks families have to learn to be separated. England suffers from it as much as Ireland and does not complain. This is quite true. But if when the famine came we had said to the Irish peasants, 'Through no fault of yours, a terrible calamity has fallen upon you; there are more of you living on the land than the land will support, and we take blame to ourselves, for we ought (or those who by our means are placed above you ought) to have prevented the multiplication of you where the decay of a single root might be your destruction; when we look back upon our management of Ireland, we cannot acquit ourselves of being responsible for you; and, therefore, as you must go away, we will give you land elsewhere; we will take you there and settle you, and help you to live till you can maintain yourselves,' – if we had said this, there would have been at least a consciousness that we had done our best to soften their misfortunes.

The million that we might have sent to Canada or Australia would have drawn after them the millions that have followed. Our colonies would have doubled their population, and there would have been no Irish vote in America for party demagogues to flatter by threats of England, and no Fenianism at home.

We are told that Government has no business with emigration; that emigration, like wages, prices, and profits, must be left to settle itself, according to laws of nature. Human things are as much governed by laws of nature as a farm or a garden, neither less nor more. If we cultivate a field it will yield us corn or green crops. The laws of nature will as assuredly overgrow it with docks and nettles if we leave it to govern itself. The settlement of Ulster under James I. was an act of government; yet it was the only measure which ever did good to Ireland. The removal of a million poor creatures to Canada and the establishment of them there, would have been under present circumstances considerably more easy. It was a question of money merely. To send them to Canada might have cost, perhaps, as much as the Abyssinian war. Had we feared they might cross the border after all into the States, and had preferred Australia or the Cape for them, it might have cost a little more, and it would have probably turned out on the whole a profitable investment. Trade follows the flag. We consider the Americans to be good customers, but they import only ten shillings' worth of our manufactures per head in proportion to the population. The imports of the Australian colonies are at the rate of 10*l.* per head. English capital is locked up waiting for profitable investment. The high rate of interest in America is due wholly to the extent of land there, which yields profits: so enormous and so certain when reclaimed and cultivated. We have the same resource in no less abundance. We have land, we have capital, we have labour. Yet we seem to have neither the ability nor the desire to bring them together, and develop their results. We are told persistently by a powerful school of politicians that the colonies as colonies are of no use to us, that we can look with entire indifference on their separation from us, and on their adoption of any future course which may seem best to themselves.

What is the meaning of so strange a conclusion?

Many explanations can be given of it. There is a certain vague cosmopolitanism growing up among us. Patriotism is no longer recognised as the supreme virtue which once it was believed to be. 'Prejudice in favour of England,' that proud belief in England which made men ready to sacrifice themselves and all belonging to them in the interests of their country, is obsolete and out of fashion. It is not uncommon to hear Liberal politicians express an opinion without much regret, that England has had its day; that her fighting days are over, that like the old Témeraire, she has nothing now to look for but to be towed into her last resting-place; that a hundred years hence her greatest achievement will be considered to be having given birth to America. A more respectable theory is that we are still sufficient for ourselves, that we have enormous resources still undeveloped at home if Government will but let the people alone and leave trade and manufacture to take their course. There is the overwork of public men, who catch gladly at an excuse for shaking off unnecessary trouble. And there is the constitution of the Colonial Office, which undoubtedly has shown itself incapable of managing effectively our distant dependencies, the chiefs of the Colonial as of all other departments being selected not for special acquaintance with the subject, but for the convenience of political parties, being changed repeatedly with changes of Government and being unable therefore to carry out a consistent policy, or even to gain intelligent insight into their business. Again, there has been an impression that in case of war the colonies would be an embarrassment to us; that Canada as long as it is ours is a possible cause of quarrel with the United States, and that if we were quit of it we should be at once in less danger of war, and if war came should be better able to defend ourselves.

On the whole, however, there are two main causes underlying the rest which beyond all others have alienated public opinion from our colonies generally, and have created that general apathy of which the attitude of statesmen is but a symbol.

The first is the position recently assumed towards us by some of the colonies themselves; the second an opinion deliberately conceived on the political situation of England and the future which we should anticipate and labour for. The colonies no longer answer the purposes for which, when originally founded, we made them useful. When the States of the Union were British provinces, we sent there not so much our surplus population as those whose presence among us was inconvenient, our felons, rebels, and political and religious refugees.

As they prospered, we made them profitable to us. They were the chief markets for our African negro trade, and we paid no attention to their objections to it. We went on to tax them. They revolted and were lost to us. We supplied their places. In Canada, Australia, New Zealand, the Cape of Good Hope, and elsewhere, we possessed ourselves of territories as valuable as those which had separated from us. In these places, or in some of them, so long as they would allow us, we continued to dispose of our convicts. Taught by experience we avoided our past faults – we avoided them, that is, in the identical form for which we had paid so dearly – but so far as we dared we still managed them for our own convenience. We held their patronage, we administered their waste lands, we became involved in endless disputes with them, and this too came to an end. They refused to be demoralised by our felons: we submitted and kept them to ourselves. They claimed their lands, we abandoned them. They desired to fill their public offices with their own people: we parted with what had been an agreeable provision for younger brothers or political partisans. We surrendered all the privileges which had been immediately profitable; and finally, to close all disputes, we left them to govern themselves in whatever way seemed good to them. We gave them constitutions on the broadest basis which popular philosophers recommended. We limited our rights over them to the continuance of the titular sovereignty of the Crown, to the nomination of a Governor whose powers were controlled by the local legislature; and we maintained regiments among them to fight their battles when they fell into trouble with their neighbours. The advantage now was all on their side. They became a weight upon the English tax-payer. They relieved us of our emigrants, such of them as they could get, but America was ready to take our emigrants and to ask nothing of us in return. Their Governments, the creation of universal suffrage, embroiled us in wars, putting us to expense in defence of proceedings which we neither advised nor approved. The Canadians, while they expected us to protect them against the United States, levied duties on English manufactures for their own revenues. Relations such as these could not and cannot continue, and English politicians living from hand to mouth, and courting popularity by anxiety for English pockets, have declined to subsidise the colonies further or relieve them of expenses or duties which they can discharge for themselves. We have told the New Zealanders that if they covet the Maoris' lands, they must raise troops of their own to take them. We have said generally that we will not undertake the defence of the colonies except in wars of our own making, and that if the colonies do not like the condition they are welcome to sever the connection.

Undoubtedly there is much in this way of putting the case which is primâ facie reasonable. The colonies are offended. They declare themselves ardently attached to England. They say they are proud of belonging to us, and they call on England to reciprocate their affection, and they are astonished and hurt at what they regard as an injurious return. Rejected love, they tell us, curdles into enmity. A distinguished Australian reminds us that the Alabama quarrel is even now embittered by a remembrance of the tea duties. The *Times* asks with wonder what possible resemblance can be found between taxing colonies against their will and leaving them to the absolute disposal of their own fortunes. Still the colonies are not satisfied. They fail in any way to answer the argument, unless by reproaching us for being blind to what they conceive to be our own interests, but there is a rankling feeling of injustice somewhere. They make common cause with one another. Australia takes up the wrongs of New Zealand, and both resent the frankness with which we discuss a probable separation of Canada. If they have to leave us in their present humour they hint that they can no longer be our friends. Affection cannot subside into indifference. The *spretœ injuria formœ* festers into ill will.

When there are differences of this kind the right is seldom wholly on one side. Taken literally, nothing can be more just than the reply of the *Times* to Mr. Wilson. Yet situations never exactly repeat themselves, and the same spirit may exhibit itself in more forms than one. In our present relations with our colonies as well in our past we are charged with considering or having considered nothing but our own immediate interest. It is true that we have never yet acknowledged that the colonies are of more than external moment to us. Till now, and especially since the establishment of Free Trade, there has been room in England itself for the expansion of the people. The colonies see or think they see that we have gone as far as we can go that way; they consider themselves infinitely important to us, and our determined blindness adds point to the offence.

We taxed New England, they say, for our own convenience: for the same reason and equally unwisely we are throwing off them. We made use of them, while they left us their patronage and consented to be convict stations: when we cannot use them any more in this way, we bid them go about their business, although they are Englishmen like ourselves, as if Englishmen might be told prudently that if they had real or imagined grievances we did not want them, and that they were free to change their allegiance. Interest, however, is not the only bond by which nations are held together. The Frenchman prefers poverty at home to prosperity under an alien flag. Patriotism may be sentimentalism, but it is a sentimentalism nevertheless which lies at the root of every powerful nationality, and has been the principle of its coherence and its growth. Our practical differences with the colonies would have been found easy to set right had there been a real desire to adjust them, but we have not recognised their attachment to us as of serious consequence. We lost the North American States. The world thought that we were ruined, and we found ourselves as strong as before. We have come to believe that we are sufficient for ourselves, that we can keep our Indian empire and maintain our rank among other nations out of the resources of our own two islands. We imagine that all our colonists can do for us is to become purchasers of our manufactures, and whether dependent or independent they will need equally shirts and blankets and Sheffield and Birmingham hard-ware.

The England of the future as pictured in the imagination of the sanguine Liberal statesman is to be the emporium of the world's trade, and an enormous workshop for all mankind. With supplies of the best iron or coal which if not inexhaustible will last our time and our children's and grand-children's, with the special aptitude of the English atonce for mechanical art and for navigation, we consider that we can defy competition, and multiply indefinitely our mills and furnaces and ships. Our great cities are to grow greater; there is no visible limit to the development of our manufactures; we can rely upon them with confidence to supply a population far larger than we have at present. Our exports in 1862 were more than double what we exported in 1842. They may have doubled again twenty years hence, and once more by the end of the century. Civilisation spreads with railroad speed; each year opens new markets to us; and with the special advantages which no other nation combines in equal measure we imagine that we have nothing to fear. Trade may occasionally fluctuate. There may be years when our prosperity may seem arrested or even threaten a decline – but in all instances such partial checks have been followed by a splendid rebound. The tide is still seen to be flowing steadily in our favour, and we see no reason to fear that English commercial enterprise in any direction whatever is approaching its limits. Confident in ourselves we have thus looked with indifference on our dependencies in other continents, or on the opposite side of the globe. If they prefer to adhere to us we do not propose to drive them off. If they wish to leave us we are prepared neither to resist nor remonstrate. We make them understand that whether they go or stay they are masters of their own fortunes. They are practically self-governed, and with self-government they must accept its responsibilities; above all things they must make no demands on the heavily burdened English tax-payers.

The first question to be asked about all this is, whether our confidence is justified; whether the late rate of increase in our trade is really likely to continue. There are symptoms which suggest, if not fear, yet at least misgiving. Success in trade on so great a scale depends on more than natural advantages: it depends on the use that is made of them: it depends on our reputation for honesty; and English reputation, it is needless to say, is not what it used to be. The rage to become rich has infected all classes. Railway companies, banking companies, joint-stock trading companies have within these few last years, fallen to shameful wreck, dragging thousands of families down to ruin. The investigation into the causes of these failures has brought out transactions which make ordinary people ask whither English honesty has gone. Yet there has been no adequate punishment of the principal offenders, nor does any punishment seem likely to be arrived at. The silk trade is said to be in a bad way, and the fault is laid on the French treaty. It was shown a year or two since, that fifty per cent. of hemp was worked up into English silk. May not this too have had something to to do with the decline? It was proved, in the *Lancet*, after a series of elaborate investigations, that the smaller retail trade throughout the country was soaked with falsehood through and through. Scarcely one article was sold in the shops frequented by the poor, which was really the thing which it pretended to be. Last year there was an outcry about weights and measures: attention was called to the subject in the House of Commons by Lord Eustace Cecil; and perhaps, of all the moral symptoms of the age, the most significant is the answer which was given on that occasion by the President of the Board of Trade. The poor were and are the chief sufferers by fraud of this kind. Mr. Bright has risen to distinction as the poor man's friend; and those and the analogous complaints, with the general approbation of the great Liberal party, he treated with impatient ridicule. He spoke of adulteration as a natural consequence of competition. For false weights and measures, he said that accuracy was practically impossible; and with a courage inspired doubtless by contempt of his audience, he dared to add, that tradesmen were as often found to have their weights too large as too small. Of course they have; and well the police know why. The dishonest retail dealer keeps one set of weights by which he buys, and another by which he sells: and Mr. Bright's defence did but double the weight of the accusation. If a grocer gives me fourteen ounces of tea, when I pay him for a pound, I am indifferently consoled by learning that a dealer in my spare garden produce had got a hundred weight and a half of potatoes out of me, when I suppose myself to be selling him but a hundredweight. If I buy what professes to be a silk umbrella and I find myself in possession of an umbrella which is two parts hemp, I am as much robbed as if a thief had picked my pocket. I am told that I must take care of myself; that it is not the business of Government to save me from making a bad bargain. What is the business of Government? If *caveat emptor* is to be the rule, then why not *caveat viator*? Why the expense of maintaining a police? Many fine qualities are developed in men – courage, prudence, readiness, presence of mind, skill in the use of weapons – if they are left to defend for themselves their persons and their purses. Mr. Bright's reply to Lord Eustace Cecil will not have tended to remove the misgivings with which foreign purchasers are watching the symptoms of English commercial morality.

Once more: do we see our way so clearly through the growing perils from the trades' unions? We are told on all sides that English manufacturers cannot hold their ground against foreign competitors if the unions are to dictate the wages at which the artisans are to work. Our monopoly of trade depends on our powers to undersell the foreigner in his own market: a very slight margin makes the difference. If the dictation of the unions is allowed to destroy that margin by insisting on an advance with the revival of demand, the manufacturer's profits are eaten up. His occupation passes from him to countries where men and masters can work together on terms more satisfactory to both of them. Has the solution of the problem been found so easy? Has the faintest ray of light as yet been thrown upon it? The unions and the master employers are in a state of war, either open or at best suspended; and war is the most wasteful and ruinous of all means by which human differences can be adjusted. Every strike is a battle – a battle which determines nothing – in which there is no glory to be gained and no victory to be won which does not widen the breach more irreparably, while the destruction of property and the resulting ruin and devastation are immediate and incalculable. Where is there a sign that labour and capital are beginning to see their way to a reconciliation? Political economy is powerless; and the statesman who relies for the stability and progress of England on an indefinite expansion of trade, must either possess an insight marvellously deeper than that of common mortals, or must have a faith in economic principles in which, for our part, we are unable to share.

But let us grant his conclusions. Suppose these difficulties overcome; suppose Manchester, Liverpool, and Glasgow swollen till they have each a million inhabitants; suppose Lancashire a universal workshop – a hundred thousand chimneys, the church spires of the commercial creed, vomiting their smoke into the new black heaven spread above them; Lancashire calico and Yorkshire woollen clothing every bare back in Asia; the knives and forks of Europe supplied from Sheffield; and Staffordshire furnishing iron for the railways of four continents. Let Sir Samuel Baker convert the interior of Africa into an enormous cotton-field, and the Nile become a highway, through which five million bales shall annually make their way into the Mersey. Let London expand to twice its present unwieldy size, its mendicancy and misery be absorbed, and the warehouses on the Thames become the emporium in which the produce of the world is absorbed and again dispersed among mankind. Let the most sanguine dream of the most enthusiastic political economist be realised. Let us imagine our people so enlightened by education as to understand and act upon the policy of honesty; harmony be established between employers and employed on an enlightened recognition of their mutual interests; adulteration be thought as wicked as adultery, and the English brand on steel and calico once more accepted as a passport for excellence. Let us make an effort of imagination and concede that all this may be – well, and what then?

For a certain class of people – for the great merchants, great bankers, great shopkeepers, great manufacturers, whose business is to make money, whose whole thoughts are set on making money and enjoying the luxuries which money can command – no doubt, it would be a very fine world. Those who are now rich would grow richer; wealth in the modern sense of it would be enormously increased – suburban palaces would multiply, and conservatories and gardens, and further off the parks and pheasant preserves. Land would continue to rise in value, and become more and more the privilege of those who could afford the luxury of owning it. From these classes we hear already a protest against emigration. Keep our people at home, they say we shall want them when trade revives. There may be no work for them at present. Their wives and little ones may be starving with cold and hunger. They may be roaming the streets in vagrancy crowding the casual wards or besieging the doors of the poor-houses; but still keep them – all will be well by and by. Meantime let the poor-rate rise; let the small householder in Whitechapel, himself struggling manfully for independence on the verge of beggary, pay six shillings in the pound to feed his neighbour who has sunk below the line. The tide will turn; labour will soon be in demand again. Our profits will come back to us, and the Whitechapel householder may console himself with the certainty that his six shillings will sink again to three.

But these classes, powerful though they may be, and in Parliament a great deal too powerful, are not the people of England; they are not a twentieth, they are not a hundredth part of it; and what sort of future is it to which under the present hypothesis the ninety-nine are to look forward? The greatness of a nation depends upon the men whom it can breed and rear. The prosperity of it depends upon its strength, and if men are sacrificed to money, the money will not be long in following them. How is the further development of England along the road on which it has been travelling at such a rate for the last twenty years likely to affect the great mass of the inhabitants of this island? We have conquered our present position because the English are a race of unusual vigour both of body and mind – industrious, energetic, ingenious, capable of great muscular exertion, and remarkable along with it for equally great personal courage. If we are to preserve our place we must preserve the qualities which won it. Without them all the gold in the planet will not save us. Gold will remain only with those who are strong enough to hold it; and unless these qualities depend on conditions which cannot be calculated, and which therefore need not be considered, the statesman who attends only to what he calls the production of wealth forgets the most important half of the problem which he has to solve.

Under the conditions which I have supposed, England would become, still more than it is at present, a country of enormous cities. The industry on which its prosperity is to depend can only be carried on where large masses of people are congregated together, and the tendency already visible towards a diminution of the agricultural population would become increasingly active. Large estates are fast devouring small estates; large farms, small farms; and this process would continue. Every economist knows that it must be so. Machinery will supersede human hands. Cattle breeding as causing less expenditure in wages will drive out tillage. A single herdsman or a single engineer will take the place of ten or twenty of the old farm labourers. Land will rise in value. Such labourers as remain may be better paid. Such as are forced into the towns may earn five shillings where they now earn three; but as a class the village populations will dwindle away. Even now while the increase has been so great elsewhere, their number remains stationary. The causes now at work will be more and more operative. The people of England will be a town bred people. The country will be the luxury of the rich.

Now it is against all experience that any nation can long remain great which does not possess, or having once possessed has lost, a hardy and abundant peasantry. Athens lost her dependencies, and in two generations the sun of Athens had set. The armies which made the strength of the Roman republic were composed of the small freeholders of Latium and afterwards of Italy. When Rome became an empire, the freeholder disappeared. The great families bought up the soil and cultivated it with slaves, and the decline and fall followed by inevitable consequence. Tyre, Carthage, or if these antiquated precedents are to pass for nothing, Venice, Genoa, Florence, and afterwards the Low Countries had their periods of commercial splendour. But their greatness was founded on sand. They had wealth, but they had no rank and file of country-bred men to fall back upon, and they sunk as they had risen. In the American civil war the enthusiastic clerks and shop-boys from the eastern cities, were blown in pieces by the Virginian riflemen. Had there been no western farmers to fight the south with men of their own sort, and better than themselves, the star banner of the Confederacy would still be flying over Richmond. The life of cities brings with it certain physical consequences, for which no antidote and no preventive has yet been discovered. When vast numbers of people are crowded together, the air they breathe becomes impure, the water polluted. The hours of work are unhealthy, occupation passed largely within doors thins the blood and wastes the muscles and creates a craving for drink, which reacts again as poison. The town child rarely sees the sunshine; and light, it is well known, is one of the chief feeders of life. What is worse, he rarely or never tastes fresh milk or butter; or even bread which is unbewitched. The rate of mortality may not be perceptibly affected. The Bolton operative may live as long as his brother on the moors, but though bred originally perhaps in the same country home he has not the same bone and stature, and the contrast between the children and grandchildren will be increasingly marked. Any one who cares to observe a gathering of operatives in Leeds or Bradford and will walk afterwards through Beverley on a market day, will see two groups which comparing man to man are like pigmies beside giants. A hundred labourers from the wolds would be a match for a thousand weavers. The tailor confined to his shop board has been called the ninth part of a man. There is nothing special in the tailor's work so to fractionise him beyond other indoor trades. We shall be breeding up a nation of tailors. In the great engine factories and iron works we see large sinewy men, but they are invariably country born. Their children dwindle as if a blight was on them. Artisans and operatives of all sorts who work in confinement are so exhausted at the end of their day's labour that the temptations of the drink-shop are irresistible. As towns grow drunkenness grows, and with drunkenness comes diminished stamina and physical decrepitude.

The sums spent by English town operatives on gin and beer almost equals a second revenue; while every shilling swilled away is so much taken from the food and clothes of their children. In the country villages habits of life are different. The landlord can use his authority to remove or diminish temptation; but restraint in towns is with general consent regarded as impossible; no parish board, no government dares interfere; education, religion, philanthropic persuasion are equally powerless, and the rate of consumption of intoxicating liquors (usually at present poisonous as well as intoxicating), in proportion to the population, increases every year. The conditions under which the town operative works all encourage a reckless tendency: many occupations are themselves deadly, and the cry is for a short life and a merry one. Employment at best is fitful. The factory hand is generally perhaps earning overflowing wages. Then bad times come, and he works but three days a week, or four, or none. He is improvident in his abundance. His hand to mouth existence is unfavourable to the formation of habits of prudence. As a rule, he saves little, and the little is soon gone. The furniture goes to the pawnshop, and then comes want and starvation; and any shilling that he can earn he carries to the gin-palace, where he can forget the hunger-stricken faces which he has left at home. His own fault, it is said; but when particular tendencies show themselves uniformly in particular bodies of men, there must be causes at work to account for them. And besides drunkenness there are other vices and other diseases, not peculiar to towns, perhaps, but especially virulent and deadly there, which tend equally to corrupt the blood and weaken the constitution. Every great city becomes a moral cesspool, into which profligacy has a tendency to drain, and where, being shut out from light, it is amenable to no control. The educated and the wealthy live apart in their own streets and squares. The upper half of the world knows nothing of the under, nor the under of the upper. In the village the squire and parson at least know what is going on, and can use authority over the worst excesses; where men are gathered in multitudes it is impossible. Disease and demoralisation go hand in hand undermining and debilitating the physical strength, and over-civilisation creates in its own breast the sores which may one day kill it.

I have spoken of the effect of modern city life upon the body: it would be easy were it likely to be of any service to say more of its effect upon the mind. In those past generations, when the English character was moulding itself, there was a virtue specially recognised among us called content. We were a people who lived much by custom. As the father lived, the son lived; he was proud of maintaining the traditions and habits of his family, and he remained in the same position of life without aspiring to rise from it. The same family continued in the same farm, neither adding to its acres nor diminishing them. Shop, factory, and warehouse were handed down with the same stationary character, yielding constant but moderate profits, to which the habits of life were adjusted. Satisfied with the share of this world's goods which his situation in life assigned to him, the tradesman aspired no higher, endeavouring only in the words of the antiquated catechism, 'to do his duty in that state of life to which it had pleased God to call him'. Throughout the country there was an ordered, moderate, and tempered contentedness, energetic – but energetic more in doing well the work that was to be done, than in 'bettering' this or that person's condition in life. Something of this lingers yet among old-fashioned people in holes and corners of England; but it is alien both to the principles and the temper of the new era. To push on, to climb vigorously on the slippery steps of the social ladder, to raise ourselves one step or more out of the rank of life in which we were born, is now converted into a duty. It is the condition under which each of us plays his proper part as a factor in the general progress. The more commercial prosperity increases, the more universal such a habit of mind becomes. It is the first element of success in the course to which the country seems to be committing itself. There must be no rest, no standing still, no pausing to take breath. The stability of such a system depends, like the boy's top, on the rapidity of its speed. To stop is to fall; to slacken speed is to be overtaken by our rivals. We are whirled along in the breathless race of competition. The motion becomes faster and faster, and the man must be unlike anything which the experience of humanity gives us a right to hope for, who can either retain his conscience, or any one of the nobler qualities in so wild a career.

Is such a state of things a wholesome one? Is it politically safe? Is it morally tolerable? Is it not certain for one thing that a competition, of which profit is the first object, will breed dishonesty as carrion breeds worms? Much of it is certain to continue, unless England collapses altogether. Nothing but absolute failure will check the growth of manufactures among us; but is it absolutely necessary that the whole weight of the common-wealth should be thrown upon it? Is there no second or steadier basis to be found anywhere? I for one cannot contemplate the enclosure of the English nation within these islands with an increasing manufacturing population, and not feel a misgiving that we shall fail in securing even those material objects to which our other prospects are to be sacrificed. We shall not be contented to sink into a second place. A growth of population we must have to keep pace with the nations round us; and unless we can breed up part of our people in occupations more healthy for mind or body than can be found in the coal-pit and workshop – unless we preserve in sufficient numbers the purity and vigour of our race – if we trust entirely to the expansion of towns, we are sacrificing to immediate and mean temptations the stability of the empire which we have inherited.

If we are to take hostages of the future we require an agricultural population independent of and beside the towns. We have no longer land enough in England commensurate with our present dimensions, and the land that we have lies under conditions which only a revolution can again divide among small cultivators. A convulsion which would break up the great estates would destroy the entire constitution. It is not the law of the land, it is not custom, it is not the pride of family which causes the agglomeration. It is an economic law which legislation can no more alter than it can alter the law of gravity.

The problem is a perfectly simple one. Other nations once less powerful or not more powerful than ourselves, are growing in strength and numbers, and we too must grow if we intend to remain on a level with them. Here at home we have no room to grow except by the expansion of towns which are already overgrown, which we know not certainly that we can expand. If we succeed it can be only under conditions unfavourable and probably destructive to the physical constitution of our people, and our greatness will be held by a tenure which in the nature of things must become more and more precarious.

Is there then no alternative? Once absolutely our own, and still easily within our reach, are our eastern and western colonies, containing all and more than all that we require. We want land on which to plant English families where they may thrive and multiply without ceasing to be Englishmen. The land lies ready to our hand. The colonies contain virgin soil sufficient to employ and feed five times as many people as are now crowded into Great Britain and Ireland. Nothing is needed but arms to cultivate it, while here, among ourselves, are millions of able-bodied men unwillingly idle, clamouring for work, with their families starving on their hands. What more simple than to bring the men and the land together? Everything which we could most desire exactly meeting what is most required is thrust into our hands, and this particular moment is chosen to tell the colonies that we do not want them and they may go. The land, we are told impatiently, is no longer ours. A few years ago it was ours, but to save the Colonial Office trouble we made it over to the local governments, and now we have no more rights over it than we have over the prairies of Texas. If it were so, the more shame to the politicians who let drop so precious an inheritance. But the colonies, it seems, set more value than we do on the prosperity of the empire. They care little for the profit or pleasure of individual capitalists. They see their way more clearly perhaps because their judgment is not embarrassed by considerations of the Chancellor of the Exchequer's budget. Conscious that their relations with us cannot continue on their present footing, their ambition is to draw closer to us, to be absorbed in a united empire. From them we have no difficulty to fear, for in consenting they have everything to gain. They are proud of being English subjects. Every able-bodied workman who lands on their shores is so much added to their wealth as well as ours. An emigration even by millions would be infinitely welcome to them. They will absorb our people as fast as we can send them out, while in desiring to remain attached to England they are consulting England's real interests as entirely as their own. Each family as it establishes itself will be a fresh root for the old tree, struck into a new soil.

And yet statesmen say it is impossible. Wealthy England cannot do what wretched Ireland was able to do, and transport those whom she can no longer feed to a place where they can feed themselves, and to herself be a support instead of a burden. Impossible! The legislative union with Scotland was found possible, and there were rather greater difficulties in the way of that than those which obstruct a union with the colonies. The problem then was to reconcile two nations which were hereditary enemies. The problem now is but to reunite the scattered fragments of the same nation, and bridge over the distance which divides them from us. Distance frightens us; but steam and the telegraph have abolished distance. A Cornish miner and his family can now emigrate to the Burra Burra with greater ease, and at a less expense, than a hundred years ago they could make their way to a Lancashire coal-pit. St. George's Channel at the time of the union with Ireland was harder to cross in stormy winter weather than the Atlantic is at present. Before the Panama railway was opened, and the road to California lay round Cape Horn, London was as near it as New York: yet California was no less a State in the American Union. England would not hold the place which now belongs to her had there not been statesmen belonging to her capable of harder achievements than reattaching the colonies. It is not true that we are deterred by the difficulties. If there was the will to do it, if there was any real sense that the interests of the country required it, the difficulties would be found as unsubstantial as the proverbial lions which obstruct the path of the incapable. We are asked contemptuously how it is to be done. We ask in return, do you wish it to be done? for if you do your other question will answer itself. Neither the terms of the federation, the nature of the Imperial council, the functions of the local legislatures, the present debts of the colonies, or the apportionment of taxation, would be found problems hard of solution, if the apostles of *laissez-faire* could believe for once that it was not the last word of political science.

For emigration, the first step is the only hard one; to do for England what Ireland did for itself, and at once spread over the colonies, the surplus population for whom we can find no employment at home. Once established on a great scale, emigration supports itself. Every Irishman who now goes to the United States, has his expenses paid by those who went before him, and who find it their own interest being settled where there is such large elbow-room to attract the labour of their friends. It would cost us money – but so do wars; and for a great object we do not shrink from fighting. Let it be once established that an Englishman emigrating to Canada, or the Cape, or Australia, or New Zealand, did not forfeit his nationality, that he was still on English soil as much as if he was in Devonshire or Yorkshire, and would remain an Englishman while the English empire lasted and if we spent a quarter of the sums which were sunk in the morasses at Balaclava in sending out and establishing two millions of our people in those colonies, it would contribute more to the essential strength of the country than all the wars in which we have been entangled from Agincourt to Waterloo. No further subsidies would be needed to feed the stream. Once settled they would multiply and draw their relations after them, and at great stations round the globe there would grow up, under conditions the most favourable which the human constitution can desire, fresh nations of Englishmen. So strongly placed, and with numbers growing in geometrical proportion, they would be at once feeding places of our population, and self-supporting imperial garrisons themselves unconquerable. With our roots thus struck so deeply into the earth, it is hard to see what dangers, internal or external, we should have cause to fear, or what impediments could then check the indefinite and magnificent expansion of the English empire.

There is one more element in the question which must not be passed over. These are not days for small states: the natural barriers are broken down which once divided kingdom from kingdom; and with the interests of nations so much intertwined as they are now becoming, every one feels the benefit of belonging to a first-rate Power. The German States gravitate into Prussia, the Italians into Piedmont. While we are talking of dismembering our empire, the Americans have made enormous sacrifices to preserve the unity of theirs. If we throw off the colonies, it is at least possible that they may apply for admittance into the American Union; and it is equally possible that the Americans may not refuse them. Canada they already calculate on as a certainty. Why may not the Cape and Australia and New Zealand follow? An American citizen is a more considerable person in the world than a member of the independent republic of Capetown or Natal; and should the colonists take this view of their interests, and should America encourage them, what kind of future would then lie before England? Our very existence as a nation would soon depend upon the clemency of the Power which would have finally taken the lead from us among the English speaking races. If Australia and the Cape were American we could not hold India, except at the Americans' pleasure. Our commerce would be equally at their mercy, and the best prospect for us would be to be one day swept up into the train of the same grand confederacy.

It is easy to say that we need not quarrel with America, that her interests are ours, that we mean to cultivate friendly relations with her, with such other commonplaces. From the day that it is confessed that we are no longer equal to a conflict with her, if cause of rupture should unhappily arise, our sun has set: we shall sink as Holland has sunk into a community of harmless traders, and leave to others the place which once we held and have lost the energy to keep.

Our people generally are too much occupied with their own concerns to think of matters which do not personally press upon them, and our relations with the colonies have drifted into a condition which it is agreed on all sides must now be modified in one direction or another. Statesmen who ought to have looked forward have allowed the question to take its own course, till they have brought separation to the edge of consummation. The breaking up of our empire, however, cannot be completed till the country has had an opportunity of declaring its pleasure, and if the nation is once roused into attention, pricked it may be into serious thought by the inexorable encroachments of the poor-rate, it may yet speak in tones to which the deafest political doctrinaire will be compelled to listen. A very short time will probably see some decision taken for good or evil. Representatives from the colonies are said to be coming here in the spring,[1] to learn what they are to look to, and the resolutions then arrived at will be of immeasurable moment to their fortunes and to ours. It is no party question, all ranks, all classes are equally interested; manufacturers in the creation of new markets, landowners in the expansion of soil which will remove, and which probably alone can remove, the discontent with their increasing monopoly at home. Most of all is it the concern of the working men. Let broad bridges be established into other Englands,

[1] Unfortunately they are not coming. Since this article was written, Lord Granville has pushed separation one step nearer by throwing cold water on the proposal. He says that he does not desire the colonies to leave us, but he takes pains to exhibit his indifference whether they go or stay; and it is this indifference, so ostentatiously displayed, which is the active cause of alienation.

and they may exchange brighter homes and brighter prospects
for their children for a life which is no life in the foul alleys
of London and Glasgow; while by relieving the pressure at
home they may end the war between masters and men, and
solve the problems of labour which trades unions can never
solve.

That emigration alone can give them permanent relief the
working men themselves will ultimately find out. We cannot
save the millions of Irish. That portion of her volumes the
sibyl has burnt already. Are we to wait till our own artisans,
discovering the hopelessness of the struggle with capital, and
exasperated by hunger and neglect, follow in millions also the
Irish example, carry their industry where the Irish have carried
theirs, and with them the hearts and hopes and sympathies of
three quarters of the English nation?

Flectere si nequeo superos, Acherenta movebo!

If Mr. Gladstone and Mr. Odger are indifferent, we appeal to
Mr. Disraeli. This is one of those Imperial concerns which
the aristocracy, lifted by fortune above the temptations and
necessities of trade, can best afford to weigh with impartiality.
They too may find motives of prudence to induce them to turn
it over in their minds. There are those who think that if the
colonies are cut off, if the English people understand that they
are closed in once for all within the limits of their own island,
that they have no prospects elsewhere unless they abandon
their country and pass under another flag, the years that the
present land laws would last unmodified may be counted on
the fingers of a single hand.

THE COLONIES ONCE MORE*
James Anthony Froude

The storm which has burst over the Continent may clear away as rapidly as it has risen, or it may rage till it has searched out and destroyed every unsound place in the organisation of the European nations. Providence or Nature, or whatever the power is which determines the conditions under which human things are allowed to grow and prosper, uses still, as it has ever used, fierce surgery of this kind for the correction of wrong-doing; and if Providence, as Napoleon scornfully said, is on the side of the strongest battalions, it provides also, as Napoleon himself found at Leipsic, that in the times of these tremendous visitations the strong battalions shall be found in defence of the cause which it intends shall conquer. England for the present lies outside the lines of conflict. Whether she can escape her share of it depends on causes which she can but faintly control; and whether at the close of this present summer France or Germany lies exhausted, unable to strike another blow, or whether the circle of conflagration is to widen its terrible area till the whole world is again in arms, it behoves us equally to look to ourselves. We have obligations on the Continent which we cannot disclaim without dishonour, and dishonour tamely borne means to England political ruin.

A nation of thirty millions, inferior in mental and physical capabilities to no other people in the world, moated by the sea, defended by a powerful fleet, and united in themselves by hearty loyalty to their country, ought to be in no fear of the strongest force which could be hurled against them. But it is on this point of loyalty, of which it has been the fashion of late to speak contemptuously as a sentimental virtue, that the result of such an attempt would perhaps eventually depend. At this moment, if we were taken by surprise as Prussia has been, and a hostile power could by any means obtain twenty-

* From *Fraser's Magazine*, vol. 82 (September 1870), pp. 269–87.

four hours' command of the Channel, London would inevitably be taken; but if we are sound at heart, if England is to us all a home which high and low among us are alike determined to defend, as the treasure-house which contains all that we value in life, the loss of London would but nerve us to a more determined struggle, and we might still look forward to the last result with confidence. We might lose fearfully in life and property, but we should keep our honour untarnished, and our great place in the world unshaken. Have we, then, a right to expect a spirit in the great masses of our people which would carry us successfully through such a crisis? The English are instinctively brave and noble-minded. The traditions of the past are powerful, and there is a prestige attached to the present condition of the British Empire which for a time at least would raise all classes to a level with the demands on their endurance. How long their resolution would last, what amount and what duration of privations they would be contented to endure, depends, however, on the further question, what interest many of us have in England's stability – what each man would lose which is really precious to him if she fell from her place.

The attachment of a people to their country depends upon the sense in which it is really and truly their home. Men will fight for their homes, because without a home they and their families are turned shelterless adrift; and as the world has been hitherto constituted, they have had no means of finding a new home for themselves elsewhere. And the idea of home is inseparably connected with the possession or permanent occupation of land. Where a man's property is in money, a slip of paper will now transfer it to any part of the world to which he pleases to send it. Where it is in the skill of his hands there is another hemisphere now open to him, where employers speaking his own language are eager to secure his services. Land alone he cannot take with him. The fortunes of the possessors of the soil of any country are bound up in the fortunes of the country to which they belong, and thus those nations have always been the most stable in which the land is most widely divided, or where the largest number of people have a personal concern in it. Interest and natural feeling coincide to produce the same result. Ridicule as we please what is now looked upon as sentimentalism, we cannot escape from our nature. Attachment to locality is part of the human constitution. Those who have been brought up in particular places have a feeling for them which they cannot transfer. A family which has occupied a farm for one or two years will leave it without difficulty. In one or two generations the wrench becomes severely painful. To remove tenants after half a dozen generations is like tearing up a grown tree by the roots. The world is not outgrowing associations of this kind. It never can or will outgrow them. The *aroe et foci*, the sense of home and the sacred associations which grow up along with it, are as warm in the new continent as in the old. It is not that every member of a family must remain on the same spot. The professions and the trades necessarily absorb a large proportion of the children as they grow to manhood; but it is the pride of the New Englander to point to his namesake and kinsman now occupying the farm which was first cleared by his Puritan ancestors. The home of the elder branch is still the home of the family, and the links of association, and all the passions which are born of it, hold together and bind in one the scattered kindred.

England was once the peculiar nursery of this kind of sentiment, and thus it was that an Englishman's patriotism was so peculiarly powerful. It has seemed of late as if all other countries understood it better than we. In France, in Germany, in Russia, even in Spain and Italy, either revolution or the wisdom of the Government has divided the land. The great proprietors have been persuaded or induced to sell; when persuasion has failed they have been compelled. The laws of inheritance are so adjusted as to make accumulation of estates impossible. Two-thirds or at least half the population of those countries have their lives and fortunes interlinked inseparably with the soil; and their fidelity in time of trial is at once rewarded and guaranteed by the possession of it. England is alone an exception. When serfdom was extinguished in Russia, each serf had a share in his late owner's lands assigned to him as his own. The English villein was released from his bondage with no further compensation, and is now the agricultural labourer – the least cared for specimen of humanity in any civilised country. In France there are five million landed proprietors. In England there are but thirty thousand. Such property as the rest of us possess is movable. Thirty thousand favourites of fortune alone possess that original hold on English soil which entitles England in return to depend upon them in the day of trial; and thus it is that to persons who think seriously there appears something precarious in England's greatness, as if with all her wealth and all her power a single disaster might end it. No nation ever suffered a more tremendous humiliation than France in the second occupation of Paris, yet France rallied rapidly and is now stronger than ever. Her population remained rooted in the soil to which they are passionately attached, and their permanent depression is impossible. If she be defeated in the present struggle it will be ultimately the same. Forty millions of people can neither be destroyed nor removed; and where the people are, and where the land is their own, their recovery is a matter of but a few years at most. They may lose men and money, and possibly a doubtful outlying province, but that is all the injury which an external power can inflict on them. With England it is difficult to feel the same confidence. If the spell of our insular security be once broken; if it be once proved that the Channel is no longer an impassable barrier; and that we are now on a level with the Continent, the circumstances would be altered which have given us hitherto our exceptional advantages; and those of us who can choose a home elsewhere, who have been deprived of everything which should specially attach us to English soil – that is to say, ninety-nine families out of every hundred – will have lost all inducement to remain in so unprofitable a neighbourhood.

Let it be said at once that we are not blaming Government or blaming the laws because the small estates are absorbed into the large. It is the result of economic social and moral conditions which cannot be interfered with on a scale large enough to produce a sensible effect without paralysing the entire system of our national industry. It is a state of things, however, for which provision was instinctively made in past generations: As English soil became visibly too strait for its increasing population, not the Government, but the English themselves, by their own courage and energy, secured to the flag enormous slices of the waste places of the newly discovered world; enormous areas of soil in which ten times as many people as are now choking and jostling one another in our lanes and alleys might take root and expand and thrive; and the question is whether these spaces may not be utilised; whether, without rude changes at home, we may not exchange England for an English Empire in which every element shall be combined which can promise security to the whole. The fairest part of this vast inheritance was alienated from us by one set of incompetent ministers, it is now a rival, and may one day be a hostile power. The country, not the Government, explored and took possession of fresh dominions almost as splendid as what had been lost for them. What is to be done with these, whether they are to remain attached to us, or are to be affronted or encouraged into separation and what is called independence, is a matter on which Government may blunder a second time; the nation itself is alone competent to form and pronounce an opinion.

We make no apology for returning to a subject which was discussed in this Magazine a few months back when the political sky was comparatively clear; and the subsequent treatment of which in Parliament makes an appeal to the country itself more than ever necessary.

It is well known that to a particular school the colonies appear only a burden. Young communities cost money before the resources of a new country can be adequately developed. It is held that to part with them will be an immediate relief to the English taxpayer, that we can employ our people at home by developing our manufactures, and that the Government, untroubled with the responsibility of defending our remote and scattered dependencies, can provide cheaply, easily and certainly for our own security at home. The promulgation of these opinions has created much uneasiness in the colonies themselves, whose own almost universal wish is to remain under the sovereignty of the Queen. At home also to some persons they have seemed singularly shallow. Without colonies the natural growth of our population must overflow into foreign countries. The indifference with which we have allowed Irish emigration to drift into America has created an element dangerously hostile to us across the Atlantic, while it has embittered the already alienated feelings with which we are regarded in Ireland itself. In our own emigrating artisans, if we allow them passively to become parts of another community, we are losing elements of strength which might be of more worth to us than the gold mines of Ballarat.

The present Government, however, has been suspected of secretly favouring the views of the separatists. They have been several times called on during the late session to explain their real views, and the tone which they have taken in their replies indicates at any rate most signally the estimate which they have formed of the political magnitude of the question. Lord Granville has again and again repudiated all intention of shaking off the colonies. He insists that the policy which he pursues is that which on the whole gives most satisfaction to the colonists themselves, and tends more than any other which could be pursued to secure their attachment. He has said also, and whenever challenged he has repeated, as if with a consciousness that he was wronged by the suspicions entertained of him, that he admits the duty in case of war of defending the colonies against aggression with the whole force of the empire. The assurance is good in itself, but it is little to the point. No one suspects the Government of meditating treason, and it would be nothing less than treason wilfully to abandon the protection of any part of her Majesty's dominions. But whereas there are two possible colonial policies – one to regard them as integral parts of the British Empire, as an inheritance of the nation in which the crowded hive at home may have room to expand and strengthen itself, in which English families may receive portions of the land belonging to us in which to take root though circumstances deny it to them at home; the other, to concentrate ourselves in these islands, to educate the colonies in self-dependence, that at the earliest moment they may themselves sever the links which bind them to us – of these two policies it is believed that the Government deliberately prefer the second, and nothing that Lord Granville or any other member of the Cabinet has said upon the subject leads us to suppose that the belief is unfounded. A few words would have sufficed to remove the uneasiness, but those words have not been spoken.

Lord Granville is transferred to another department, but it is evident that there is to be no change in the colonial policy. Lord Kimberley's language is identical with his predecessor's. It is quite certain that in the opinion of Mr. Gladstone's Administration the colonies are rather elements of weakness to us than of strength, that they belong to themselves rather than to us, and that any endeavour on our part to develop their resources or transport the overflow of our people there will be wasted effort and money thrown away.

We say nothing of the withdrawal of the troops. That is an entirely secondary matter. No civilised nation in the world pays so much for its army as we do, and in none is there so miserable a result; and if there were any chance that our scanty regiments would be maintained in full efficiency at home, and would not be allowed to dwindle into skeletons under the blight of our military mismanagement, it might be wise to concentrate at the heart of the empire such means of defence as we possess. The self-governed colonies are perfectly capable of taking care of themselves, and they will defend to the last each their own portion of the British Empire, if they may be assured that they are to continue to belong to it. But the entire drift of the action of the Colonial Office points to a desire on our part that as soon as possible they should rid us of all responsibility for them. Our statesmen avow in their conduct what in words they are still compelled to disclaim. Our leading colonists are not invited to a share in the established dignities of the empire. They are not made members of the Privy Council. They are not admitted to the Bath, still less to the high distinction of the Garter. A new order is created especially as the reward of colonial merit. A difference in its flag is forced upon Victoria. The unanimous desire of the Australians for the annexation of the Fiji Islands is refused; as if to goad them into separate action on their own account, lest those islands should be appropriated for a naval or a penal station by some other power. When the Dominion of Canada was proclaimed, the Government organs declared, with no uncertain voice, that British North America might now be independent when it pleased. The present Governor-General, though he afterwards explained away his words, expressed a distinct wish that the gift of independence might be soon accepted. It is incredible that he would have dared to use such words unless they had been prompted from home. The late Governor, when Lord Granville disclaimed any desire to part with Canada, and denied that his policy tended towards separation, said in his place in the House of Lords that it undoubtedly had such a tendency, and for that reason he hoped the Government would persevere in it. The new Knighthood was bestowed osten- tatiously on a Canadian statesman who had avowed publicly his desire that Canada should be annexed to the United States. It was precisely as if Mr. Smith O'Brien had been made a peer when he went to Paris to ask the Provisional Government to undertake the protection of Ireland. A few weeks ago the *Times* spoke no less pointedly of the proposed confederation of the Australian Colonies and New Zealand as the birth of a new nationality. All this can bear but one interpretation. Such confederations in themselves may be good things or bad. They need not necessarily involve a separation from England, but the separation is what the party at present in power desire to promote, and the purpose is but faintly concealed in a few reluctant and partial concessions to public opinion, the guarantee of a loan to New Zealand and the delay in the complete evacuation of the Canadian Dominion till the Red River disturbances shall have been composed.

We do not believe that such a policy can be approved by the country in general. Were the issue fairly before the people it would be instantly repudiated. The fear is rather that they will look on inattentively, supposing that all is going well, till the mischief is consummated. It will then be past remedy, and the vengeance which will assuredly fall on the authors of it will be a poor compensation for an irreparable disaster. We choose the present moment, therefore, when the position of England must be causing serious thought to everyone who is capable of understanding it, to recall attention to a question which appears to us to be one of life or death.

It has two branches, which in the past session have unfortunately been argued apart, though, in fact, they cannot be separated; the political relations of the colonies with the mother country, and the possibility of the desirableness of a sustained and methodical emigration supported in part by the State in the general interests of the nation. These two subjects are factors in the same problem, for the only practicable means of attaching the colonies to us is by feeding them intelligently with emigrants who leave England grateful for the assistance which removes them from our surfeited towns to a situation where they can have a fairer prospect of a healthy and useful existence. No one in his senses proposes to reclaim for the discredited Colonial Office the control over dependencies which the home officials do not care to understand, and in the welfare of which they have no genuine interest. The object is to create or foster those natural links of affinity between Great Britain and her distant provinces which, to the disgrace of our political sagacity, we have permitted to grow unchecked between Ireland and the United States of America. At present, from causes far from honourable to us, those who emigrate on their own account prefer any flag to ours. The natural outflow is to New York, and every family which settles in the republic carries with it enmity to the home from which it has been driven, and leaves the germs of disloyalty behind in its kindred. The hope of those who see these things and dread their consequences is to turn the stream before it becomes too late to prevent the spread to England and Scotland of the same process which in Ireland has been so fertile in mischief; to relieve our towns of a plethora of people which is breeding physical and moral disease, and in furnishing our colonies with the supply which they most need, to give them an interest in maintaining their connection with us.

That a great State emigration is in itself possible, possible in the sense that there are no insurmountable obstacles created by the nature of things, and that if carried into effect in union with the Colonial Governments it would, beyond all other means, tend to bind them to us, even Lord Granville himself would hardly deny. The extent of our dependencies is so vast, and the wealth waiting to be drawn out there by human industry so enormous, that with proper provisions and preparations they could receive among them at present at least a quarter of a million of our people annually. The number for whom work could be found would increase in geometrical proportion. The Irish who go to the States send for their families; the English would necessarily do the same; and the strain upon the State, which even at first would be comparatively slight, would in a short time disappear. That the emigration question, therefore, and the political question should have been argued separately, has been a serious misfortune. It has enabled those who wish to keep things as they are to break the sticks each by itself, to represent emigration to our colonies as of no special consequence to us because our relations with them are uncertain, and to argue the impossibility of drawing those relations closer from experience of the bad results in the past of the mother country's interference.

In the early part of last spring a deputation waited on the Prime Minister to represent the distress in the manufacturing towns, and to recommend the establishment of an emigration system at the cost of the State. The Prime Minister gave a courteous but hesitating answer. He left it to be implied that he was himself in favour of the deputation's object, but that he must consult the Colonial Minister and the Chancellor of the Exchequer. He spoke, perhaps, in some irony, for the opinions of Mr. Lowe and Lord Granville might have been anticipated without difficulty. Lord Carnarvon followed in the House of

Lords. There had been an expectation that a subject of so much importance would have been alluded to in the Speech from the Throne, and the absence of it was significantly noticed by Lord Cairns. Lord Cairns, however, left England immediately after. Lord Carnarvon, as an ex-Colonial Minister, took upon himself to represent those who were dissatisfied with Lord Granville's proceedings; and he had an opportunity of rising above the position of a party leader, and treating the matter on the broadest grounds of statesmanship. Lord Russell, in the preface to an edition of his Speeches, had introduced a censure on Lord Granville so emphatic as to imply that if his policy produced its natural result, though he escaped impeachment, he would deserve and receive eternal infamy. Lord Carnarvon, however, confined himself to strictly political criticism. He evaded the larger bearings of the subject. He spoke merely as a member of the Opposition, anxious to avail himself of an opening to attack the Government in power. He gave Lord Granville an easy victory, for he had himself in office been no wiser than his antagonist. Lord Salisbury and Lord Derby were silent, and the discussion dropped as an unsuccessful party move.

A petition, very largely signed, from the working men of the metropolis was afterwards addressed to the Queen. It spoke the language of unbewitched common sense. It set out that England was overcrowded, that work for the people was not to be found at home, that they were loyal to the Crown and wished to remain British subjects, and that her Majesty possessed dominions in other parts of the world where there was room and to spare for them. They therefore besought her Majesty to close her ears to those who advised her to part with those dominions, to declare emphatically that the colonies were integral parts of the empire, and that the State would assist those who were willing to remove to them.

This petition was received by the Home Minister in behalf of the Queen, and a reply was returned more than usually characteristic of what Mr. Dickens called the 'Circumlocution Office'. Sympathy was of course expressed with the distress of the people. The value of emigration was ardently acknowledged. The Government, the petitioners were assured, would do everything in its power to promote their welfare. There were, however, as Mr. Bruce contended, laws of nature which it was hopeless and idle to resist. Emigration, like all other human movements, obeyed tendencies which were inherent in the order of things. Those who left their old homes in search of new, selected, necessarily, those countries to which access was most easy, where the climate was most favourable, and the land richest and most readily obtained. The United States, he said, possessed advantages in these respects superior to those of the English colonies, and therefore into the United States the main tide of emigration from these islands must continue to flow.

That Mr. Bruce's view of these advantages is in itself incorrect, and that other causes operate besides these supposed laws of nature, may be proved by the increasing pressure of the American population upon the border of the districts between Chicago and the Red River, which are as fertile as any lands in the world, and which, it is notorious, would, if annexed to the Union, be immediately and densely occupied. The Americans are kept out by the British flag. In them it seems the sense of nationality is something not so wholly unsubstantial. We are inclined to think, too, that in assuming allegiance to be a mere word, and personal interest their solitary principle of action, Mr. Bruce is passing a satirical comment on the character of the English which they have not yet deserved. Political economy, though supreme in the House of Commons, has not so far entirely superseded more old-fashioned motives; nor are we as a people so completely different from all other nations in the world, present or past, that it is a matter of indifference to us whether we do or do not become subjects of an alien power. The Russians do not emigrate at all, though their climate is not less severe than that of British North America. The sense of home is always strongest in the inhabitants of northern latitudes, and with it the more robust qualities which are developed by their more energetic habits of life. The northern nations of the old world have been larger-limbed and stouter-hearted than the children of those effeminate regions where the soil yields its harvest without labour and warmth generates indolence and languor. The future of America it is likely will resemble in this respect the past of Europe, and the hardy race which will hereafter dominate in that vast continent will probably be the men bred in New England and in that Dominion in which Mr. Bruce tells us it is impossible to persuade English emigrants to remain.

Mr. Gladstone, similarly taking up the other side of the

matter in the House of Commons, stated as a reason why a closer union with the colonies was impossible that the nearest of them, Canada, was divided from us by nature, by a waste of rolling water – and that what God had placed asunder it was vain for man to try to join. The objection can be forgotten when there is a desire to overlook it. New Zealand is at least as difficult of access from Australia, yet a South Pacific confederation is considered not only not as an impossibility, but is recommended as feasible and good. The ocean of which the Prime Minister speaks so fearfully is a highway, almost a railway, made ready by Nature to our hands. To a nation like the English, whose strength is on the water, whose wealth is in its trade, Nature herself could have devised no fairer means of communication. Every fraction of the empire is easily accessible, and to speak of Canada as necessarily separate from us because the Atlantic intervenes is less reasonable than it would have been seventy years ago to make St. George's Channel an objection to the union with Ireland.

But it was reserved for Mr. Goschen to speak the last and most instructive words as the opinion of the present Cabinet. Mr. Torrens, on the 17th of June, called the attention of the House of Commons to the want of employment in the great towns, and the increasing distress of the people. He pointed to the effect of voluntary emigration as tending, if left to itself, to strengthen rival nations at the expense of England. He showed that the movement so much to be dreaded had actually commenced; that the English artisans were already following largely the Irish example, and that of 167,000 working men who had left this country during the past year, 133,000 had become citizens of the United States. He invited the Government to assist those among them who were willing to remain Englishmen, still to preserve their allegiance. He recommended the establishment of cheap lines of communication with the colonies – cheap ships as we had cheap railway trains – and to enable any man who by contributing part of his passage money would give a proof that he was not a pauper, to remove in preference to Australia or to Canada. The adoption of such a scheme, he said, would, more than any other measure, attach the colonies to us, while the development of the colonies would as certainly be the surest means of increasing English trade. Lord George Hamilton spoke on the same side, but scarcely with the same effectiveness. He injured his argument by a side blow at the Irish Land Bill, and a proposition Imperial in its conception was degraded into a House of Commons movement intended only to embarrass the Government. In so plain a matter, however, it was difficult to go very far wrong, and his main arguments, like those of Mr. Torrens, expressed the convictions of almost every reasonable man. Mr. Goschen on the part of the Cabinet replied; and his speech will hereafter be looked back upon as we look back upon other strange utterances of men whom the tide of politics at critical times has drifted into power. Mr. Goschen insisted that no case had been made out for Government interference. The supposed distress had been exaggerated. The people had been suffering slightly from one of those accidental fluctuations to which the commerce of the country was periodically liable, but the worst part of the trial was already over. Trade was fast reviving. The prosperity of the working classes was returning, and as an infallible index of improvement he stated, amidst the cheers of the House, that they were consuming increasing quantities of beer, gin, and tobacco. The population was growing – growing at the rate of 300,000 a year – but England was not yet filled, and there was ample room for them all. The mills and mines would find them employment. The great towns would grow bigger. Great Britain tended more and more to become the workshop of the world, and the limit, if limit there was, to the capacity for internal expansion was still far off and invisible. Those who wished to emigrate at their own cost were of course at liberty to go, but Mr. Goschen protested against doing violence to the acknowledged principles of political economy by attempting to divert the outflow to one country rather than another. The United States would not like it, and that was sufficient.

Plainer language of its kind has not been heard in Parliament within the present century, and the reformed House of Commons illustrated its origin and justified Mr. Lowe's prediction of the effects to be anticipated from an extension of the suffrage, by the delight with which it listened.

All was well with the English working man because he was drinking more beer and gin. The Government was not at liberty to assist English subjects from one part of the Queen's dominions to another because it might happen to displease a foreign government. The last argument, we were told after-

wards by the *Times*, 'went to the root of the whole difficulty'
– truly a remarkable confession.

It is not to be supposed that such arguments as these express
the real conviction of men so able as Mr. Gladstone, Mr. Bruce,
or even Mr. Goschen. Their offhand answers may have served
the purpose as tricks of defence to parry the attacks upon
them, but the true ground of their resolution must be looked
for deeper down. They must have convinced themselves that
it is safe and desirable to allow the multitude of people which
is now crowded into this island to become denser than it is –
the feverish race for wealth, which is at present the sole motive-
power of English industry, to grow yet hotter and more
absorbing. We are to reap the harvest of manufacture while
our coal and iron hold out, and to leave the future to care for
itself. Mr. Gladstone is not a cynic, still less is he in himself a
mere worshipper of wealth. With one side of his mind he
shares in the old convictions of wise and serious men. He
'thinks nobly of the soul.' He believes with Plato – at any rate
he thinks that he believes – that the first aim of a well-ordered
commonwealth should be the moral improvement of the
human beings which constitute it. He would admit that the test
of a wholesome condition of things in any country is not the
balance-sheet, but the character of the people; that sobriety,
prudence, honesty, chastity, fear of God, and a physical existence healthy and happy because natural and good, are better
than all the cotton bales from all the mills of Lancashire. We
must suppose him, therefore, to think seriously that the
children of an English artisan dragged up among the gutters
of Sheffield or Spitalfields amidst Mr. Goschen's gin and beer
and their detestable concomitants have as good a chance of
growing up into healthy and worthy manhood as under the
free sky of Canada or New Zealand, where land is to be had
for the asking, and waits only for the spade to yield its crops.
These may be sentimental considerations, but Mr. Gladstone,
at any rate, is not insensible to them. What can be the arguments, then, which are outweighing them in his mind?

It is easy to understand the cheers of the House of
Commons. It is a house of rich men. Each Parliament that
meets is richer than its predecessor. The present – returned by
the enlarged constituency – is the wealthiest which has ever
sat in England. To a rich man no country can be more agreeable, no system of things more convenient or delightful, than

that in which we live. Inevitably, therefore, all that is going on will appear to him to be reasonable and just. The Noble Lords – I speak of some, not yet, happily, of all – are grown wise in their generation, and acknowledge the excellence of what they once despised. The growth of manufacturers has doubled, quintupled, multiplied in some instances a hundredfold the value of their land. Their rents maintain them in splendour undreamt of in earlier generations, which has now become a necessity of existence. They have their half-dozen parks and palaces; their houses in London, their moors in Scotland, their yachts at Cowes. Their sons have their hunters at Melton, their racing stables, their battues. In the dead season of sport they fall back to recruit their manliness with pigeon shooting at Hurlingham. These things have become a second nature to them, in which they live and move and have their being. Their grandfathers cared for the English commonwealth. It is hard to say what some of these high persons care for except idle luxury. To them, therefore, the system most commends itself which most raises the value of their property. The more densely England is peopled the greater grows the value of their acres without labour to themselves, and they well understand how to keep at arm's-length the inconveniences of the pressure. That such as they, therefore, should look with little favour on emigration is no more than might be expected. Still less favourably will those regard it who rank next to them, and who aspire to rise into their order – the great employers of labour. To the manufacturers abundance of labour means cheap labour, and cheap labour is the secret of their wealth, the condition of their prosperity, the means by which they undersell other nations and command a monopoly of the world's markets. Political economy, the employer's gospel, preaches a relation between themselves and their workmen which means to them the largest opportunity of profit with the smallest recognition of obligation to those upon whose labour they grow rich. Slavery, beyond its moral enormity, was condemned economically as extravagant. The slave born on the plantation was maintained while he was too young to work at his master's expense. His master had charge of him when he was sick, and in his old age when he could do no more he was fed, clothed, and lodged for the remainder of his days. The daily wages system, besides having the advantage of being a free contract, leaves the master at the day's end discharged of further responsibilities. He is bound to his workman only so long as it is his interest to retain him. While trade flourishes and profits are large he gives him full employment. When a dead season supervenes he draws in his sails. He lies by till better times return, and discharges his hands to live upon their savings, or ultimately to be supported by the poor rate till he needs their services again. The State, therefore, in assisting emigration interferes to rob him of his living. 'Keep the people at home,' said a noble Lord, 'we shall want them when trade revives.' Poor rates can be borne with, for those who are themselves little more than paupers share the burden of them. Even trades-unions and strikes can be borne with so long as the men confine themselves to higgling over the wages rate. Hunger will bring them to terms in time. Anything but a large emigration, for with emigration wages will rise in earnest and profits lessen. The man by whose toil the master has prospered has gone where his toil is for himself, where he is taking root upon the land, a sturdy member of the commonwealth, and the home market is relieved of his competition. The nation is richer for the change so long as he remains an English subject, but the capitalist employer loses a percentage of his profits.

Thus arguments of all kinds are pressed into the service to blind the working man to his obvious interest and prevent him from demanding what if he asks for resolutely cannot be refused. He is told that emigration supported by the State will lay an additional burden on the already heavy-laden taxpayers; that we shall be robbing the operatives who stay at home of part of their hard-won earnings, and making a present to others of what it is not ours to give. The objection is valid against the poor-rates as they are at present levied. There is something monstrous in compelling the petty shop-keeper, barely able to keep his own head above water, to contribute to the support of the discharged workman from whose labour when employed the shopkeeper drew no penny of advantage. But the advocates of State emigration do not contemplate a tax which shall touch the poor. The annual savings of this country are estimated by Lord Overstone at something near a hundred and forty millions. Mr. Gladstone points to the fifteen millions contributed voluntarily by the Irish peasantry for their own exodus, and asks who can be so sanguine as to dream of any such sum being raised by rate for the emigration of the English working men? The fifteen millions are an index, on one side, of the affectionate feelings of the Irish people. One active member of a family is sent to America by a subscription among the rest. Out of the abundance which he finds there he sets apart a sufficient sum to bring his brothers and sisters after him. This is the fairer aspect of it, but it is not all. Another and a darker passion animates the Celtic peasant to his efforts and his sacrifices, and that is hatred of England – hatred of the country which he charges unjustly with having been the cause of his misery, but which may be more fairly challenged for having attempted so little to remove it. The consequences of our long neglect of Ireland we have already experienced to our sorrow. The Church Act and the Land Act are the price which we have already had to pay for Fenianism, and they are probably not the last payment. If we escape (as we may not escape) being embroiled in this present war, yet if we allow an English voluntary exodus in the same spirit as the Irish, and directed to the same quarter, a statesman who can look beyond the next five years or ten has cause to tremble at the too certain consequences. Suppose that out of these hundred and forty millions a fourteenth part was taken to divert the stream to Australia and Canada and the Cape, to carry off annually a quarter of a million people, settle them on vacant lands, maintain them for the first year till the first crop was grown; if instead of letting them become so many thousand hostile citizens of the American Republic, we preserved them as loyal citizens of the British Empire, and secured with it the regard and gratitude of the working millions whom they left at home; if the masses of the English people were made to see at last that those in power were not wholly forgetful of them; it would be a not unwise investment if only as an insurance for the rest. What is the use of enormous wealth if we cannot defend it? and how can we defend it unless the whole nation has an interest in the stability of the country?

I shall be told that the cost will fall on the operatives at last; for capital requires investment. The hundred and forty millions provide fresh labour, and find fresh multitudes in food. It is not wholly so, for more and more of English savings goes abroad in loans to foreign governments, in maintaining French and Prussian armies, or finds labour, not for English artisans, but for Russians, Americans, or Turks. But the money that remains at home does not improve the condition of our people who remain upon our hands, it only multiplies their number.

It merely creates fresh manufactories, fresh workshops, fresh courts and alleys in our huge sweltering towns, and swells further the vast and weltering tide of human life in a space already grown too strait for it. Mr. Goschen ridicules the idea of a maximum. Where, he asks, is the line to be drawn? When can it be said that England is so full of men that it can safely hold no more? The maximum we should say had been reached when the population had passed beyond all rational control; when, if religion and morals have not grown to be unmeaning words, the population has swollen into a bulk which is the despair of minister and priest, of the schoolmaster and even the policeman; when hundreds of thousands are added annually to our numbers to grow up heathens in a country calling itself Christian. We should point to that very torrent of drugged beer and poisoned gin, the increased consumption of which Mr. Goschen and the House of Commons regard with such admirable complacency. Let but a severe war, or any one of the thousand calamities which nature has at its command, cripple or paralyse trade for a few successive years, and half our people will be left to immediate starvation, and to the furious passions which hunger will necessarily breed. If statesmen wait for other signs, the signs may come at last in the shape of catastrophes in which it will be too late to cry out for a remedy. There is, however, another symptom among us which we commend to the consideration, if not of Mr. Goschen, yet of his chief.

A few years ago the English public was shocked by the discovery of an institution at Torquay for the murder of babies. A woman named Charlotte Windsor undertook, for certain small sums of money, the charge of inconvenient infants, promising so to provide for them that their parents should be no longer troubled with the burden of their maintenance. The provision was a pillow or a handkerchief pressed upon their mouths, and a grave in Torbay or on the hill-side. The murderess was detected, but escaped execution by a legal subterfuge, and the example remained either to deter or encourage further experiments in the same line of business. On the 20th of last June, two other women were brought before the Lambeth Police Court on a charge somewhat similar. Charlotte Windsor was old. Many years had passed since she had 'given suck' or seen a baby smiling on her face. Such restraint as animal emotions can exert no longer served as a check on her calculated ferocity. These women were still of an age to be themselves mothers. One of them, the elder, had a child of her own at the breast. Their proceedings, therefore, were of a milder kind, and will save them too from the penalty which the Torquay assassin escaped so nearly. They put advertisements in the newspapers offering a home and a mother's care to any child whose parents desired to part with it; and for the small sum of five pounds they undertook to bring it up as their own, and educate it for service or a trade. The infants which passed into their hands were not smothered, but were allowed to die for want of nourishment, or were assisted out of the world by laudanum, lime water, or paregoric elixir. When death was evidently near, but before it arrived, they were carried away, the servants in the house being told that they were going back to their friends, and the next thing that was heard was that little dead bodies had been found by the police lying about in baskets or brown paper parcels.

Much natural horror is expressed at the exposure of so infamous a trade, but the trade itself is a mere bubble on the surface, an indication merely of a pervading poison at work everywhere in the under-currents of society. The population of this country increases at the rate of something like a thousand a day. The increase would be nearer two thousand a day if the average mortality among the children of the poor was no greater than among the more prosperous classes. Vast numbers of the human creatures brought into life in this island die before they are five years old, who would have survived with adequate food, clothing, shelter and care. We may be told that it is a law of nature. One pair of magpies would fill the globe in a century if four out of five that are hatched were not starved when they left the nest. Society cannot provide for the issue of improvident marriages or illicit concubinage. We have more children already on our hands than we know what to do with, and must be grateful that we are relieved of their presence by causes for which we are not responsible. All civilised nations have experienced the same difficulty, and dealt with it as they could. The Greeks and Romans exposed their superfluous babies. The Chinese do the same at present. The English as a Christian people leave it to nature. Child-murder remains a crime, but we none the less congratulate ourselves that an abstraction which we can disguise under the name of a law provides a relief for our overburdened system. Natural selection decides who shall live. The robust survive to contribute to the sinews of society. The sickly drop off and are spared a struggle to which they would have been unequal.

The enlightened persons who form public opinion in these matters do not usually belong to the classes which suffer, or they might acquiesce in these arrangements with less equanimity. Their children for the most part live and assist to keep down the averages. We can be wonderfully submissive to laws of nature while others only suffer from them. When our own shoes pinch we discover that with a little effort the shape can be altered. It is a law of nature that the strong shall prey upon the weak. It is a law of nature that if a house is not drained, the occupants of it shall be in danger of typhus fever. But there are very few laws indeed affecting man which are not conditional, and the chief purpose of human society is to control the brutal and elemental forces by reason and good sense. If the country cannot afford to rear more than a certain number of children, means ought to be attempted to prevent them from coming into existence. The infinite wretchedness produced by the present state of things ought not to pass for nothing. It has become not uncommon in these days to hear of miserable fathers and mothers unable alike to support their families or see them starve, destroying their children and themselves, and making an end of their troubles thus. Again, if we please, we may call in Providence. The classes which suffer most are toughest-hearted. The poor old Devonshire woman with eight hungry mouths about her, and nine shillings a week to feed them, looks with envy on the Lord's mercy to her neighbours whose babies die in arms, and sighs out, 'We never have no luck;' but this callousness itself is frightful, and is in itself one of the causes of the enormous mortality.

Put it as we will, half the natural increase of the population of this country is made away with by preventible causes – by causes which are prevented in the more favoured classes of society, and might therefore, so far as the nature of things is responsible, be prevented in all. Part of the destruction is caused by positive crime; part by unavoidable distress; part, and by far the largest part, by indifference and neglect. Omitting for the present those who are starved and those who are murdered, and confining ourselves to the great bulk of infant mortality, let us ask whether any means exist by which it can be successfully encountered. Encountered, I presume it ought to be if possible; we have not yet wholly outgrown the idea that there is something in human life more sacred than in the lives of animals, and a murrain among the cattle is considered a sufficient subject for an Act of Parliament. Men say impatiently that the parents are to blame; if the father spent the money which he wastes at the ginshop in providing better clothes and food for his family, this alone would save half of those who die; but duty is a matter of conscience, and you cannot make people moral by statute. We commend the consideration to the better thoughts of Mr. Goschen. Children, however, are the property of the State as well as of their parents; were it a question of sheep and oxen we should look about for some other answer. Unhappily, the supply of human creatures is in excess of the demand as English society is now constituted; and there is no interest public or private in keeping more babies than necessary alive. The fathers and mothers find them a burden, and statesmen with their hands full of other matters look on unconcerned. The neglect on both sides is monstrous, unnatural, and requires explanation; and the explanation lies in the organisation or disorganisation of modern industry; in tendencies at work alike in town and country, which increase in force in geometrical proportion with the extension of the modern conditions of labour. The artisans in the great cities, the agricultural labourers driven out of the old-fashioned hamlets and huddled into villages, are heaped together in masses where wholesome life is impossible. Their wages may be nominally rising, sufficiently, perhaps, to keep pace with the rise of prices, but wages form only a small part of the matter. The labourer lodges now many miles from his work. He leaves his home in the early morning, he returns to it late at night. The ground in town has become so enormously valuable that the factory hand and the mechanic can afford but a single room, at the best two. When his day's toil is over he has no temptation to return to the squalid nest which is all that society can allow him, and he finds the beerhouse and the gin palace a grateful exchange. The wife, obliged herself to work to supply the empty platters, must be absent also many hours from home; she has no leisure to attend to her children, and they grow up as they can, to fall a prey to disease and accidents which lie in wait for them at every turn.

A stranger travelling on a railway from end to end of England would think that there was no civilised country in the world where there was so much elbow room. He sees enormous extents of pasture land and undulating fallows cultivated to the highest point of productiveness, with only at intervals symptoms of human habitations. He sees the palaces of the noble and the wealthy set in the midst of magnificent parks, studded with forest trees and sheets of ornamental water, or maintained for game preserves and artificial wildernesses. In Scotland he sees whole counties kept as deer forests and grouse moors that the great of the land may have their six weeks' enjoyment there in the autumn. Room enough and to spare he would naturally think there must be in a land where ground could be devoted so lavishly to mere amusement. If he is guest at one of these grand mansions he will be told, as Mr. Goschen says, that over-population is a dream. He gazes across the broad-reaching lawns, or down the stately avenues. Miles distant he sees the belt of forest which bounds the domain and holds the outer world at bay. His host tells him with pride that from his own coal and iron are made the rails which shall link together the provinces of India, that there is no limit to English production, to English wealth, to English greatness. True enough, there never was in any country such productiveness, never any system which extracted larger material results from the loins and sinews of human beings, and never any which recognised less obligation to those beings by whose toil all this wealth has been created.

What would you have? it is impatiently asked. What ought to be done? I should say at any rate do not let the present condition of things develop further till you have learnt better how to govern it, and how to apportion better the moral and material proceeds of it. Remove as many of the people annually as will make room for the natural increase. You will then have breathing time to look about you and overtake the confusion which is every day becoming now more intolerable. At best you will succeed but imperfectly in reducing the numbers, for as you relieve the pressure at home many of the children who now die will survive. The employer may take heart. When we have done our utmost we shall make no depletion in the labour market. But the rate at which our moral disorders are growing will at least be checked. If nothing else we shall have saved a moiety of infants from a miserable death; and if England itself is to remain the land of those burning contrasts which are now so appalling we shall be planting a race of Englishmen elsewhere who may grow up under the happier conditions which belonged to our fathers. The aged oak may decay at the heart and yet still stand for centuries, when it is fed by healthy juices from its extremities. Two alternatives lie palpably open to us at this moment. Shall there be a British Empire of which the inexhaustible resources shall be made available for the whole commonwealth? Shall there be tens of millions of British subjects rooted in different parts of the globe loyal all to one crown, and loyal to each other because sharing equally and fairly in the common patrimony? Or shall there be an England of rich men in which the multitude are sacrificed to the luxuries of the few, an England of which the pleasant parks and woodlands are the preserves of the great; and the millions, the creators of the wealth, swill and starve amidst dirt and disease and vice and drunkenness and infanticide?

Every day makes it more clear that the true objection to emigration, the true cause of all this feeling so lately broken out among us that England is sufficient for itself, and that the colonies are a burden to it, is the interest of the landowners and the employers of labour. The time may come, perhaps may be very near, when their wealth may not be tenable on those terms. If we are put to the test we shall require all our strength, and it will be well for us if we have a nation to fall back upon whose loyalty we have deserved, and whose tempers we may safely trust. But we cannot have everything. We cannot have patriotism in the people, and political economy the sole rule of statesmanship. Money will not save us. We cannot buy off invasion as the failing Roman Empire tried to buy off the barbarians. We must rely upon the sentimental virtues, and we must take means to foster those virtues. If we tell the people in the name of our Government that they and theirs have no inheritance in the land of their fathers, that the world is a great market where they must higgle for themselves, and make their own bargains, the mill hand or farm labourer will be a mere fool if he risk his life or bear taxation for a country which disowns concern in him.

We are not particularly sanguine that a large Imperial policy will receive consideration, at this time especially, when there may be peril at our doors. Nor even were the horizon as clear as a few weeks since Lord Granville believed it to be, is it likely that the wealthy part of England would consent to a self-denying ordinance which would demand immediate sacrifices. Ten millions would be a cheap investment even now if it secured the attachment of the colonies, and taught our people that the commonwealth, in the old sense of that most meaning word, was still the care of English statesmen. After all, what are those hundred and forty millions of savings? They are savings from what? The whole of it is the produce of English labour, the earnings of the working men themselves, deposited in the hands of their employers. It is no very great thing to ask that a portion of this great sum should be expended in their interests.

Doubtless, however, a Parliament which would take this view of the matter would be a Parliament returned by the working men themselves, and the working men if they take the power into their hands will not use it for such a wholesome purpose as emigration. The working men have set far different ends before them. They see their masters growing in splendour and luxury. They see their own condition unimproved, and under the existing system unimprovable. They see the soil of England becoming the demesne of an ever-diminishing number of for-tune's favourites, and their cherished idea, it is well known, is a redivision of the land, and their own restoration to a share in the general inheritance. They know that the land laws of England are different from the land laws of any other country in the world. They do not ask how far the monopoly which they deprecate may be due to causes which legislation did not produce and cannot remedy. They do not enquire what the effect would be of a violent disturbance of landed tenures, or how far they would obtain from a division of the soil the happiness they anticipate. They look at France, once absorbed by the great as England now is; they see it now partitioned among five million families, each living free and independent among their own fields and gardens. They conceive that with just laws the same would be possible here.

Men possessed with an idea cannot be reasoned with. Divide England, Scotland and Ireland as they will, two-thirds of our thirty millions could not live on the produce of the land, and an interference with the rights of property would paralyse manufactures and destroy the means of support for the rest. As little can the trades-unions do for the distribution of the profits of labour with their arbitrary restrictions upon work and their wild notions of a dead level of reward, where the idle and incapable shall share alike with the skilful and industrious. The problem as they approach it is insoluble. They are like children grasping at the moon.

Nevertheless it is in these directions that their thoughts are running, and sooner or later the organisation of the unions will be turned upon politics, and upon securing a majority in the House of Commons to carry out these notions. The gin and beer are doubtless elements of conservatism. Mr. Goschen's satisfaction at the increased consumption of such things is not without reason. The thriftless vagabond who carries his week's wages on Saturday afternoon to the pothouse, and emerges out of his bestiality on Tuesday morning to earn the materials for a fresh debauch – this delightful being has nothing politically dangerous about him. He will sell his vote to the highest bidder, and look no farther than his quart of half-and-half. The working men, however, as a body, are alive to the disgrace of their order. Some day or other they may check for themselves what they have vainly petitioned the Legislature to assist them in restraining; and whether or no, the present elements of confusion in English society are sufficiently threatening. If we allow our industrial system to extend in the same manner and at the same rate of increase as hitherto, every feature most fraught with danger must increase along with it. The boundary line between rich and poor will be more and more sharply defined. The number of those who can afford to hold land must diminish as by a law of nature. The wealthy will become more wealthy, the luxurious more luxurious, while there will be an ever enlarging multitude deeply tinctured with mere heathenism, left to shift for themselves, and resentful of the neglect, with the cost of living keeping pace with the advance of wages, and therefore in the presence of an enormous accumulation of capital, condemned, apparently for ever, to the same hopeless condition, and yet with political power in their hands if they care to use it.

No one who is not wilfully blind can suppose that such a state of things can continue. Human society is made possible only by the observance of certain moral conditions; and tendencies which, if not positively immoral, are yet not positively moral, but material and mechanical, must and will issue at last in a convulsive effort to restore the social equilibrium.

England, itself, is committed for good or evil to be a great manufacturing country. Let her manufactures cease, and her political greatness is at an end. It is not equally necessary that they should be extended beyond their present limit. It is not equally necessary that the stability of the Empire should exclusively depend on them. Providence or our fathers' energy has brought splendid territories under the British flag, where fresh communities of us may spring up dependent on less precarious terms. The millions to be hereafter added to our numbers may be occupied in the cultivation of land, whilst our efforts at home may be turned, for the future, rather to improving the quality of what we produce than multiplying the quantity of it, and to bringing under control the dirt, and ignorance, and disease, and crime which are making our great towns into nurseries of barbarism. The employers might allay their alarms. The initial loss, if loss there was, would compensate itself in the goodwill of the employed, and in the improved work in which that goodwill would show itself. The surest road to the development of trade, it has been proved to demonstration, lies in the development of the colonies.

Little sanguine as we are, therefore, we conclude, as they say in the House of Commons, with a motion – we invite the Ministry not to follow Mr. Goschen in his satisfaction with the revival of trade, but to look upon it merely as a reprieve, as a breathing time in which they may take precautions against the return of evil days. We invite them to reconsider the political effects of the exodus of the Irish, and to regard it not as an example but as a warning. We invite them to reflect that, although our colonies might be considered an embarrassment to us if they were embedded in continents and accessible only through the territories of other nations, yet that with a water highway to their doors they are so disposed as to contribute to a mercantile state such as ours not weakness but enormous strength; that the ten millions by whom those colonies are now occupied might become fifty millions, yet the addition be felt only in providing openings for yet vaster numbers; that the sovereign of this country would be possessed of so many more devoted and prosperous subjects; and that by providing this outlet, the only sure measures would have been taken for the improvement of our people at home.

We invite them, therefore, to set themselves at once in communication with the authorities in the self-governing colonies, and learn from them how many emigrants annually, and on what terms, each of them is ready to receive. And for the Crown colonies, turning their backs resolutely on land jobbing and the scandals of the old mismanagement, to use the power which they have retained in the true interests of the commonwealth. A change in the political relations, if change is necessary, will follow hereafter of itself. Healthy confederations must grow, and cannot be made. The only stable bond of union is mutual goodwill.

GREATER OR LESSER BRITAIN*
Julius Vogel

About the end of the year 1869 much anxiety was felt, not only in political circles but throughout the country, on account of the supposed desire of several members of the Liberal Government to detach the colonies from the Empire.[1] The denials which were made and the discussions in Parliament which ensued are matters of history. They did not very much change the impression which previously existed, except to remove apprehension of immediate hostile action against the colonies.

Mr. Disraeli, in the address which he delivered to the Conservative Association at the Crystal Palace on the 24th of June, 1872, commented on the action which the Liberals had taken towards disintegrating the Empire. He said:

> If you look to the history of this country since the advent of Liberalism forty years ago, you will find that there has been no effort so continuous, so subtle, supported with so much energy and carried on with so much ability and acumen, as the attempts of Liberalism to effect the disintegration of the Empire.

He then commented upon the ability with which the effort

---

* From *Nineteenth Century*, vol. 1 (July 1877), pp. 809–31.

[1] 'If there is any lesson which we should draw from the loss of the United States, it is the misfortune of parting from those colonies in ill-will and irritation. We parted with those great colonies because we attempted to coerce them; and if we now part with our present colonies it will be because we expel them from our dominion. The circumstances are different, but the result will be the same, and that result must be the bitter alienation and undying enmity of these great countries. For my own part I see with dismay the course which is now being taken, a part at once cheeseparing in point of economy, and spendthrift in point of national character. I will be no party to it, and I beg to enter my humble and earnest protest against a course which I conceive to be ruinous to the honour and fatal to the best interests of the Empire.' – Lord Carnarvon in the House of Lords, February, 1870.

was sustained. Self-government, he considered, was granted to the colonies as a means to the end. He continued:

> Not that I for one object to self-government. I cannot con-
> ceive how our distant colonies can have their affairs
> administered except by self-government. But self-govern-
> ment, when it was conceded, ought, in my opinion, to have
> been conceded as part of a great policy of Imperial consoli-
> dation. It ought to have been accompanied by an Imperial
> tariff, by securities to the people of England for the enjoy-
> ment of the unappropriated lands which belonged to the
> Sovereign as their trustee, and by a Military Code, which
> should have precisely defined the means and the responsi-
> bilities by which the colonies should have been defended,
> and by which, if necessary, this country should call for aid
> from the colonies themselves. It ought further to have been
> accompanied by the institution of some representative
> council in the metropolis, which would have brought the
> colonies into constant and continuous relations with the
> Home Government. . . . Well, what has been the result of
> this attempt during the reign of Liberalism for the disinte-
> gration of the Empire? It has entirely failed. But how has it
> failed? By the sympathy of the colonies with the mother
> country. They have decided that the Empire shall not be
> destroyed, and in my opinion no Minister in this country will
> do his duty, who neglects an opportunity of reconstructing as
> much as possible our colonial empire, and of responding to
> those distant sympathies which may become the source of
> incalculable strength and happiness to this land.

Probably there was no part of the Conservative programme that more powerfully appealed to the masses of the people than this indirect pledge to respect the integrity of the Empire, for the feeling was very general that the Liberals did not care how soon it was broken up. Since the accession of the Con-servative Government to office they have scarcely ever failed on any available public opportunity to express the high con-sideration in which they hold the colonies.

It will be interesting to consider whether those utterances have had more meaning than mere grace and compliment. Seven years since, the feeling was wide-spread that the Government desired to detach from the Empire the colonies[2] not held for military purposes. New Zealand was virtually given to understand that she was at liberty to secede from the Empire; and in Canada and at the Cape of Good Hope[3] the respective Governors discussed the separation of the colonies as a contingency neither remote nor improbable. Lord Kimberley, the Secretary of State for the Colonies who preceded Lord Carnarvon, has, however, frequently stated that it was not the policy of his Government to throw off the colonies. No one would presume to doubt his Lordship's assertion, and it was made in a manner meant to convey that it expressed the truth both in letter and spirit. It is generally understood that individually some of the members of the late Government looked upon the colonies as sources of weakness, and it is scarcely unfair, in the face of these supposed individual opinions, and of Lord Kimberley's specific declarations, to come to a conclusion that the subject was discussed in Cabinet, and at some time or other a decision arrived at, that whatever the individual opinions of some of Her Majesty's Ministers might be, the Government should not adopt as their policy the disintegration of the Empire.[4] But without any policy of the kind, and with

---

[2] Throughout the rest of this paper, unless when the context otherwise implies, the word 'colonies' will be used to designate the constitutional colonies and the dependencies which are likely to become constitutional colonies.

[3] In North America, we have unmistakable indications of the rapid establishment of a powerful independent State. In Australia, it is probable that its several settlements, with their great wealth and homogeneous population, will see their way to a similar condition. In New Zealand the severance is being accomplished under very painful circumstances. In Jamaica, where responsible government was wholly inappropriate, it has ceased to be. In this colony I cannot think that any desire exists for its transfer to the rule of another power, neither can I think that, with its scanty resources and its divided population, it would desire to stand alone.' – Extract from Speech of His Excellency the Governor of the Cape of Good Hope (Sir P. Wodehouse), delivered January 25, 1870.

[4] Even the *Spectator*, one of the most able, earnest, and thorough-going supporters of Mr. Gladstone's Government, felt constrained to accept this view of the situation. Take the following passage for example:—

   'Ministers have changed their policy, have changed it very abruptly, and have changed it for the best of all reasons – because they had begun to discover that their line was not the line of the people of England, and would, if pushed to its logical results, end in events which would bring down the bitter displeasure of the people of England. Unless the colonies clearly understand this, we shall not reap half the benefit of the change, and therefore it is that we wish the only reasonable and intelligible *rationale* of

the intention to administer the law as it stood, a strong conviction might have been entertained that the colonies would in course of time be detached from the Empire, and that the sooner that result ensued the better.

Now Lord Beaconsfield's utterances mean otherwise. He looks forward to the colonies becoming more valuable to the Empire. He had nothing, he said at a banquet given to Her Majesty's Ministers by the Lord Mayor in 1875, to add to his previously expressed views, 'that we should develope and consolidate our colonial empire; that we should assimilate not only their interests, but their sympathies, to the mother country; and that we believe they would prove ultimately, not a source of weakness and embarrassment, but of strength and splendour to the Empire.' In Lord Kimberley and Lord Carnarvon we have the representatives of opposite points of view. Lord Carnarvon administers the Colonial Department as if he thought the colonies would remain with the Empire. He has asserted on several occasions an authority for the Colonial Department which his predecessor would not have claimed. It would be wrong to attribute to Lord Kimberley either indolence or indifference. He administered the Colonial Office not without exerting authority, but exerting it in a manner that indicated his aim to fit the colonies for a career of independence. Lord Carnarvon administers the department not only without a thought to such a change, but he constantly gives recurring evidence that he considers the colonies permanently bound to the Empire. South Africa has presented to him a most delicate and difficult problem. He might have temporarily dealt with it by refusing to recognise its gravity. But he has conscientiously grappled with it, and its various phases have found him not unprepared. It is probably reserved to him to complete the work of consolidation in Africa which he has so well begun. Then will belong to him the proud reflection that

this sudden change of front to be clearly understood there. This is in fact a death-bed repentance of the Ministry, by which we do not of course mean that it is a repentance made in the moment of its dissolution – far be it from us to anticipate that distant event – but a repentance that came only just in time to secure its salvation, to assert the most emphatic popular condemnation of its policy towards New Zealand. Had the colonial agitation and request for peaceable separation come, we at least entertain no doubt that even Mr. Gladstone's popularity would not have sufficed to save the Ministry.' – *Spectator*, May 21, 1870.

he stands alone in the character of his work – that no one before him by peaceful means has ever succeeded in consolidating such vast territories as those of Canada and South Africa. The reflection may nerve him to the larger task of consolidating the Empire. The annexation of Fiji and of the Transvaal Republic strikingly illustrates the difference, wide as the poles asunder, between the policies of the Liberals and Conservatives. The two administrations to which we have so lengthily referred thus typify opposite points of the colonial question.

It is not, of course, to be supposed that the desire to see the colonies separated, or indifference to such a result, is shared in by all Liberals. On the contrary, amongst the Liberals the colonies have strong supporters. There has been no more powerful utterance in favour of confederation than the address delivered by Mr. Forster, at Edinburgh, in November, 1875, though much of the force was lost by the unfortunate declaration that if a colony wished to separate he would be no party to preventing it. Mr. Childers, again, must be credited with a high opinion of the value of the colonies. He has never abated the early interest he took in them, and probably commands from them more personal support than any other English statesman. Mr. Magniac, Sir R. Torrens, Mr. Mundella, Mr. McArthur, and Mr. Kinnaird have stood forward at various times as earnest advocates of colonial interests, and Sir John Lubbock has lately given evidence of the same goodwill by laborious investigations, the results of which have been published in these pages. It is generally understood by the colonists that the colonies remain colonies because it suits them and the mother country that they should so continue. It is equally generally supposed that if the colonies wished to secede they would not be forced to remain – that they are free to go. From this has followed the wide-spread feeling that the independence of the colonies is merely a question of time; and the colonists are insensibly imbibing that belief. If it is meant to retain the colonies, can any words do justice to the folly and the wickedness of training the people to a false belief as to their future institutions, of teaching them to expect that for which they ought not to look; of leading them along a path at some point of which the destiny they are taught to believe in must be overthrown?

The practical follows the theoretical, and the colonies involuntarily exercise their power in the direction in which they believe their destiny tends. It is difficult to establish that the question is urgent. It cannot be made to appear urgent in the ordinary sense. It cannot be said. 'If you neglect to deal with this question during this or that session, calamity will arise before you meet again.' But is that not urgent, the delaying to do which means in years to come a compound interest of calamity? The question is urgent in the sense that the forest-planting question is urgent. You may destroy forests and neglect to replace them, and the middle-aged may not live to suffer in consequence. But the time will come when the country will suffer, when regularly flowing rivers will become fitful torrents, when the earth, deprived of its moisture and its soil washed into the ocean, will cease to produce as it did before the hand of man commenced to destroy without concurrently reproducing. Who could point to the exact time when destruction exceeded desirable limits and reproduction became an imperative necessity? Even so, who can say when it may be too late to deal with the colonial question? In calmness and repose it may be easily dealt with. But when immediate urgency appears, when angry passions are aroused, when it will be perceived that the course of legislation during the long past, and the direction in which men's minds have been trained, have all converged to a future disintegration, what hope then without disaster to preserve the unity of the Empire?

The colonists, as a rule, are ardently loyal, and those who emigrate to colonies recall to themselves in the reproduction of the institutions to which they have been accustomed the scenes and the ties they have left behind them. They love to think that they have not abandoned their country, but merely removed to another portion of it. The young persons born in the colonies are taught to venerate and love the mother country. Yet the idea prevails alike amongst those who are born in or who emigrate to the colonies that the time will come when these will be independent. If this assumption is wrong, and it is not meant to break up the Empire, is it not vicious to educate these young communities to a false view? And if this false view continue, if this national independence always looms in sight, must not the time come when it will be imperatively demanded, and even the most trifling incident at any moment may cause the demand to arise? Nor is the idea that the colonies are growing into nations confined to the colonists. The originators of colonial constitutions had it largely in their minds. It finds favourite expression in after-dinner speeches, and not unfrequently in the House of Commons, when speakers launch into patronising remarks describing the colonies as young nations. From that point of view which regards the colonies as integral and inseparable parts of the Empire prognostications of the kind are little short of treasonable. They are and should be open to the same exception as would be taken in the several countries concerned to advocating the separation of Ireland from Great Britain, Hungary from Austria, Alsace from Germany, or the reinstatement of Poland as an independent kingdom.

A settlement one way or other should be arrived at, so that the nature of their future position should be made known to these communities. If the colonies are to understand that they have not, and will not have, the power to deprive the Sovereign of these realms of portions of her dominions, and that every inch of territory is dear to the Crown, let it be so declared. There is one very difficult point to be considered – would the colonies have the right to complain of a decision which would deprive them of the prospect of future independence? If the question were put before them of immediate independence or continuing to remain with the Empire, the election would probably be favourable to the latter. But a feeling more or less strong has grown up, that independence has been placed at the disposal of the colonies, and it might be to some extent felt that they have a right to the choice. In other words, the education in the direction of independence already alluded to has made progress, and the question is, ought it to be recognised? There are those who will say that the very fact of this question having to be asked is a proof that it would be better to leave the subject alone. We might agree with this view if we held that ultimate separation was a conclusion to be desired. But if the nation should, as we believe, recoil in horror from such an eventuality, it is clear that the longer the impression is allowed to continue that the colonies have the right to expect future independence, the more difficult will it be to remove or deal with it.

Here it may be aptly asked, why alone of all nations is Great Britain to hold her dominions by ties so slender, that their disruption is virtually invited? In the greatest of her difficulties, and in spite of all temptation, Spain has refused to relax her grasp on Cuba. The United States, carved by force of arms from out another nation, was not long in learning the lesson that the first duty a country owes to herself is to preserve her own integrity. Hence the later, and perhaps the grander, of her two great wars. Is it because Great Britain, having first provoked the war by her own misconduct, failed to come off victorious in the struggle, that she is for all time to come to be so cowed, so timorous, as to submit to her Empire being broken up by any one who succeeds in persuading her subjects in any part of her dominions that they will do better to set up on their own account? If Great Britain is indeed to become a second-rate power in the scale of nations, let her people have the gratification of carrying with them into obscurity the recollection that they renounced the colonies, not these renounced Great Britain.

Before considering the details of a scheme of confederation, it would be well to further pursue the point of the right of the mother country to impose it on her colonies. It might be considered expedient to give to the colonies separately the power of deciding within a definite and early time whether each would join the confederation or prefer an independent career; but it is to be doubted whether the colonies have at present the right to demand such an option. True, the acts of constitution seem to lead to future independence; true, such an idea was in a measure present in the minds of their framers; and true moreover that it has been offensively pressed on the colonies by the doubts freely expressed as to whether they are sources of strength or weakness to the Empire. But, on the other hand, property is property, and the right to it ought not to be prejudiced by inexact and inferential obligations. The designs of a political school, and the quiet success with which such designs have been worked out, cannot be held to bind or commit those who have not been a party to them. The property of the sovereign in the dependencies of the Empire should be more firmly asserted in consequence of any doubts thrown upon it. To give to the colonies this option would in itself be an admission of a right to which, notwithstanding they have been deceived, they can scarcely be said to be entitled. But there is a limit to all things, and if they are too long allowed to remain under a false impression, something of a right must grow up.

If the union is to continue only so long as both the colonies and the mother country are contented with it, if the mother country or any colony at any time can end the connection, then it is impossible that the union can be more than temporary. The time must come when one side or another will see, or think it sees, an advantage in separation. The doctrine that the union should depend for its continuance upon the pleasure of either party to it affords a comfortable excuse for inaction. Meanwhile it serves the purpose of those statesmen who strongly desire to see the colonies abandoned, and do their best in various ways to promote that end without declaring their purpose, without the knowledge of their sovereign or the support of their country. There is no more disagreeable phase of existence than that of a feeling that a quiet but powerful movement is being exerted in a direction contrary to one's wishes, but with such concealment and denial that it is nearly impossible to rouse others to the sense that a counteracting movement is necessary. Like the Italian dungeon that slowly contracted round its inmate till it crushed him to death, but the diminishing volume of which it was difficult to perceive, so are many subjects crushed into unwelcome shape by a force unapparent in its action until the effect approaches completion. A union, lasting only as long as all parties to it please, means a union open to be insidiously undermined by opponents, means one liable to be broken by innumerable accidents, means one which even its friends assist to destroy, for in contemplating the contingency of its future disturbance they shape their course to meet that consequence. If the union is desirable, it should not be open to question. The institutions, the policy, the legislation, the habits and the thoughts of the people should grow round and about it till the unity of the Empire becomes embodied in the inmost affections and traditions of the nation.

It will be very suggestive to consider what are the prevailing ideas concerning the colonies entertained in the mother country. It would be idle to pretend to determine with even approximate accuracy the numerical strength of the supporters of the various views. But the attempt to do so will have its use; for the proportions can be guessed with sufficient exactness to lead to the conclusion that the present position of public thought upon the subject is eminently unsatisfactory. Probably two-fifths of the population of the United Kingdom have friends or relations in one or more of the colonies. Inasmuch as these two-fifths comprise in great measure the adult population, it is a larger proportion of the thinking population than at the first glance appears. But only a small number of those who have friends or relations in the colonies have an accurate knowledge of more than one colony. Even the particular colony to which their connections belong is often known to them but slightly. A substantial knowledge of the colonies is mainly confined to those who have resided in them, or who have political or business relations with them. But interest in the colonies is not confined to those who have a knowledge of them. A very large proportion of the adult working classes hold the colonies in high, though mystical, veneration. The colonies, to them, are places where, if they ever resolve to leave their native towns or villages, they may find all the comforts denied to them at home. They think of the colonies as lands of plenty – as lands where the labouring man is held in high estimation – as lands where a career is open to him, where he can become an employer instead of a servant, above all where he can become an owner of land, and where his children will be well educated and have great positions within their reach. For the higher classes the colonies have less attraction. To them, the colonies are lands in which it may or may not be desirable to try to make money. Some emigrate with the hope of bettering their positions, but hoping also to return to the mother country, although it is commonly the case that they remain there by preference after they have earned the means to live at home. A great many who never visit the colonies try to make money through their business connections with them.

But, whatever may be the feelings entertained concerning the colonies themselves, the minds of the vast mass of the people are quite colourless on the question of the relations between the mother country and the colonies. They recollect that disintegration was talked of some years since, and are under the impression that it was abandoned on account of its unpopularity. They think it was a freak of a small body of politicians, and that it was finally disposed of by the Conservative reaction. They are less disposed to struggle about it now than they were seven years ago, when the question was more before them. They have no knowledge of the changes constitutional government has worked in the colonies. If they were questioned on the subject, they would probably say England is essentially a colonising country, and they suppose will continue to hold her dependencies. Why should she give them up? If she could afford them before steam and electricity made communication easy, why should she now get rid of them? Even of those who most prize the colonies, few will look upon the subject as pressing. Of those who really do consider the question, and with whom therefore its practical decision rests, a powerful section believes that it would be well, both for the mother country and the colonies, that the connection should be severed. They think that to propose the severance would be unpopular, but that, if the matter be left alone, the result will work itself out. A much larger section shares the belief as to what the result will be, without desiring it. They look upon the matter as decided, and they think it only a question of time when these young nations will declare themselves. The zealous longers for separation, and those who believe it must come whether they like it or not, compose nearly all of those who have thought about the question. There remain a few very ardent men who long for confederation, who believe it to be possible, but who hesitate to commit themselves to the course which must be taken when it is desired to initiate a great political crusade. They are not wanting in earnestness. It may be they are not agreed as to what is to be done; and it is useless to preach a theory without indicating the practice that should flow from it.

The case here presented is less hopeless for confederation than at first sight might appear. If the vast body of the people, whose minds are now colourless on the question, are favourably predisposed to retaining the colonies, there is good material to work on if the case be vigorously taken up. Given those who are willing to become advocates of the cause, they will find multitudes ready to follow them; and large as their object is, they may reduce it to the simple proposition that it is the duty of the mother country to declare that she holds, and will hold, the colonies as part of her territories – that throughout the Empire the people must grow up in that belief, and must shape their legislation, their institutions, and their aspirations accordingly.

The question of whether confederation is desirable is another way of asking if it is desirable to retain the colonies. But although the declaration of the unity of the Empire must pave the way to confederation, it is not to be supposed that the work of confederation will end with such declaration. When once the unity is declared, a serviceable machinery must follow for giving to the colonies a share in the government of the Empire proportioned to their importance. What might have been without the constitutions the colonies enjoy it is useless now to consider. They have been made in large measure self-governing communities; and if they are not to be independent, they must have, as an alternative, a share in the government of the country.

In considering, from an imperial point of view, the policy of retaining the colonies, let us ask ourselves what positions the colonies fill, and of what consist their charms and counter-charms. It has already been said that to the great mass of the people of this country the colonies have an engrossing and peculiar fascination. It is not to be supposed that this arises from a conviction or impression that they are better governed than the mother country. The colonies have not the leisured classes that really govern the United Kingdom. The masses generally are not inclined to undervalue the ability and unselfishness of the leisured classes. To those whose very exist-ence depends on daily toil, the charm of a life to which all toil is unnecessary assumes an exaggerated character. The spectacle, then, is most forcible which constantly meets the view of the workers by compulsion – the spectacle of work, hard, absorbing, laborious work, performed by those who, but for ambition, a love of doing good, and an innate sense of the *noblesse oblige*, might lead lives of Epicurean ease. This volun-tary hard work is not confined to those holding positions of conspicuous power. The willingness to labour, the desire to do good, the determined mastery of special knowledge for pur-poses of philanthropy, the devotion of time and means, and the subordination of ordinary engagements to the pursuit of many varied objects, are sufficiently common to make the bulk of the people think they are not unfortunate in the classes which mainly wield the governing power. It would be an injus-tice to the discernment of the people to suppose that they are of opinion that amidst the absorbing pursuit in the colonies of pecuniary gain abler governing men are to be found. They may be pleased at the idea that the government of the colonies is more generally distributed amongst all classes of the popu-lation, but they do not feel that therefore that government is abler. It is the space, the unoccupied room, that the colonies enjoy, which speaks to the hard-worked denizens of a densely

populated country. Next to Belgium, England, in proportion
to its area, is the most heavily populated country in the world.
It has a population per square mile nearly double that of India
and Japan, and more than three and a half times that of the
Chinese Empire. Taking Great Britain and Ireland together,
the population per square mile, though much less than that of
England and Wales alone, exceeds very much the population
per square mile of any country in the world excepting Belgium.
Can it be wondered at that the colonies have such charms to
those who most suffer from the crowding? The colonies are
the safety-valves of the poorer classes, and the affection which
they feel for them is to be justified by logical considerations.
Recent developments, which point to the permanent loss of
foreign markets for many different articles of British manufacture, have increased the hardships of the crowded state of the
country, and much enlarged the desire to seek new homes in
the colonies. Of course this desire is controlled by the cost of
emigration. It is the fashion to speak of the vast improvement
in the condition of the labouring classes. In instituting a comparison between the then and now, no consideration seems to
be given to the growth of new wants. If a similar comparison
were to be made between the past and present conditions of
the middle classes and of the upper classes, it would be recognised that so many new necessities had become inseparable
from their lives that the requirements which sufficed for their
predecessors would be insufferably insufficient for them. The
lower classes are amenable to the same argument. For them
also new necessities and wants have arisen, as sternly
demanded for their comfort as were the recognised wants of
bygone times. As man continues to live, his wants increase
with the improved knowledge of how to supply them. The
denial of the new wants inflicts as much hardship as the denial
of the old. A great deal of the so-called improvement in the
condition of the working classes has to be qualified by the consideration of the demands necessary to insure the same amount
of comfort and happiness. If an abstract standard could be set
up, we might compare the condition of the working classes
now with that of the early inhabitants of the country, who
found in the woods and forests a larder and wardrobe, with
which they were satisfied till they learned to require something
better.

The dread of the producing power and the population of the

mother country being reduced is unreasonable, if the subjects of the nation, their wealth, industries, and resources are merely transferred from one part of the Empire to another. It is otherwise if the mother country has no external possessions, and the wealth and population that she loses pass to other countries, making them proportionally more and her less powerful.

The landed proprietors are generally supposed to feel little interest in the colonies, and to be opposed to emigration to them. At first sight such a feeling seems natural, but on reflection its short-sightedness is apparent. The emigration of agricultural labourers may, it is true, raise the rate of agricultural labour, or, perhaps it is more correct to say, prevent it from falling. The landed proprietors, again, are not likely to be swayed by those sentiments of personal liking for the colonies so deeply sunk in the minds of the working classes. A colony may become the home of the working man and his family. The landed proprietor does not look forward to anything of the kind. Even if some junior members of his family go to the colonies, their ambition in commencing is to make enough money to be able to live at home, although frequently, as has been said, a residence in the colonies changes this feeling to one of preference for the new home. But if the landed proprietors have not the same personal interest in the colonies as that possessed by the working classes, they have indirectly a very deep interest, and one with which the coming years are likely to vividly impress them. The maintenance of those institutions they most prize, the safety of their order, of their lands and their family possessions depend upon the colonies remaining as outlets for surplus home population. If England is to be kept within herself, it cannot be long before the conditions of land tenure are rigidly scrutinised, and the question asked if the nation has not the right to buy up the land for redivision into smaller holdings. But revolutionists would vainly raise such questions whilst the means to become possessors of estates in the Empire is more open to the poorer classes of to-day than it was to those who in times past, from the humblest beginning, founded some of the greatest families in the country. The landed proprietor should see in the colonial outlet his best guarantee of safety, and, with the humblest classes, should sturdily resist the decolonising policy of the international school. Lord Beaconsfield has at various times vigorously asserted the common interests that bind together the extreme classes – the landed and the labouring classes. Probably in no sense is this more remarkably true than in that great interest which the labouring and landed classes jointly have in upholding the colonies against the machinations of the politicians who reduce everything to a pounds, shillings, and pence denomination, and whose chief notion of the future is compound interest.

The probable increase of the population of the colonies is a subject full of interest. In a masterly speech recently delivered by Sir Hercules Robinson, the Governor of New South Wales, on the subject of intercolonial federation, some calculations were given as to the increase of the population of Australia. Sir Hercules is of opinion that he is below the mark in the following estimate:

> Supposing, however, that only the recent New South Wales increase of 4 per cent. annually is maintained, the population of this continent at that rate at the end of the present century – twenty-five years hence – will be over 5,000,000; twenty-five years later it will be 12,500,000; while in the year 1950 it will be 31,250,000, which was the population of the United Kingdom by the last census taken in 1871.

Mr. Forster believes he will be within the mark in estimating the population of the British North American, the Australasian, and the South African colonies at the end of this century at 15,000,000, and accepts as a certainty that before the middle of next century 'our colonies within the temperate zones' will outnumber the population of the United Kingdom. Sir Hercules and Mr. Forster are both moderate in their prognostications, and we venture to predict that their estimates will be immensely exceeded if, in the meanwhile, the colonies are constituted inalienable portions of the Empire. In the face of a declining foreign trade, it is of the utmost importance to commercial Great Britain to cultivate the colonial trade. But it is by some denied that the trade follows the flag. We are of those who believe otherwise. It is incontestable that there is scarcely a civilised nation whose ambition or jealousy or economical policy does not prompt it to desire to use as little as possible British manufactures. Great Britain has, with equal liberality, preached and practised free trade, but it is to be doubted if she has gained two nations to her opinions. In each country a few advanced men adopt free-trade principles, and very much they are glorified in return in English publications. But the nations themselves do not yield, and perhaps, if the governments stated exactly what they thought, they would say that they know what suits their respective countries better than the English who so kindly volunteer their advice. England's foreign trade is falling off, and is likely to continue to do so, because she is dealing with unwilling customers. In the colonies she may be sure of constantly increasing trade and willing customers.

A very interesting paper on the colonies was read by Mr. Archibald Hamilton in 1872 before the Statistical Society, in which he specially set himself to show that the trade followed the flag. He adduced the instance of the conquered colonies. For example, the French Canadians, who have never been absorbed into the British colonial population, consume a very small proportion of French as compared with British goods, without the latter enjoying any protection. The Dutch population at the Cape affords a similar example, whilst conversely the trade of Java is essentially Dutch. Mr. Hamilton gives some interesting figures as to the consumption of British products per head of population in British possessions and in foreign countries. He takes the average of three years, viz. the year of census with the preceding and succeeding years. The consumption of the North American colonies 1*l.* 5*s.* 8*d.* per head; Australia and New Zealand, 8*l.* 10*s.* 3*d.*; Cape and Natal, total population 2*l.* 6*s.* 4*d.*, white 8*l.* 12*s.* 2*d.*; West Indies, 2*l.* 8*s.* 7*d.*; Mauritius, 1*l.* 14*s.* 7*d.*; United States, 17*s.* 10*d.*; France, 6*s.*; Spain, 2*s.* 1*d.*; Portugal, 10*s.* 4*d.*; Germany (Prussia, Hamburg, and Austria), 6*s.* 11*d.*; Italy, 4*s.* 3*d.*; Russia, 11*d.*; Holland, 2*l.* 16*s.* 2*d.*, a portion of which probably belongs to Germany; Belgium, 11*s.* 10*d.*; and Brazil, 11*s.* 2*d.* Mr. Forster, three years later, pursued the same subject at Edinburgh. He said:

> I must ask you to look into the facts for yourselves, and if you do so I think you will incline to believe that the balance of evidence shows that the trade does follow the flag. Remember, all that is required to justify this opinion is to have ground to believe that we have more trade with the colonies than we should if they were foreigners. Take these figures. We find by the parliamentary returns that our exports last year were in value to

		£
Australia (including New Zealand)	more than	20,000,000
France	less than	30,000,000
British North America	more than	10,000,000
The United States	less than	33,000,000
The Cape and Natal	about	4,700,000
China	less than	5,000,000

He went on to point out that the seven millions of colonists are not bad customers. 'Our import from them is about 11 per cent., and our export to them about 12½ per cent., of our import and export to and from all foreign countries.'

An important point, to which Mr. Hamilton calls attention, should be remembered. The British trade with the colonies is not represented only by British exports and imports. There is a great deal of indirect trade under British auspices. The colonies draw supplies from all parts of the world. In a majority of cases these are paid for by British exports to the supplying countries. The whole course of colonial trade is in connection with British houses and British joint-stock companies. Let the colonies cease to be British, and we may be certain that, to whatever extent they are able, they will endeavour to divest their trade of its British character.

The colonies already absorb large amounts of British capital, and would absorb much more if it were understood the union was to continue. Doubts as to the colonies separating from the mother country alone stand in the way of larger investments. The *Times* recently published a return of the sums owing by certain defaulting States for principal and interest, by which it appears that no less an amount than 335,000,000*l*. is due to credulous England, of which she is likely to recover very little. With consummate irony the *Times* headed the paragraph 'English Charities abroad'. Whilst the colonies continue to belong to Great Britain it is scarcely possible for them to default. The interest and principal of their public debts are made first charges on their whole yearly revenues. The governor, the government, and the audit department would be guilty of a gross infraction of the law if they allowed a penny of public money to be paid away for ordinary services whilst any of the legally constituted first charges remained unsatisfied. The colonies, therefore, must pay their debts before their ordinary services can be carried on. As far as private affairs are concerned, the laws of the colonies offer as much security as the laws of Great Britain. It is urged we are aware that the colonies are no more friendly than foreign countries to British commerce. This is deduced from the supposed leaning of the colonies to Protection. A great deal of misapprehension exists on the subject. It may safely be said that the bulk of the colonial discussions about Free Trade and Protection are of a *doctrinaire* character. Whether the colonies are avowedly in favour of Free Trade or Protection, their actual policy is much the same. New South Wales, for example, is a colony firmly imbued with the principles of Free Trade. The Colonial Treasurer in his last Budget proposed that tobacco manufactured from colonial leaf should be subject to an excise duty of 6*d.* as against 1s. 3*d.* chargeable on tobacco manufactured from imported leaf. He hinted also that at some future time there should be an excise duty on wine and sugar. He does not propose this at once. He knows that colonial wine and sugar would never have been produced and manufactured if at the commencement they were subjected to an excise duty. But he wisely foresees that in the course of time they will be able to compete with imported articles of the same kind, and contribute to the revenue. Meanwhile, like his Protection-favouring neighbour Victoria, he relies on his customs revenue to supplement the revenue derivable from sales of land, from railways, and from other sources. He has more land revenue than Victoria, so he does not require so much customs revenue. His stamp and succession duties may be a little more severe than those of Victoria, but practically they do not come to much, and otherwise he has no direct taxation. Canada, assumed to be favourable to Protection, has heavy excise duties which yield an amount equal to a third of the customs duties and one-fifth of the entire-revenue. But none of the colonies, we believe, have a property or an income tax, and it is not difficult to discern the reasons which lead to their avoidance. The colonies depend little upon any feeling for or against Free Trade, but much upon a keen appreciation of the immediate interests to be served. The annual profits in the colonies of almost every business or profession are, as a rule, unequal. To reckon these profits as income, and not to regard a considerable part of them as capital, would be imprudently to forget the possibility of lesser earnings in succeeding years. Hence there is not that well-defined distinction between capital and income that is to be found in older established countries, and an income tax would be regarded as to some extent a tax on capital. A great deal of foreign capital is invested in the colonies in various enterprises. By foreign is meant capital not belonging to owners residing in the colony. An income tax would very much discourage the introduction of such capital which is generally considered to be of service in promoting undertakings which otherwise might be neglected. To a property tax there are even stronger objections. In most of the colonies a large part of the country is still unsettled and unsold Crown lands. A property tax on sold land would more than by its own amount reduce the value of the land which remained to be sold. There is a popular idea that such land should be given away, but no one who has watched the experience of several land systems in different colonies can doubt the subtle force of Gibbon Wakefield's dictum, that even if the money is to be thrown into the sea it is better to exact for the lands from which the Crown parts a fair price. A property tax would not only affect the value of unsold Crown land, but discourage settlement. The cultivation and improvement of land are of paramount importance in these young countries, and a property tax would have a deterring effect. By means of rates property is made to contribute to local purposes. This, however, is not regarded as a hardship, for the return for the payment is more apparent than if the money went to the Treasury. The Government of Victoria lately went to the country on the policy of a property tax to be levied with the object of enabling the customs duties to be reduced. From a late telegram it is to be inferred this object has not found favour, since after the election the Government tendered their resignation. Both sides, however, appear to incline towards some kind of property tax, and there is little room to doubt that such a result is approaching. That it is so rather confirms the arguments which have been used. Victoria has given away, or parted with very cheaply, an immense quantity of her best land. Strangely enough, a conception of maintaining, and benefiting by, the value of her public estate has never found a place in the policy of her public men, so that the fear of a property tax injuring that value does not deter them. Besides, if they really gave heed to that consideration, the colony having divested itself of so much land has approached the margin beyond which the returns from a property tax may more than compensate for the injury to the value of the unsold estate.

The colonies, then, find it on the whole convenient and expedient to chiefly rely upon the customs as a means of raising revenue, apart from any considerations in favour of protection. Discussions take place as to which articles should be taxed, which admitted duty free, and a great deal is frequently said about Protection. But if a certain amount of revenue has to be raised through the custom-house, and this end be kept steadily in view, the details are not of very much importance. There is every reason to believe that, if confederation took place, the colonies would readily lend themselves to the consideration of a Customs union or agreement. They rather lean to the opinion that the mother country was unmindful of what she owed to her children when in respect to their trade she placed them on the footing of foreign countries, and claimed from these credit for the unselfish manner in which she was willing to deal with her own possessions. For the rest, if a colony does sometimes legislate in a manner which shows more anxiety for its own than for the mother country's interest, let what has already been said be remembered, that the colonies are being educated into the belief of future independence.

It has been urged that, whether or not the colonies continue to be united with the mother country, they will receive emigrants from it. To such an extent as this is the case, the arguments as to the separation of the colonies closing the outlets of emigration from Great Britain and reducing the rate of wages are modified. The separation of the colonies would not altogether close emigration to them, but the emigration would be very different in nature and extent. From a national point of view the emigration to colonies which had become independent nations would be the reverse of beneficial. Granted that the evil of an overcrowded population is great, yet it is only a lesser evil to a nation to lose large numbers of its subjects. The emigration to the United States during the last twenty-five years has lost Great Britain more of her subjects than the wars of the whole of the century. It has not been the removal of so many of her subjects to other portions of her dominions with the purpose of extending the power and prosperity of the country, but it has been the departure of hostile subjects, who, besides hoping to find a more congenial home, have to a greater or less extent carried away with them unfriendly feelings to the country they have left. The Irish emigration to the United States nearly caused Great Britain, and possibly in the future may yet do so, a war which would cost more than the most lavish liberality could devote to the material improvement of the colonies.

It is very much to be questioned if it is possible for Great Britain and her colonies to separate with mutually friendly feelings, although, as has been said, they are being educated into expecting separation. If, at the last, separation proceed from the action of the mother country, the colonies will vividly retain a feeling of soreness at the slight they will consider put on them. If the separation arise through the action of the colonies, there will remain with Great Britain the bitterness arising from the conviction that the lofty aspirations of the past are frustrated, and that a small career remains to take the place of a great destiny. The progress of the released colonies would be so many reproaches to the country that had been deprived of them. Inasmuch as, whenever separation occurs, it will not be clear to whose fault it will be due, and each will blame the other, the probabilities are that the bitterness of feeling will exist on each side.

Suppose the colonies detached, emigration to them will mean emigration to a foreign country. To Great Britain it will mean the loss of so many subjects, with the not unwarranted suspicion that each subject lost means one gained by a not very friendly nation. True, to whatever extent such emigration may proceed, it may serve as an outlet for an overcrowded country driven to great straits. But how vastly different the ebb and flow from one part of the same dominion to another of a friendly population, seeking in less crowded areas more scope for industry and enterprise, to driving people from their country under the oppressive influence of actual want, or, as in the case of the Irish proceeding to America, under the influence partly of want and partly of a feeling of strong resentment against the Government of the country they are leaving.

Even if it were statesmanlike to view with complacency the loss of so many of a country's subjects, it is not to be supposed that as a mere outlet the colonies when independent will suit the interests of the poorer classes as they do now. Emigrants from the mother country land in the colonies amongst their fellow-subjects on a footing of perfect equality. Let those who know the feelings with which the native-born Americans receive the Irish emigrants deny that the position of persons seeking in a new country a new nationality is widely different from that of emigrants who proceed from one portion of their own dominions to another. Although, too, if the colonies were independent, assisted emigration from the United Kingdom might not altogether be stopped, it would be fallacious to expect it would continue on the same scale. Some of the colonial governments now assist German emigrants, but such assistance is small in proportion to that which they render, and are likely to render, to their own countrymen. In brief the whole character of the interchange of population would be altered if the colonies became independent nations. In the one case emigration means the beneficial dispersion through the Empire of friendly subjects, in the other an outlet for the disaffected to swell the ranks of the unfriendly of other nations.

The confederation of the Empire would largely encourage the investment of capital in the colonies. Great Britain finds the money for the wars of other nations. When two countries determine to fight, they look to Great Britain for the money they require. She aids in keeping up the immense armaments of the Continent; she finds the means for the employment of the labouring population of foreign countries; she opens up those countries by railways and other modes of communication. It is natural that capital should seek investment. But how much would be absorbed by the colonies if it were understood they were to continue parts of the British dominions! We have already said that investors in colonial securities and colonial enterprises have before them the contingency of separation. With separation the value of property in the colonies and of colonial securities would for a long while be much depressed. As new nations, they would be subject to the difficulties, the changes, and revolutions, from which young countries are seldom free.

If new territory were to spring up from the sea, adjoining Great Britain, as soon as it could safely be visited, it would be covered with works. British capitalists would eagerly invest their means in what they would regard as beyond doubt their own territory. Declare the colonies inseparably portions of the Empire, and they will be so many provinces added to Great Britain. Enterprise, population, and capital would fly to them, not only in the shape of joint-stock enterprises, but in that of enterprises personally conducted, or conducted on personal behalf. At present, such is the want of confidence in the permanency of the connection with the colonies, that trust funds (notwithstanding that in the deeds of trust no prohibition is contained) are not allowed to be invested in colonial lands or colonial securities, although such investment is permitted in some Indian securities not enjoying an imperial guarantee. The want of means of investing trust funds is notorious, but their colonial investment has been obstinately opposed – the principal ground being the doubt whether, in course of time, the investment might not prove to be made in a foreign country. The rise in the value of their securities, and the flow of capital, enterprise, and population which would follow confederation, would no doubt greatly benefit the colonies, and reconcile them to a position which, to some people, might appear the lesser one of being part of a great confederation, instead of becoming separate and independent nations. The colonies now believe, and many people in Great Britain share the belief, that they may at their option cease to be parts of the Empire. Is that a position a great nation should accept, to be exposed to dismemberment at the pleasure of her dependencies? The favourite dictum is, that England will never burn another ounce of gunpowder to retain a colony that wishes to be free. Is it possible to fail to see that such a condition is only compatible with the belief that the time for secession will come?

If the great colonies are to continue parts of the Empire, it is utterly unreasonable that they should be free from all contribution towards national expenditure. The fleet belongs to the nation, and is essentially for the service of the nation, and nothing can justify freeing the colonies of British America, South Africa, and Australasia from contribution towards its cost, except the intention to free them from the nation. Whilst they possess so little property and population, their proportionate contribution would not be large, and, with the intention of getting rid of them, the anti-colonial party may think it wise to forego the present contribution to lessen the difficulty of severing the connection. But consider what those colonies will be fifty years hence, and the extent to which they might and should relieve the tax-payers of the mother country, while helping to maintain an irresistibly powerful fleet. If Great Britain will be stronger without her colonies, it seems to be clear that she would be stronger without India. The possession of the latter is at least as likely to lead to complications which might commit the nation to an exercise of power or the necessity of expenditure. The United Kingdom should either divest itself of all external dominions, or make the scheme of the nation march with their continued possession.

Humanitarian influences might be appealed to. It is at the least probable that if the colonies become independent they will for a considerable period be subject to all those ills of internal and external war which overtake young countries. They will fight amongst themselves sometimes empire; they will combine to fight against others; they will in some cases, before their institutions attain to the age which commands reverence and veneration, experience a great deal of internecine dissension and bloodshed. The United States may be considered very fortunate in having had only one great civil war, but what a destructive war that was! If the colonies of Great Britain become independent, they cannot hope to escape war and war's consequences. A confederation, on the other hand, whilst it would be free from civil war, would, in time, own such a powerful fleet that it would escape war with foreign countries. To no class of persons should confederation more appeal than to those who desire to abolish the horrors of war.

Concerning the plan of federation we have already said that the mere declaration of the continued unity of the Empire would arrest its disintegration. But before the declaration was made some heed would have to be given to the conditions of that unity. Even were it desirable, it could not be expected, after all that has taken place, that the mother country would retrace her steps, and the colonies submit to such an alteration in their prospects, without a knowledge on each side of what the change meant. The colonies have been too much advanced on the road to self-government to submit to a total exclusion from a share of control in the affairs of the Empire, and we have already admitted that they should contribute to the national expenditure by bearing a portion of the cost of the navy. Obviously the share of control should increase with the share of contribution. It is not to be supposed that the contribution would be very large at first, though made on strictly fair terms. The proportions of population and property in different parts of the Empire should rule the rate of contribution. A census throughout the Empire might be taken every five years, and on the results the payments of the next five years be based. Although there should be so much payable on account of population and property, it should be open to each part of the Empire to make up its contribution in the way it determines. It need hardly be said that it should be no part of the policy or scheme of the confederation to interfere with the local government of either the mother country or her confederated dependencies. Some difficulty might be experienced in deciding whether and to what extent native population and property should contribute.

The references made to the fleet required for the Confederated Empire presuppose a very powerful naval armament – one so powerful that it would be safe from all attacks, and that it would, as far as could reasonably be expected, relieve the Empire of the dangers and risks of protracted or even brief wars. The Confederated Empire could afford to pay for any fleet that could possibly be found desirable. Each portion of the Confederation would probably have its own local forces, and as it became necessary, provision could be made to give to those forces a combined and consolidated character. It is often argued that the colonies would be sources of weakness to the mother country in case of war. Too much weight is probably attached to this idea. If Great Britain and America were at war, Canadian territory would very likely be involved, but it would be just as well to make Canada the battle-field as any other territory; somewhere the fight would have to be fought out. With this exception, the colonies, for a long while to come, are not likely to be prominently affected by war. No nation would desire to permanently occupy or wantonly injure them. They might be placed under contribution, but any amount so obtained would wait the settlement of the war. If victorious, Great Britain would exact restitution; if not victorious, the loss inflicted on the colonies would form a small fraction of the total bill of costs. It really comes to this, then, that, to the extent of their value as strategical points, the mother country should encourage the fortification and defence of the colonies. Those which remained unfortified would suffer little if a clear understanding existed as to the consequences of war being shared by the whole Confederation. The money the colonies have expended, and are continuing to expend, on fortifications, shows they are not afraid of their proper share of responsibility.

To resume, the control or representative power should correspond with the contribution. The question of representation is the great stumbling-block in the way of confederation, not on account of its real, but of its fancied difficulties. What! swamp the House of Commons with colonial votes, add to the many embarrassments of party another perhaps as troublesome as the Home Rule combination? Anything is better than that, and thus many who have large views of what a confederated empire might be shrink from the subject. If their fears were to be justified, there would be small hope of federation, for it is easy to see how great would be the objection to relinquishing for the United Kingdom a thoroughly local government. But it should be quite as vital a point to maintain the ordinary government of Great Britain as the ordinary government of any dependency. The aim should be to build up a federal government without impairing the machinery of ordinary government. If this were well understood, there would be no inconvenience from haste on the part of the colonies. Whilst they would not consent to be excluded from a prospect of either independence or of control in federal affairs, they are by no means eager for immediate representation. For some time to come they would be well content with representation at a Board of Advice to the Secretary of State for the Colonies. This, at any rate, would not be a revolutionary step, for it would be only following the example of the Council of the Secretary of State for India. After a time, which could easily be designated in advance, the population, wealth, and importance of the colonies would entitle them to more direct representation, and their representatives should form part of the Federal legislative body. The constitution of the Federal Legislature would not involve much difficulty. The House of Lords, as one chamber of it, would equally be available for the Federal Legislature as for the ordinary Legislature of Great Britain. There is nothing to prevent persons who may reside in the colonies from being called to the peerage, and already many peers possess considerable colonial estates. The House of Commons, as the House of Commons for Great Britain, should not be disturbed. It is a question very important, but which need not be decided at the moment of confederation, whether the Federal Lower Chamber should be the House of Commons plus the colonial representatives, or whether the Federal representatives of Great Britain should be distinctly and separately selected. The Imperial Parliament, until the Federal Parliament grew into being, should, as it now is, be superior, and the Government of the United Kingdom would be the executive of the Confederate Empire. There are two familiar instances of exceptional representation that show how easily particular requirements can be dealt with. In the French Legislature the colonies of France are represented; in the House of Representatives of the United States, territories are allowed to be represented by delegates.

The measure of confederacy, then, which we advocate, is a declaration that the colonies are inseparably portions and provinces of Great Britain; that all parts of the Empire should contribute to the cost and maintenance of the fleet; and that, in course of time, as the importance of the outlying dominions warrants it, all parts of the Empire shall be represented in the Federal Legislature; and that, in the meanwhile, the colonies be represented at a Board (or Council) of Advice to the Secretary of State for the Colonies.

Many references have already been made to the advantages the colonies would enjoy from federation, while it has not been concealed that possibly they may to some extent think that their independence has been so guaranteed that they have the right to complain of its being denied to them. But it is to be supposed they would be consulted during the passage of the measure; and, whatever the hopes held out to them, they are not entitled to set up the result of the machinations of a few statesmen against the wishes of the vast masses of the people. And the colonies have much to gain. There will be preserved to them a national feeling – a desire to be great amongst the great, not amongst the little, to be parts of a powerful Empire instead of being powerless independent countries. They will save themselves from the risks of small States – the risk of external wars with countries like themselves, or internecine wars as various parties in the State energetically try to assert the supreme control. Nor will the colonies be pecuniarily losers. Against the actual contributions they would make might be set the increased value of colonial securities and colonial property already mentioned. They might indeed regard their payments as premiums of insurance on their possessions, which in consequence of such payments would be more than proportionately increased in value.

And what does confederation mean to Great Britain? It means that, instead of sinking into a small money-loving State – a second Holland – she is to retain in her own dominions her subjects and their wealth, and not to drive them abroad. The enterprise of her people is to be devoted to enlarging the power of their country, instead of their diminishing it by becoming the subjects of other nations. The trade which she is losing, as other nations are able to supply themselves with their own manufactures, she will more than regain through the wants of millions of her people dwelling within her various dominions which she will have to satisfy. She will look forward not to declining trade, but to its unlimited increase. For the great mass of her population, the toiling millions, she will retain the possessions which will open to them and their children and children's children the means of rising to distinction and wealth if their ambition so prompts them. The most powerful of nations, with irresistible naval armaments, she will be able to stay war. The pauperism of the country will be reduced by the increased demand for labour; and portions of the British possessions, which are now wildernesses, will be covered with useful works and teem with prosperous communities.

The endeavour has been made to show in this paper –

1. The unsatisfactory nature of the relations between the mother country and the colonies.

2. The urgent necessity for doing something to arrest the disintegration towards which progress is being made.

3. That a union, depending upon the pleasure, for the time being, of the different parts of the Empire, means separation sooner or later.

4. That, under the union-during-pleasure condition, much is being done to hasten separation.

5. That the mother country is entitled to retain and consolidate her possessions.

6. That confederation is desirable, and would be fraught with advantage both to the parent country and the colonies in the shape of increased trade, increased value of property, the augmented happiness of the people, and the saving of much misery and disaster.

7. That its accomplishment does not present great difficulties.

THE VALUE TO THE UNITED KINGDOM OF THE FOREIGN DOMINIONS OF THE CROWN*
Robert Lowe

In ancient times the value of a territorial acquisition to the country that obtained it was a very simple affair. The colonies of Greece were considered by the parent state mainly in the light of outlets for the redundant population of a poor and mountainous country. The colonies of Rome were planted almost entirely for military purposes, and, if they answered these, nothing else was demanded from them. But as regards territories acquired by conquest or by cession the case was very different. After undergoing a spoliation more or less complete they settled down into a miserable and abject dependence a tribute was wrung from them regulated rather by the greed of the exactors than by the ability of the tributaries, and the choicest of their youth were enrolled in the armies of their cruel and rapacious conquerors. The measure of the value of such an acquisition was just what could be wrung from it in men and money without destroying its power of further contribution. The Spaniards did not even observe this rule. In their greed for gold they exterminated the natives of Hispaniola in working the mines, and were thus driven to the humane suggestion of Las Casas, the importation of Africans to supply the race which they had murdered. The value of these acquisitions was therefore the realised property and the labour of the race, whether extorted from them in the character of slaves or tributaries. From this sum there was very little deduction for the expense of government. A few magistrates exercising indiscriminately executive and judicial functions without diligence and without appeal or revision, sufficed for the government of such a society, which may be best described as

* From *Fortnightly Review*, vol. 22 ns (November 1877), pp. 618–30.

a state of collective slavery. Whatever may be thought of the morality of such a proceeding, we cannot wonder that the acquisition of a state to be held on such terms was regarded as a source of wealth to the conquerors. What we seek to discover is, what in the absence of all these cruel and unjust means of acquisition, and after allowing for the expense of a thoroughly efficient and good government, is the value to the paramount state of a foreign dependency. We are not aware that such an inquiry has ever been attempted, nor can we regard it as a mere matter of curiosity. Occasions are continually arising when it is of the utmost importance to know accurately the worth of the interests with which we have to deal, and the statesman can no more dispense with this knowledge than the trader can deal with wares of which he has not ascertained the value.

The foreign dominions of the Crown may be divided for the purposes of this inquiry into three parts. 1. Places which are held for purely naval and military purposes, such as Gibraltar and Malta. 2. Those which are more or less fitted to be the residence of English labour, such as Canada, the southern parts of Australia, the Cape, Tasmania, and New Zealand. 3. Those whose climate renders it impossible that they should ever become the residence of a labouring population composed of persons of European descent, such as India, the West Indian Islands, and the northern parts of Australia. The value of the first division is a matter purely for soldiers and sailors – our concern is with the two last alone. If this inquiry had been made a hundred years ago, there can be no doubt as to the answer that would have been given. In the absence of any actual experience on the subject, it was then universally believed that the loss of the American colonies was a fatal blow from which the nation could never recover. Of course this was in some degree owing to the mistaken views which were then entertained as to the value of the monopoly of the colonial trade. But even when allowance has been made for this exploded error, there still remains a great amount of terror and despondency which we now know to have been utterly groundless, and which can only be accounted for by a gross mistake of words for things. The Englishman of a hundred years ago believed, as we believe at the present day, that the elements which constitute the indispensable conditions of the greatness of a State are inhabitants, territory, and capital.

He saw that the American Revolution deprived us, as far as America was concerned, of all three, and he looked no farther. Had he dived a little deeper into the matter, he would have seen that the value of all these things depends entirely on the degree in which they can be made useful to the State which is the nominal owner of them.

Now, as to the territory, it is quite clear that its loss is a very inconsiderable evil so long as it is (as is the case with all civilised nations) just as accessible to us as if it were our own. The United States, since their separation from us, have received far more British emigrants than our remaining colonies. Our people have settled and thriven on the land that they are said to have lost in North America.

Then as to the inhabitants. The English Crown lost three millions of thriving and industrious subjects; but then the question arises, Did the English Crown ever possess them in the sense which could make their loss a serious misfortune? Why are subjects a support to a State? Because the wealth which they possess is a fund from which the State can draw, and on which it can borrow for the supply of its necessities. Subjects are also a support to a State, because they are the natural defenders to whom it looks in war for protection. We venture to suggest that the reason why the loss of the American colonies was so little felt by those who expected to feel it so deeply was, that the colonists of North America had never, or only in a very slight degree, felt or discharged either of these duties. They never assisted us in our wars in Europe or anywhere except where they themselves were concerned, and so little idea had they of aiding us with money, that they separated from us rather than contribute to our revenue. They never performed towards us the duties of full citizenship, and reason as well as experience shows that we could not be injured by the withdrawal of services which we never enjoyed. But this is not all. A country may incur very heavy liabilities on account of subjects who make her no return. Our Consuls in the East could tell us of the great relief which they would experience if the Maltese, for instance, were not as much entitled to the protection of the British power as the inhabitants of London. Subjects are not always a support, but they very often become a burden. We spent ten millions in order to rescue from captivity three or four British subjects detained in Abyssinia, and we did this mainly to keep up our influence in India, which did not give a man or a rupee for the service. We do not put forward these considerations as showing that there are not many advantages in a colonial empire such as we now hold, and may, we trust, long continue to hold. The close union that still exists between us and our present colonial dominions is highly honourable to both parties, and has an obvious tendency to promote trade and cement friendship. But it is idle to attempt to conceal from ourselves that this union is in its very nature temporary and precarious, and may, and probably will, be put an end to without any misconduct on either side.

In the first place the union is one-sided. In case of war we are bound to defend Canada and Australia just as much as we are bound to defend Great Britain and Ireland. But there is no reciprocal obligation. The colonies do all that we require, and more than we expect, if they defend themselves. The cause of war is almost sure to be one in which all, or at any rate many, of the colonies have no interest. They will naturally feel regret that they are exposed to loss and injury in a cause which is not theirs, and we ought not to blame them if they prefer their own interests to ours. The present is essentially a fair-weather plan. Like Don Quixote's Helmet, it has broken down once, and we shall do wisely not to be too confident in it for the future.

It is besides not likely that the colonies will ultimately be content without having a voice in those deliberations by which their welfare may be so seriously affected. To gratify this reasonable desire would amount to a remodelling of Parliament on a federal principle. To this there are two insuperable objections: one the impossibility of persuading England and Scotland, and perhaps even Ireland, to consent to such a change; the other the difficulty which is sure to arise among the colonies themselves. We will not dwell on the first, but refer our readers to the masterly essays of Mr. Goldwin Smith in this Review, and Lord Blachford in the *Contemporary Review*. On the second point, which has hitherto escaped observation, we will offer a few remarks.

Every colony is, by the ties of Government, trade, and a certain degree of common interest, connected with the Imperial Government. The colony looks back to her origin and her history, inseparably intertwined with our own.

'And Rome may bear the pride of him of whom herself is proud.'

Much may and doubtless would be conceded to the mother-country which would be conceded to no one else; with her there is no spirit of rivalry. But of an assembly composed partly of representatives of the mother-country and partly of the representatives of other colonies, each colony would be utterly intolerant. They would say, and with some justice, that they recognise the right of England to a voice in matters affecting their welfare, but that they utterly deny the right of any one colony to exercise any influence over the affairs of another.

Every one whose lot it has been to be practically acquainted with the sentiments and aspirations of a colonial community, is well aware that one colony seldom errs on the side of over-estimating the advantages or good qualities of its neighbour. They are apt to regard each other more as rivals than as co-operators. The products of those that lie near each other are mostly similar, and they are competitors for custom in the London market. Many reasons may be given why it would be very much for the interest of the Australian colonies to form a confederacy somewhat on the pattern of the United States, or at least to join in a Zollverein, and thus save the expense and delay of inter-colonial custom-houses. But though no one can deny this in the abstract, these reasons have hitherto been urged in vain. There is but one really efficacious motive to draw them into a confederacy, and that motive is fear. Where that is present the thing may be forced upon the colonies, as in North America and South Africa; where this is wanting, as in Australia, minor inducements are tried in vain.

But if this repulsion exists so strongly between neighbouring colonies, what will it be between colonies separated from each other by the diameter of the earth? Will Canada accept laws from New Zealand? or Australia submit to the legislation of Jamaica? And yet the only conceivable scheme by which the colonies can possibly be admitted to share in imperial councils is an assembly in which the Crown and the colonies shall be alike represented.

Whenever, therefore, the time shall arrive for the colonies to claim a voice in the general policy of the empire, there is nothing for it but separation, since the only alternative that can be suggested is utterly unworkable. The result is that we shall act most wisely by looking the question fairly in the face, whenever the inevitable day shall arrive when our larger colonies shall make the claim to have a voice in imperial affairs, and solve the question by submitting patiently and graciously to the inevitable alternative of separation, instead of exaggerating the mischief by futile efforts to avert it. It is not natural that nations which are destined, probably in the lifetime of some persons now in existence, to become more numerous than our own, should submit to be for ever in a state of tutelage. Our wisdom is to defer the change as long as possible, and when it does come to throw no captious obstacles in the way, but to console ourselves by the reflection that the experience of a hundred years ago shows us that it is very easy to exaggerate the mischiefs that arise from such a separation; above all, we should be on our guard against such phrases as 'the decline of the empire', the 'setting of the sun of England', and other poetical and rhetorical expressions, which have really no application to a change that only marks an inevitable period in a singularly wise and beneficent policy of which we have every reason to be proud.

To those who view the probable separation of the colonies from the mother-country at some period more or less remote as a proof of our degeneracy as compared with those who founded them, it may be some consolation to observe that hardly any of these settlements at the present day are answering the purposes with which they were founded. The great object in founding a colony was undoubtedly to secure the monopoly of its trade, and so long as we confined ourselves to that the American Colonies were among the most loyal of our fellow-subjects. Australia was originally occupied as a penal settlement. The West India Islands were desired as fields for the employment of slave-labour; and India, as we shall see presently, was acquired for objects very different from those which are now assigned for its retention.

There remains for consideration the third and by far the most important part of our inquiry, the question, namely, of the amount of injury which we should sustain by the loss of those dominions of the Crown which, being situated within the tropics or in their vicinity, can never become the home of a laborious and quickly multiplying European population. Our sugar islands were acquired as labour-fields for slaves, and with emancipation they lost the greater part of their value.

Nature is so bountiful and life so easy in these lovely isles, and indolence so irresistible, that we lose greatly instead of gaining by the change from slave labour to free. To add to the depression in these once flourishing possessions, it pleases the Government of France, in addition to one hundred and nine millions which the nation has to pay for Government and the interest of debt, to raise another million, which is employed in bounties to enable the beetroot sugar of France to undersell the sugar of the tropics. No one, we think, will say that any considerable loss would be sustained if these islands were separated from the British dominions. There can, in fact, be no reason for retaining them except the honourable feeling that it would be disgraceful to England to allow some of the fairest spots of the earth to relapse into utter sloth, ignorance, and barbarism, after she has once taken them into her hands.

Only one other question remains for consideration according to the plan which we have laid down for ourselves, and that is to appreciate as fairly as we can the loss which we should suffer were we to be deprived of the dominion which we now exercise without contest or rivalry over a territory as large as all of Europe that is not Russia, inhabited by two hundred and fifty millions of the human race. So strong is the feeling on this subject, that the House of Commons, which can listen with patience and toleration to proposals for a virtual separation between England and Ireland, shows unmistakable symptoms of impatience and displeasure at the bare supposition that such a catastrophe is possible. There is, we fairly admit, in the possession of such a country as India everything that can gratify our vanity and excite our imagination: the language, whose history is lost in unfathomable antiquity, but which is so like our own that many words are almost identical, and the single fact that a company of English traders conquered a country which Alexander the Great was never permitted to reach, are alone sufficient to excite our interest and gratify a natural and excusable pride. We may well be pardoned if our eyes are dazzled and our heads a little turned by such an acquisition; especially when we remember how powerful was the attraction which the notion of the conquest of India exercised over the mind of Napoleon, and how he chafed at the check at Acre, which according to him changed the destiny of the world. Still the possession of India by England is a hard and prosaic reality, and the gain and loss ought to be weighed and measured with perfect fairness and accuracy, like any other public transaction. It is now nearly a hundred and twenty years since the battle of Plassey left us without a rival in India, and handed over to us the key of this enormous treasure-house, and we have before us the fullest means of judging of the value, the cost, and the probable durability of the wonderful acquisition.

No one can deny and no one can exaggerate the immense value which the ordinary Englishman attributes to the possession of India by this country. The feeling is not, we apprehend, founded on any very careful study of the history of its acquisition, nor yet does it appear to spring from any very minute estimate of the advantages which we derive, compared with the price that we pay for them. But of its reality and intensity there can be no doubt. In the present struggle in the East, if there is any enthusiasm it certainly is not evoked on the side of the Russians. The public does cold justice to their merits, and unsparingly criticises their defects. One of the severest checks our arms ever underwent was our defeat in Affghanistan; a defeat caused mainly by what we now know to be an utterly groundless apprehension of a Russian invasion of India. The Russians are, perhaps, the only people in the world to whom we are not fair and just, whose faults we systematically exaggerate, and whose difficulties we persistently underrate. Unanswerable geography and incontrovertible demonstration are employed in vain. It is a sentiment, and therefore above or below argument, and the foundation of that sentiment is the fear of losing India.

We must concede to those who laid the foundation of our Indian dominion, that their views, at any rate, were not warped or disturbed by over-refinement or over-conscientiousness. Whatever they fought and plotted for, it certainly was neither the honour of England nor the well-being of the people of India. Their objects were less elevated and much more substantial. The agents of a trading Company, they had made the discovery that in the then state of India, more was to be made by the sword than by the pen. Countries were devastated, governments overthrown, plunder practised on the largest scale, the troops of England farmed out to do the work of hired banditti, inoffensive women plundered, all laws, human and divine, trampled under foot in the pursuit of wealth. There is not an article in the impeachment of Warren Hastings that is not supported by the most conclusive evidence. The success was as complete as the means by which it was obtained were cruel and disgraceful. The only praise that the founders of our Indian Empire are entitled to is that they thoroughly knew their own minds, and adapted the means to the ends with skill and unscrupulousness. The policy was cruel, rapacious, and wicked, but it was perfectly intelligible. If Clive or Hastings had been asked what was the object which he had in view in India, he would have had no difficulty in answering that his object was to enrich the East India Company, and, if in a candid humour, he might, perhaps, have added, 'not wholly forgetting myself'. The whole transaction had an antique air about it, and puts one more in mind of a Roman pro-consul or procurator than an English general or governor. But this was not to last. It was a rather gross anachronism; and, though Hastings was acquitted, the disclosures of the trial roused at last the conscience of England. Step by step these gross iniquities were corrected, and the rule of equity and justice replaced the rule of violence and cruelty. The conquering Company first became virtually a department of the Government, and has ceased to exist for nearly twenty years. The Romans would have drawn thirty millions per annum from India, the English Government does not draw a single farthing. Nay, it may be doubted whether, if we take into account unpaid services which the English navy performs for India, we have not in fairness a right to demand a payment from India on this, and perhaps on other accounts. So far are we from treating India as a tributary, that, although India raises a revenue of fifty millions sterling annually, to which the rich contribute little or nothing, we not only raise private subscriptions to assist the Government of India in performing a duty (the relief of famine) which it has the means and the power to perform for itself, but we hear a good deal of a project to guarantee a loan to India for the purposes of the Famine, with the view of saving one or two per cent. in the interest, and something of a proposal to present her, on behalf of the English taxpayers, who support their own poor, with a round sum of five millions.

India has not only ceased to be plundered, oppressed, and trampled upon, we are in great danger of being plundered, if not by her, on her behalf. She has become our pet, our darling, our spoilt child. Not only is she destined to a state of perpetual tutelage, she is petted and subsidised, while the colonies of our own planting are left to go on their way without notice, aid, or sympathy.

Such being our disposition with regard to India, we may reasonably ask what are the peculiar advantages which we derive from the possession that justify our extreme sensitiveness and tenderness on this subject? One reason undoubtedly is, that, in our present dealings with India, we exhibit ourselves to the world in a thoroughly beneficent and unselfish attitude. In our present treatment of India we have certainly done all in our power to atone for the crimes of our forefathers. We may also justly be proud of the spectacle which we present to the world, of a small number of Europeans diffusing the benefits of peace, order, and good government among so many millions of the human race, and thus raising them to a position, moral, social, and intellectual, which they never could have attained for themselves, and which they could not retain for a year without our assistance. If there were a prize of virtue for nations, as there is at Paris for individuals, we might enter into the competition with considerable hopes of success. But our inquiry is of a humbler and more practical nature. We do not ask what is the degree of moral approbation which our attitude in India deserves, but what are the material advantages which we obtain from a position of which we are so proud and so tenacious?

One advantage which we derive from our possession of India is the patronage of a number of places of considerable dignity and value, which serve as the rewards of merit and good service for which there is no adequate distinction at home. Another and far more important benefit which we derive from India is the great stimulus which has been given to education, and the brilliant prize which is held out to industry and ability by throwing open the Indian service to competition. This great experiment has not only provided India with the best Civil Service in the world; it has also gone a great way towards solving the problem of the best way of promoting the highest education. The standard idea of promoting education which found favour with our ancestors, and which is not yet by any means obsolete among ourselves, was to erect an expensive building, and, if there was anything over after the building had been paid for, to devote it to the payment of teachers. But Indian experience has taught us that while costly buildings avail little, and salaries which are paid whether the teacher teach well or ill are rather hurtful than beneficial, prizes held out as the rewards of superior industry and ability will create without any further machinery all that is necessary to obtain them. The Indian experiment has created for us the best Civil Service in the world; it is the pattern on which our own Civil Service is being remodelled, with every prospect of a similar result; and, if the United States are really in earnest in their profession of a desire to rescue their country from the mischiefs of their Civil Service, they have nothing to do but to study the Indian model and copy it as closely as possible.

We cannot look upon Indian finance with unmixed satisfaction. It is disgraced by the cruel and unstatesmanlike salt tax, by the imposition of export duties, and by the almost absolute immunity of the rich from taxation. But these blots are the result rather of real or supposed necessity than of choice. On the other hand, we may fairly claim credit for having kept India free from those gross violations of sound economical principle which disgrace the tariffs of most of the leading States of Europe. We are also entitled to claim credit for keeping so large a portion of the human race in peace and order, and turning to industry and commerce energies which might have been wasted in mutual outrage and destruction. Something also we may perhaps hope that we have achieved towards setting up among nations not under our immediate control a higher standard of the duties of a government towards its subjects, and of those subjects towards each other, than has hitherto existed. Such is the catalogue which we have been able to draw up of the advantages which we derive from the possession and dominion over India. The picture is not, to our thinking, a very brilliant one, but we have not intentionally omitted anything. We will now proceed to state the other side of the question – the price at which these advantages, such as they are, are purchased.

It may be, doubtless it is, in the opinion of many wise and excellent persons, a sagacious and far-sighted policy to have taken possession of India. All we can say is, that if it be so we owe it rather to fortune than to wisdom, and that for the simple reason that England found herself in the possession of that position which necessarily drew after it the possession of India without ever having been consulted on the subject. We have heard of great resolutions taken with very little delib-

eration, but here was a course in which the party principally
interested – the Parliament and people of England – had no
choice at all. Once established as a leading power in India, as
was the case after the battle of Plassey, treaties as the result of
wars and wars as the result of treaties became inevitable, till
the whole fabric of native Indian Government crumbled into
dust before our feet. We might have held aloof altogether, but
to go to a certain point and to say we would go no farther
was not in our power. It is no slight matter for a great nation
to have drifted into such a situation as this. But what follows
is still more formidable. The situation in India is one from
which it is impossible to withdraw. It is perfectly clear that,
after having taken upon ourselves the fearful responsibility of
providing for so many millions of the human race a Government in the place of that which, for our own selfish ends, we
have destroyed, we are not at liberty to change our minds, and
to abandon them to the anarchy in which we had assisted to
plunge them. Equally clear is it that there seems no probability,
even in the most remote future, that a time will arrive when
India will be able, with the least chance of success, to enter on
the duties of self-government. The only possible termination
of our connection with India will be rebellion from within or
conquest from without. A wise State is slow to take a step
which puts its future destiny out of its own power; and such
a step we have undoubtedly taken, or has been taken on our
behalf, with India.

The finances of India may also become the source of a
peculiar embarrassment. Large sums have been lent on the
credit of the Indian Government, and by an Act of Parliament
trustees have been empowered to invest in these securities.
Now suppose that the Indian Government should from any
cause be unable to meet these payments. A claim would of
course be made on the English Exchequer, which it would not
be very easy to answer. It would be said that the money was
borrowed by Ministers of the Crown directly responsible to
Parliament, and that the faith of the Crown was pledged for
its repayment.

Among the advantages which we reap, not exactly from the
possession of India, but from the peace and order which we
have established there, and which, undoubtedly, would not
exist without us, may fairly be included the large trade which
we have with her. The interest of England as a manufacturing

and trading nation is, that every country should be at peace, industrious, and thriving. But that interest rests entirely on the further assumption that we are able to provide them with something better and cheaper than they can find elsewhere. It is also very possible, in the opinion of very competent persons, that we may be raising up a very effective competition against ourselves. The Hindoo by his fine touch, his exquisite taste, and, above all, by the extreme cheapness of his labour, is a formidable antagonist. This is no reason for keeping India in barbarism, but it is, as far as it goes, an answer to the argument drawn from the trade which we derive by means of the peace which we enforce.

And now we approach the last and by far the most formidable consideration connected with this subject. What is the tenure by which we hold India? We do not speak of foreign invasion, for that, considering the vast distance and the enormous apparatus of modern warfare, is not at any rate a pressing consideration. But it is, we fear, only too true that all our well-meant endeavours to conciliate the good-will and obtain the affection of the inhabitants of India, do not relieve us from the necessity of maintaining our hold on the country by the presence on its burning plains of an army of some seventy thousand British troops. This is no temporary demand. No one conversant with the subject looks forward to the time when this force can be dispensed with or even seriously reduced. We cannot trust to native troops to defend India from foreign invasion or from native rebellion. The pay and maintenance of these English troops are reimbursed to the English Government from Indian funds, but this does not stop the drain to which we are exposed. The money which we spend can be repaid to us, but who shall give us back our men? Every one knows that the freedom of our constitution, which does not admit of conscription, places us at a terrible disadvantage with the great military powers of the Continent, who possess the power of impressment for military service. Nor is this all. Not only are we poor in men, but the great facility for finding employment at good wages, the inevitable result of our great industrial success, offers temptations to desertion which are only too often successful. We have everything in the world that is required for our defence except men, and this is exactly that of which India drains us. India does not, like Saturn, devour her own children, but she decimates her European conquerors at a rate which soon places the ravages of climate on a level with the waste of many bloody battles. Consider what happened in the mutiny of 1857. We had been engaged in a war in which our troops had seen some severe service, which had much reduced their numbers. The number of our troops in India had been reduced by the ordinary causes, and not filled up. It is needless to dwell on the result. A fearful rebellion sprung up in India, and all the bravery and self-devotion of men as brave and devoted as ever supported a desperate and almost ruined cause were only just sufficient to prevent the extinction of the English name in India, by a massacre as complete as the Sicilian Vespers. Let no one suppose that this danger is past, never to return. Should another war arise, the same want of men is sure to be felt, the same danger will have to be encountered. No great power of imagination is demanded in order to picture to our minds what must have been the result had the Indian rebellion taken place one year earlier or the Crimean War lasted one year later. Our duty to our ally, our position in Europe, would have called loudly upon us to reinforce our wasted forces in the Crimea. The duty of succouring our small and hardly-pressed army in India, and saving with it the civilian European element and the helpless women and children, would have called as loudly for large reinforcements for India. Should we have been in the position to have succoured both? and if not, which were we to abandon to destruction? There is but one weak point in our cuirass, and of that we have no cause to be ashamed, for it is caused by the mildness and freedom of our institutions. But it exists, nevertheless, and this is entirely owing to the demands of India on our military resources.

We are now, therefore, in a position fairly to estimate the accuracy of the writers and orators who represent India as the brightest jewel in the British Crown, and hold that England deprived of this, her mainstay and support, must immediately sink into the condition of a third-rate power. To us it appears that the exact contrary is the truth, and that we have in India our greatest, perhaps our only serious danger. In dealing with the great nations of Europe, we have the experience of many generations to guide us. We, to a great degree, understand each other, and there is every year a greater similarity between us in views, motives, and objects. But what progress have we made towards fathoming and calculating the motives of such a country as India? We are told that it is the belief of the Mahometans of India that we are tributary (which is in one sense true) to and dependent on the Sublime Porte. The safety of India may at any time be compromised by causes just as trivial and ridiculous as the memorable episode of the greased cartridges, or the mutiny at Vellore, which arose out of the shape of a hat.

We now believe ourselves to be in a condition to answer the question which we proposed as to the value to the United Kingdom of the foreign dominions of the Crown other than military posts. The answer seems to be that to over-estimate it is extremely easy, and to under-estimate it extremely difficult. Having considerable faith in the soundness of opinions which are very generally entertained, we have done our best to find some ground for the belief that the colonies are the mainstay of the empire, and that we have in India the secret of our greatness, our wealth, and our power. As will be seen, in this attempt we have utterly failed. The matter was extremely simple while we confined ourselves to vague generalities. As long as we limited our view to tables of imports and exports, to returns of population and numbers of square miles, the case seemed plain enough; but when we came to examine the relations in which the owners of these things stood to England, the scales fell from our eyes, and we saw that all these good things, which we are instructed to regard as elements of our strength, were really ours in words alone; and what we were instructed to rely on as our property turned out to be nothing better than a mere rhetorical flourish, in fact the property of others.

The question is not whether all these magnificent territories and swarming millions exist; nor yet whether they are set down in books of geography and gazetteers as forming part of the dominions of the British Crown; nor yet whether they are the objects of admiration to the nations of the earth. The question with which we as practical people are concerned is much simpler, and may be thus expressed. What is the relation in which the inhabitant of the British Isles stands to these possessions? Are they his in the same sense in which the wealth, the population, and the strength of the United Kingdom are his? The answer must be that they are not. And if the question be further pressed, in what respect do they differ? The answer must be: The difference is simply this, that while we are bound to defend these vast possessions beyond the United Kingdom to our last shilling and our last man, the persons to whom we are so bound recognise no corresponding obligation, and after enjoying the fruits of our power and prosperity are at liberty to part from us if they so think fit in the moment of danger and distress. And, further, the answer must be that these dominions, which we call ours, give us no strength in war, and no funds at any time towards the support of our Government, and have been in the past the fruitful causes of wars.

We look for a solid repast, and can find nothing but a banquet of the Barmecide.

THE INTEGRITY OF THE BRITISH EMPIRE*

Frederic Rogers, Lord Blachford

The Nineteenth Century of last July contains an able and interesting article by Sir Julius Vogel, recently Prime Minister of New Zealand, on a question which he is especially entitled to discuss – that of 'Colonial Independence' or 'the Integrity of the British Empire'. I ask leave to notice this paper because it developes an idea at present very popular, but which, if exaggerated, I think capable of being mischievous.

Sir Julius Vogel appears to think, and is very likely right in thinking, that in sixty or seventy years the aggregate civilised population of the British colonies in North America, Australia, and South Africa will greatly exceed that of the United Kingdom. He does not think it impossible that a political whole, composed of parts so great, so growing, so diverse in interest, so remote from each other, and so free, may, notwithstanding, be kept together under one common sovereignty; and he inquires how this can be effected, and how one, at least, of the forces tending to disintegration can be neutralised.

That force consists in the accepted belief that colonies are 'young nations', whose separation from the parent stock is a question of time. This belief, Sir Julius says, has been adopted from the mother country by the colonists, and it is everywhere steadily affecting the conduct of public men. The prevalence of such a faith among populations otherwise 'ardently loyal', he ascribes to the announcement in England of the hitherto popular principle, that if colonies wish to secede from the Empire they will not be forced to remain in it. He quotes, for reprobation, 'the favourite *dictum* that England will never burn another ounce of powder to retain a colony that wishes to be free'; and displays for our approval, and therefore imitation, not only the conduct of the United States, which has endured

---

* From *Nineteenth Century*, vol. 2 (October 1877), pp. 355–65.

a calamitous war rather than permit the disruption of a geographically compact nation – a disruption which would have established at once a hostile neighbour on their frontier, and have rendered for ever impossible the fascinating and not impracticable idea of a united North America – but that of Spain, which is fighting savagely to maintain a quasi-despotic power over a distant province.

Our first step, therefore, should be, he thinks, to recall this announcement. It should be declared to the colonies 'that they have not, and will not have, the power to deprive the Sovereign of these realms of portions of her dominions, and that every inch of her territory is dear to her'. Even prognostications of separation deserve to be viewed as 'little short of treasonable'. Overt attempts must, of course, be treated as in Cuba.

Perpetual union being thus secured, the colonists should be required to contribute to the common defence in proportion to their wealth and population, and should receive a corresponding share in directing the Imperial policy. For the present this share would be so trifling that Sir Julius does not insist on it. He only wishes that the Colonial Minister shall act with the advice of a council comprising colonial delegates. It is plain, however, that some of our juniors may live to see the population of Ireland, Scotland, or even England, equalled or outstripped by some colonial confederacies. In this case the treatment of Imperial subjects will plainly have outgrown the authority of the Parliament of the United Kingdom, and a new Imperial Legislature will be necessary. This Sir Julius Vogel provides as follows: – The House of Lords, augmented by some colonial nominations, may continue to subsist as one branch of it. The popular branch must be composed of a body in which the House of Commons, actually or by repesentation, will form a part, but in which the colonies will have a proportionate, and therefore, before long, a preponderating, representation. Parliament, as it now exists, may continue to deal with affairs of merely local interest.

This state of things, or something like it, is (to borrow a word from military correspondents) Sir Julius Vogel's 'objective'. And I entirely admit that it follows not logically only, but as a matter of necessary political sequence, from his cardinal principle – the perpetual integrity of the British Empire in its present geographical proportions – for which he claims the high authority of Lord Beaconsfield.

In an address delivered to a Conservative association in 1872, Lord Beaconsfield (then Mr. Disraeli), while admitting that the affairs of distant colonies could not be carried on except by self-government, expressed the opinion that the grant of self-government 'ought to have been accompanied by an Imperial tariff, by securities to the people of England for the enjoyment of the unappropriated lands which belonged to the Sovereign as their trustee', by a military code which should have defined precisely the respective duties of the colonies and the mother country in relation to national defence, and by the institution in London of a Council representing the colonies, and communicating confidentially with the home Government.

Holding this opinion as to the necessity of self-government, which constitutes the great colonial revolution of the present half-century, he yet appeared to suggest, that it had not been promoted by the Liberals because it was necessary, but was part of a sustained attempt to dismember the Empire.

> If you look to the history of this country since the advent of Liberalism, forty years ago, you will find there has been no effort so continuous, so subtle, supported with so much energy, and carried on with so much ability and acumen, as the attempts of Liberalism to effect the disintegration of the Empire.[1]

The attempt failed. But how? 'By the sympathies of the colonies with the mother country.' They have 'decided that the Empire shall not be destroyed'. And so it became the grateful task of a Conservative Government to 'reconstruct' what remained of the Empire which others had partially ruined.

Lord Beaconsfield, dealing with the past and present, does not rashly thrust himself far into the future, or (in this place at least) say all that Sir Julius Vogel could wish. But I venture to offer a few observations on what he does say.

And first a few words on the charge against Liberal statesmen, now disinterred, of plotting disintegration.

Lord Beaconsfield dates the revolution evidently, and rightly, from the Canadian mission of Lord Durham in 1838. And it is certain that since that date – since the times, that is, of Lord Durham, Mr. Charles Buller, Mr. Edward Gibbon Wakefield,

---

[1] *Nineteenth Century*, July, 1877, p. 809 [see p. 77 of this volume].

and Sir William Molesworth – English Ministers, as well Conservative as Liberal, have more and more recognised the fact, accepted by Lord Beaconsfield, that self-government is inevitable. The example of that recognition was set in Canada, where the suppression of a rebellion was speedily followed by the establishment of responsible government. And before long this idea of responsible government – of a colonial constitution, under which all matters of local interest should be managed by a Representative Legislature and a Ministry possessing the confidence of that Legislature – took possession of men's minds like a scientific discovery. Those who thought seriously about such matters were forced to see that this or some equivalent form of government was the destiny of a British colony properly so called; and the question of its establishment became in each case one of time. That which has to be done, and is sure to be asked for, may be done grudgingly or generously. In the present case it was plainly expedient that the grant should not only be, but appear to be, generous. The series of able administrators who presided over the Colonial Office, though they of course saw that self-government might be given too soon, must have seen also that the pressure in that direction was one of those irresistible pressures which arise out of the order of nature, and to which a wise policy must conform itself. To see this, nothing more was necessary than an honest and considerate common sense. It is surely to that exercise of common sense, and not to a subtle, continuous, and energetic effort to gratify an inexplicable passion for breaking up the British Empire, that we are bound to ascribe the steady, rapid, and peaceable progress of colonial freedom, and with it that growth of colonial loyalty to which Lord Beaconsfield ingeniously appealed as a witness against the policy to which it is really due.

And now, if this loyalty is really worth anything, I ask whether it would have been secured by a grant of self-government limited in the manner which he indicates.

If you destroy an institution, it is destroyed. Other people may deplore it – you may deplore it yourself – but it is gone. Everybody sees that it is gone, and there is an end of it. But if you establish an odious regulation, and, worse still, if you establish an odious limitation on great powers in constant action, and otherwise unrestricted, it soon becomes an object of standing complaint and resistance in which all the grace of past concession is lost, and which ultimately leads to collision or withdrawal, or both.

An Imperial tariff means a tariff imposed by Imperial authority, which, if not absolutely free-trading and uniform, is an effectual bar on any colonial tendency either to derive what we think an undue proportion of revenue from duties on foreign trade, or to use those duties for the purpose of protecting native industry.

To perpetuate the application of the Land Fund or any proportion of it to the assistance of English labourers would have been to deprive the colonies of an important branch of income, and to apply that income in a way which would cheapen colonial labour.

To do these two things would have been to establish two first-class grievances which would have combined in persevering opposition to the home Government those who desired protection to native industry, those who opposed direct taxation, those who wished the land revenue to be applied to the relief of the tax-payer, those who wished it not to be applied to reduce wages by importing labour, and those who, whatever their opinions on these subjects, held it a point of honour and interest to insure that questions of local concern should be decided by the local authority, and would thus supply a flag under which all the other malcontents would certainly rally.

I myself believe it to be unfortunate that the colonists are not all free-traders. I also believe it to be unfortunate that the Australian colonies have not maintained some equivalent for the old provision of the Land Sales Act which required half of the proceeds of land sales to be spent in immigration. That provision, if continued, would have secured a large influx of labourers, who, as they became land purchasers and employers, would constantly have replenished the fund for importing labour, and at the same time would have stimulated the demand for it. This source of geometrical increase has dwindled under Australian legislation. And it follows that the abolition of this (as I think) just and wise arrangement was a sacrifice of the future to the present – of the colony to colonists, such as the Imperial Government, while it held the reins, was bound to prevent. But it is only in the infancy of a body politic that such a control can be exercised without a balance of evil. An adult colony must and will judge for itself on such matters.

I am confident that Sir Julius Vogel would himself admit that, in his own colony of New Zealand, the grant of political power would have lost all its tranquillising effect, and would have proved not the end, but the beginning of controversy, if it had not given the colonists the power of determining their import duties and disposing of their Land Fund according to their own notions of their own necessities. And the probability of this discontent is somewhat strengthened by the facts that the different colonies, according to their different circumstances, have varied greatly in the disposal of their Land Fund, and that the Australian and American colonies have struggled, with some success, against the only restriction on their tariff legislation which survived the grant of constitutional government – the prohibition of discriminating duties. If the Acts of Parliament which established self-government had imposed an unchangeable tariff and maintained an Imperial land policy, or an Imperial distribution of the local Land Fund, the home Government would have had no peace till these two monuments of Imperial dictation were abolished. And abolished they would have been. No English Government could maintain invidious anomalies against the unremitting pressure of organised and powerful communities interested in putting them down, unless supported by an equally unremitting counter-pressure of a greater political power determined to uphold them. It is certain that the destructive pressure would have been applied by the colonists. It is surely as certain that the conservative counter-pressure would not be applied, or at any rate not sustained, by the people of England.

I contend, therefore, that as it was inevitable to give self-government, so it was wise to give that self-government unreservedly.

But with all this, it now appears, some at least of the colonists are not content. Not satisfied with governing themselves, they desire to govern us. Rather they consider that the power of governing themselves involves the right to govern us. And here it is that I for one take my stand. 'What might have been', writes Sir Julius, 'without the constitutions which the colonies enjoy, it is useless now to consider. They have been made in large measure self-governing communities; and if they are not to be independent they must have, as an alternative, a share in the government of the country', meaning the aggregate Empire or Confederation.[2]

'The colonies have been too much advanced on the road to self-government to submit to a total exclusion from a share of control in the affairs of the Empire.'[3]

We have consequently to construct 'a serviceable machinery for giving to the colonies a share in the government of the Empire proportioned to their importance.' And what that serviceable machinery is to be, we have already seen.

Now I entirely admit Sir Julius Vogel's alternative. As the colonies develope they must either become separate nations, or they must have a share – eventually the greater share – in the government of the British Confederacy. Questions might arise on the working of the Federal Constitution. It does not appear whether the Imperial Ministry (which would include at least the foreign, colonial, and war ministers) is to be controlled and practically appointed by the Imperial Legislature or by the English Parliament; nor whether India and the Crown colonies are to be considered as Imperial or English property; nor whether the stimulus given to the establishment of responsible government in Ireland, Scotland, and Wales would be advantageous or otherwise; nor whether recent experience recommends a composite Legislature; nor whether it would be possible, with the requisite promptitude, to eradicate the sentimental objection which most Englishmen would feel to reducing the old historical House of Commons to the dimensions of a local legislature; nor whether it would be worth while for the colonies to send away for the greater part of every year so large a proportion of their leading men as would be necessary to secure a proper voting power in the Imperial Councils. But, all these queries notwithstanding, I am quite prepared to admit that the integrity of the British Empire could not be perpetuated by any rearrangement less objectionable than that which Sir Julius proposes. Indeed, I would add the observation that if, in the course of fifty years, such a metamorphosis became necessary, it might be found convenient, before the century was out, to consider whether the seat of government ought not to be at Melbourne rather than London. The

[2] P. 817 [p. 88 of this volume].

[3] P. 828 [p. 100 of this volume].

relative position of Australia and India, added to the acquisitions of Oceania and New Guinea, certain to be effected under Australasian influence, appears to point to such a transfer, which by that time might be justified by the relative wealth and population of the different States of the Union. The question would be a very real one, and would have arisen before now with regard to New York, if it had been possible for us to retain our North American Provinces till now.

I do not raise any quarrel upon these details, or pursue the thoughts which they suggest: I object to the conception out of which they arise. With 'Empire' that conception has nothing to do. The Imperial relation only subsists in substance between the United Kingdom on the one hand and India and the Crown colonies on the other. It subsists in form and in form only between the United Kingdom and the constitutional colonies. For that formal and delusive relation of empire it is proposed, by steps, which, if they are taken at all, must be taken in no long time – say in the course of the next half-century – to substitute a real working confederacy. The conception is that of a close and permanent association between self-governed States, not arising out of geographical neighbourhood. To this conception I object as hollow and impracticable.

Every association of human beings must have a purpose, and the object of every association must be to combine in employing means for the attainment of that purpose, according to some understood rules. Men associate for comfort or pleasure, and become a club; for gain, and become a company; to return a member of Parliament, and become a committee; for the advancement of art or science, and become a society; for the all-embracing purpose of securing order, prosperity, and safety in the territory which they occupy, and become a State.

The proposed Confederation will be an association. What is its common purpose? Evidently to secure and further the order, prosperity, and safety of the Confederation, so far as these are to be secured and furthered by the action of a common and supreme authority. But in what sense is this a common purpose? A common aspiration it no doubt is. But a common purpose, capable of being made the principle of a confederacy, must be something which can be pursued by common efforts and a common policy. Of what common efforts and common policy will the proposed confederacy be capable? What is that sphere of combined action which is a condition of its real existence?

I understand alliances and treaties between independent powers, for specific purposes. I even understand what is in form a general defensive and offensive alliance, if it is, at bottom, based on some such specific and terminable purpose. But a confederacy affects a much closer solidarity; it aims at securing that, within certain limits, but under all sorts of unforeseen circumstances, the interests, and quarrels, and responsibilities of each part shall be the interests, and quarrels, and responsibilities of the whole. What are these limits? What are to be the functions of the confederacy as such with respect to these interests and quarrels and responsibilities?

The supreme power of a confederacy may deal either with the purely internal affairs of its component members, or with their relations to each other, or with their foreign policy.

With the first of these it is fully admitted that the intended confederacy will have nothing whatever to do. This immense department of law and government must be exclusively and jealously and properly reserved to the State authorities. The effect of this reservation in confining the functions of the central power will at once be felt if we remember how small a proportion of the legislative and administrative action of our own country relates to anything but the internal affairs of the United Kingdom.

Next come what may be called inter-provincial questions. Such, it may be said, are customs duties, ocean postage, immigration, the treatment of offences committed at sea, extradition, alienage, slavery, the treatment of natives, the machinery of common defence, and others, possibly, which do not occur to me. Each of these has called for consideration in its day, and some have presented great difficulty. But much has settled itself. Events have determined that, in respect to self-governed colonies, some of these, like customs duties and immigration, must be treated as internal. About others, like alienage, extradition, and the treatment of offences committed on the high seas, arrangements may be necessary, as with foreign countries, but no serious difficulty need be anticipated. Others are definitively settled by an accepted Imperial law, like slavery; others narrowed geographically by the course of events, like the treatment of natives. Some will remain the subject of what may be called administrative negotiation, like ocean postage and (I should say) the machinery of common defence. Great questions in this department can at present scarcely be said to exist, while small ones are generally matters of discussion between the home Government and one or more of the colonies. It is perhaps worth while to explain the mode in which such discussions are now conducted. They are conducted through the governor, through whom all authoritative communications pass, and whose advice the home Government expects in all matters to receive; but whose reports are supplemented by concurrent explanations received less authoritatively from the accredited agents of the different colonial Governments, who have full cognisance of the views of their respective Governments, free access to the Colonial Office, and full opportunities for acting in concert on any question in which any number of colonies have a common interest. This method is probably not without some inconvenience. No method is likely to be otherwise which involves negotiations of detail – sometimes in the nature of bargains – between authorities at opposite ends of the earth. But it is, after all, not very inappropriate to the work which has to be done; it is capable of adjustment to meet discovered inconveniences or altering circumstances; and I am not aware of any reason for supposing that colonial Governments would prefer to it either Sir Julius Vogel's immediate proposal of a representative Council of Advice, which, if it is to have the power of controlling the Government of England, should also have that of binding those of the colonies, or the prospect of a Confederate Legislature, which would settle questions over their heads, and whose conclusions, if they happened to be carried by English votes, would not be always well received. Assuming, however, that some two or three questions of this class would be more satisfactorily settled by a representative central authority than hammered out by piecemeal negotiation, I contend that their aggregate and decreasing bulk is plainly insufficient to strengthen materially the *raison d'être* for a Confederate Legislature.

It remains that this *raison d'être* must be found, if anywhere, in foreign politics. And here, it appears to me, the conception completely breaks down. To such a confederacy as we are imagining foreign politics may be supposed to supply a sphere of action, only till we remember that it does not supply a common purpose. For, in relation to foreign politics, what purposes are common to England and her colonies as a mass? In the course of the last thirty years we have had wars in China, India, and Abyssinia, some or other of us have talked of war with the United States in aid of the Secessionists, of war with Austria and Prussia on behalf of Denmark, of war with Germany in aid of France, and now of war with Russia on behalf of British interests in or about Turkey. In which of these questions have the colonies any interest? In what European question have they any interest? If any such question involves us in a maritime war, they will no doubt suffer, but their interest in that case will not be in the object of the war, but in the war itself. It will be a simple interest of suffering. We may fairly enough say to them that as the whole Empire may at any moment be called on to put itself into peril for their protection, so they must be content to suffer inconvenience when the Empire goes to war for its own objects. But we cannot allege that they will be suffering for any object of their own or in support of a policy from which they will derive any benefit. What have they to do with the command of the Mediterranean, or the road to India, or the balance of power, or the invasion of Belgium? One of them is interested in the cod fisheries of the Atlantic, another in the development of Oceania or the annexation of New Guinea, another in the pacification of Central Africa – objects all which have to be considered between Great Britain and the particular colony concerned, because in each case we are responsible for asserting the rights of those who depend upon us. But in the external war policy of the Empire as such no colony has any tangible share, except so far as they may suffer from a state of war. No doubt their influence in our councils would, *exceptis excipiendis*, be pacific, and this is so far good. But is it yet right that the councils of any great nation should be weighted with an element which is steadily against war, without having an interest in those objects for which war may become imperatively necessary? I admit that in some commercial matters confederation might facilitate the conduct of negotiations with foreign Powers, who cannot understand colonial independence. But this would be at the cost of enabling the colonies to obstruct, in its application to foreign countries, the principle of free trade, or any other on which England may consider her commercial prosperity to depend.

Is it possible to expect that any great Power will consent to be so weighted? Rather is it not certain that, in the absence of any prevailing purpose and consolidating bias, each member of the confederacy, finding itself unable to carry its peculiar objects, will, sooner or later, think itself ill-treated, and claim the right of taking care of itself? Can this tendency be resisted? It can only be resisted, as Sir Julius Vogel plainly proposes to resist it – by force. If force is not to be applied, the result must be that so long as the advantages of following in the train of a great nation appear to outweigh the damage and peril – or rather, for sentiment's sake, somewhat longer – these communities will remain willingly attached to Great Britain. When the connection becomes a grievance, they will disengage themselves. If I were compelled to hazard a prophecy, I should guess that our great colonies would endure manfully the inconveniences of one great war, but would shrink from the prospect of a second. But, whatever the vitality of our present relations, there is between us, I contend, no such common purpose or group of purposes as will give us a common desire to pursue a common policy. And without this I see no basis for a union between practically independent Powers.

The conclusion of the whole seems to me one which it is easier to dislike than to disprove. Our present relations with our grown-up colonies are exceedingly satisfactory, and the longer they continue the better. But there is a period in the life of distant nations, however close their original connection, at which each must pursue its own course, whether in domestic or foreign politics, unembarrassed by the other's leading. And the arrival of that period depends upon growth. Every increase of colonial wealth, or numbers, or intelligence, or organisation, is in one sense a step towards disintegration. The Confederation of Canada was therefore such a step. The Confederation of South Africa will be, in the same sense, another. All these are steps of a wholesome kind, which only facilitate separation by providing against its evils; and it is hardly a paradox to say that they may delay it by preparing for it. An agreeable but transitory relation is often prolonged by the sense that when it becomes irksome it can be terminated without difficulty. On the other hand, if it is seriously believed possible that nations internally independent, and externally divided by oceans, like England, Canada, South Africa, and Australasia, can remain for ever united in one political system for the sole purpose of determining a foreign policy in which no three of them have a common object; and if English statesmen seriously undertake to render a union under such conditions perpetual, it is to be apprehended that, in their struggles against dismemberment, they may either attempt, by a sacrifice of 'British interests', to bribe the colonies into a cohesion which cannot really be secured, or may alienate them by showing a suspicious disinclination to recognise that national manhood into which they are rapidly rising – a grudging desire to withhold what may enable them to stand by themselves. I only add, by way of illustration, that Sir Julius's reference to the value of colonial loans on the Stock Exchange, and to the effect of a closer connection in increasing that value, suggests a passing apprehension lest, among other things, of the phrase 'confederation' may be begotten the substance 'guarantee'.

For these reasons I ask those who are most keenly set on maintaining the integrity of the Empire to examine accurately what is the meaning of these words, not, of course, with regard to India and the Crown colonies, in respect to which England really possesses Imperial powers and duties, but as to the constitutional colonies which govern themselves.

THE BRITISH EMPIRE – MR LOWE
AND LORD BLACHFORD[*]
Julius Vogel

Mr. Lowe and Lord Blachford between them have disposed of about sixty-four sixty-fifths of the realms on the possession of which the less wise of their countrymen are in the habit of rejoicing. Lord Blachford is less thorough than Mr. Lowe. The first would merely let the Constitutional Colonies drift away; the second sees a weakness in all the external possessions of Great Britain excepting those held for military purposes, the value of which 'is a matter purely for sailors and soldiers'. So that it should be impossible to misunderstand his meaning, Mr. Lowe terms the Colonies and India 'the foreign dominions of the Crown'. The use of that one word 'foreign' should bring the question well home to the mind of every Englishman.

> I thank thee, Roderick, for the word!
> It nerves my heart, it steels my sword.

Those possessions which the sovereign and the people have looked upon as part of a mighty nation are foreign dominions, a source of weakness not of strength. A sixty-fifth part of the whole is alone worth retaining.

Lord Blachford's paper was a reply to one that previously appeared in these pages.[1] Incidentally both he and Mr. Lowe do much to prove the truth of one of the leading allegations in the article 'Greater or Lesser Britain', that there was reality in the generally felt fear that an important section of the Liberal party designed or were favourable to the break-up of the Empire. Were Lord Blachford still the departmental head of the Colonial Office, and Mr. Lowe Chancellor of the Exchequer, the opinions they have expressed would have produced an intense sensation. Not being in possession of

---

[*] From *Nineteenth Century*, vol. 3 (April 1878), pp. 617–36.

[1] 'Greater or Lesser Britain', *Nineteenth Century*, July 1877, p. 809.

office, their papers have excited less attention. Yet it is no slight thing to ponder over, that men, who have occupied positions of such conspicuous power, would between them be glad to see Great Britain reduced to one of the smallest of civilised nations.

A great point is gained by the unmistakable views which are now expressed. As long as the advocates of breaking up the Empire hesitated to declare themselves, or declared themselves only through the means of political platitudes or economical theories, there was difficulty in concentrating attention on the question. But now that from such responsible sources the dismemberment of the Empire is boldly defended, there can no longer be an excuse for disregarding the subject. Lord Blachford agrees so far with the paper to which his is a reply, that he admits that the Constitutional Colonies are attached to the Empire by ties that are progressively weakened. If there be no organic change, both sides concurrently believe that the United Kingdom is destined to remember only as a glorious reminiscence the vast possessions it once held. Lord Blachford's objections to a plan by which this Empire might be held together depend to some extent on details. In course of time he thinks the Colonies will be unitedly more populous than the mother-country, and therefore she may then cease to have preponderating influence. He even foresees that the capital might be removed from London, and we may be grateful to him for the argument that, if we had retained our North American provinces, New York before now would be a competitor with London for the seat of government. How readily the answer comes to such a proposition! New York has not become a competitor even with Washington for the seat of government. It is not conceivable that any city under a United Empire would have superior claims to the seat of government to London. Not only would London always be convenient to the most densely populated part of the Empire, but it would be equally convenient to the crowded countries whose proceedings would be of interest to the foreign policy of the Federation. But if it were otherwise, is the aspiration of keeping united the English-speaking people to be weighed in the scale with the paltry advantages attending the seat of the meeting of Parliament? Is there any one to declare that it would not have been better for the English race and for the world itself that the United States should have continued to be a part of Great

Britain, even though such union raised the question of the seat of government between London and New York?

But the argument to which Lord Blachford evidently attaches most importance, and which he elaborates with great skill and tact, is that between the different parts of the same Empire there would be wanting such a common interest or group of interests as would 'give a common desire to pursue a common purpose'. He considers the idea of a permanent association between self-governed states not arising out of geographical neighbourhood 'hollow and impracticable'. There was a great deal of subtle truth in the sarcasm with which Lord Beacons-field a short time since described 'cosmopolitan critics' as 'men who are the friends of every country save their own'. It is odd indeed how those who are most eager in the cause of uniting nations have the least faith in the unitedness of their own nation. It will be said some day of this period of history, that whilst there has been a tendency in most parts of the civilised world to make nations represent nationalities, there has been in Great Britain a singular exhibition of a weakened national spirit. To tempt foreign nations to open their markets to English wares, the Colonies were placed on the footing of foreign countries, and the less the bait has taken the more eagerly has the endeavour been made to show that the genuine Englishman has no national prejudices. Whilst fully accepting Lord Blachford's conditions of common purpose and common objects, the advocates of United Empire contend for it that it meets those conditions. The same language, the same tra-ditions, the same ways of thought, the same habits, the same education, the same ideas of excellence and of the reverse, the same material, territorial, financial, and trading interests – all these, it is contended, go to make up a common group of purposes sufficient to bind in imperishable ties the provinces of the Empire. The differences are differences which might be urged as between different parts of the United Kingdom. That which is said about representatives of Canada voting con-cerning matters Australian might be said with difference of degree only concerning the members for the North of Scotland voting on questions having peculiar concern for the South of England or West of Ireland.

Mr. Lowe raises the question of want of common purpose in the most material form it can assume, and therefore perhaps in the form in which it is best to discuss it in order to apply the test which Lord Blachford contends for. He asks whether in case of war Great Britain's possessions will be equally interested with herself in the causes that lead to it. The answer is emphatically Yes. Great Britain, as it has been and is known to the world, is a nation whose foreign interests are mainly if not entirely connected directly or indirectly with her exterior possessions. Within her own narrow limits she has not an interest which gives her a right to interfere with other nations or take part in their proceedings or guide their destinies. Centuries have passed since any foreign people conceived the idea of permanently establishing themselves on British soil. All questions of war must be questions in which the people in Great Britain have common interest with their fellow-subjects in other parts of the world. If the quarrel is one because of an insult to British subjects or wrong to British property, the provocation is equally felt by every subject of the sovereign of Great Britain. If the question affects British shipping, that shipping, as will be pointed out directly, is so associated with Great Britain's exterior possessions that the question affects them as much at least as the parent country. If territory is at stake, that territory is not part of the United Kingdom. We have only to look to what is passing around us. All the questions which for some time past have made war a more or less likely event are questions relating to the exterior possessions of this country, and to its exterior trade. The United Kingdom itself has in no way been menaced.

It certainly follows that Great Britain should not be at the sole cost of defence. Let it be remembered that the exemption the Colonies enjoy has not arisen out of the desire to gratify them, but out of the impression that the less complicated the ties which bound the Colonies to the parent country the more easy would be the task of dissevering the connection with them. The utterances now under consideration do away with any doubt, if any doubt lingered, that the course pursued with the Colonies was a course which was to propel them on the road to independence. With that contingency in view a joint interest in defence could only have been an embarrassment, whilst the amount of the Colonies' contributions, within a reasonable period, taking population and property together as the basis, would have been so small as to make it prudent to forego the receipt of such contributions to remove an obstruction in the way of disintegration.

It will, of course, occur to any one who reads this that in the very arguments used to show the interest that the exterior possessions have in the wars of the mother-country, there is confirmation strong of Mr. Lowe's contention that the Colonies and India are sources of responsibility and therefore of danger and possible weakness to the mother-country. Mr. Lowe smiles at the Englishman of a hundred years ago who 'believed as we believe at the present day, that the elements which constitute the indispensable conditions of the greatness of a State are inhabitants, territory, and capital'. It is reserved to the statesmen of the present day to arrive at maturer knowledge. Had this ancient Englishman 'dived a little deeper into the matter, he would have seen that the value of all these things depends entirely on the degree in which they can be made useful to the State which is the nominal owner of them'. And so Mr. Lowe argues that as the United Kingdom does not immediately control the people and the territory of her exterior possessions, she gains no more from them than if they were aliens. These are arguments in favour of a lesser Great Britain not only now but in the past; they are, moreover, arguments in favour of quite a different Great Britain to anything that the British race has been accustomed to think over, and, it may be, could reconcile itself to.

The people of Great Britain are an adventurous, hardy, enterprising race, who venture freely that they may gain largely. They have attained to a 'potentiality of riches' which has no equal in history; and, strange to say, widely as they have spread over the universe, they have yet so accumulated within the narrow limits of the parent country as to make their islands the most heavily peopled territory, with one exception, on the face of the globe. There comes a time when the difficulties that distance interposes are in large measure done away with. Steamers practically divide by three the old estimate of distance; the telegraph, for some purposes, annihilates distance altogether. The exterior possessions show themselves to be fairer lands than was anticipated; they prove their adaptability to British institutions of all descriptions – in some respects they set examples that the mother-country eagerly follows, and they cost Great Britain less than formerly, whilst they display a readiness to help each other, as witness the contributions of the Colonies to the relief of the Indian famine distress. But the discovery is made that, notwithstanding all these features

intensely favourable to the Colonial dominions, the parent
State would be better without them. Is there really anything
new in the reasons discovered? are they anything different from
the simple fear of loss which usually follows success? The
Great Britain Mr. Lowe asks for is not the Great Britain known
to its inhabitants. He wishes to change everything. The grounds
he proceeds on are those which make the rich man who has
won wealth by enterprise leave the race to others. He keeps
what he has made, he leaves to the young and to those who
have yet their spurs to win fresh risks and fresh enterprise. It
is a fair question, Has Great Britain run her race? is she to live
on herself and to stagnate on the results of the past, or is she
to carry her enterprises and her wealth to her exterior possessions until she reproduces herself many times? Mr. Lowe,
and those who think with him, have really made no advance
on the Englishman of a hundred years ago. They have made
no discovery, they have simply applied a fact that must be
patent to every one, that every source of strength is conversely
a means of weakness. All Mr. Lowe's arguments, and some
portion of Lord Blachford's, are unconsciously a testimony to
the great law which runs through the universe, that in proportion to the value of an object is the severity of any
misfortune which overtakes it. No foreign nation will injure
the Colonies because of its coveting them, but because of the
blow which would be struck at the nation which owns them.
So is a man to be affected by the loss of his children, and
machinery by injury to its principal parts. The cultivation of
valuable plants, the breeding of animals, every occupation,
every development of enterprise is equally open to the argument that its strength is its weakness, that it is most vulnerable
where its value is greatest. If such considerations affecting the
Colonies are to be allowed to reverse the policy which has
grown up with the growth of Great Britain and given to it its
place amongst nations, then all enterprise must come under
the same category. Each must keep and greedily guard what
he has and risk it no further. So entirely does an excessive fear
born of success drift from all that makes up human progress,
that its ultimate landing-place is a return to the savage condition in which individual responsibilities are lost in the animal
propensities that tyrannise over intellectual aspirations. So
utterly wanting in reason to those who know the Colonies is
the indifference to getting rid of them, that for Great Britain

to cast them off because of possible danger which may arise from them is scarcely less insane than would be the proposal to cut off one's legs and arms because of possible disease and accident. Without India and the Colonies, England would lose her arms and legs, and remain a fat, bloated body racked with internal disease. We may ask Mr. Lowe to assist us in aptly characterising those arguments which, on the ground of newly discovered vague dangers, would discourage England from preserving and federating her Empire. 'Everything', wrote Mr. Lowe to the *Times*,

> is impossible to cowardice and selfishness. . . . Those who use such arguments, however obscurely worded, satisfy all the tests of inanity. They are applicable, if true at all, to the whole human race. They are true for all ages of the world if true for any. They are good for women as well as men, and for children as well as women. They have the emptiness of the air-pump and the flatulency of the balloon. What we have a right to expect is an argument drawn from experience.

After all, the eminently successful are but few; their power, however, is enormously in excess of their numerical strength. To the vast majority the Colonies and India are directly or indirectly the land of promise. Lord Blachford, we have already observed, attaches no importance to common nationality and uniformity of language, thought, and institutions, as a bond of union and ground of common object and purpose; but it is singular that he should fail to see a significant common purpose in the large investments of British capital in the Colonies. The subject of the prospects of the Colonies as future arteries for the trade and enterprise of Great Britain is of peculiar interest now, when the question of the foreign trade of the country occupies such anxious attention. The commercial future of the country largely depends upon the choice between disintegration and federation. The vast place which the shipping of Great Britain takes in the development of the trade of the country will not be doubted. That shipping depends for its existence not only upon the trade that employs it, but upon the protection that its country is able to afford it. Whilst Great Britain owns possessions and has ships of war in all parts of the world, her merchant marine is but the embodiment of her wide-spread dominions. The loss of her shipping would inevitably follow the loss of her dominions. Such as result would not only be natural, but desirable. It would not be politic for her in her attenuated condition, wrapped up within herself, and desirous of avoiding all interference with the outside world, to court the innumerable difficulties that might arise from her distant shipping. From time immemorial ships and Colonies have been bracketed together. If the Colonies are to go down, the same prudence (let us call it) which relinquishes them will dictate the curtailment of the merchant shipping.

In a recent remarkable article the *Times* threw doubt upon the importance to Great Britain of its foreign trade. The figures used were those of the value of the exports to foreign countries and British possessions, so that the argument embraced all countries with which Great Britain trades, whether her own dominions or foreign. Why, the writer urged, is there so much alarm about the risk of England losing her foreign trade? It would not so vastly matter if she lost it all; her productions which she sends abroad are very small in comparison with those she retains for her own use. Then he shows what England's total annual earnings amount to; and after making sundry deductions well justified by the nature of his argument, he concludes that England derives a net income from her exports of about 140,000,000*l*.; and he asks, Can this be of great moment compared with the aggregate income of the country? He reasonably urges that at the worst only a portion is in jeopardy. Some part the country cannot lose. The boldness of this line of reasoning might well carry the reader with it. A country which, in a hundred different ways, is in the habit of associating its chances of existence and success with the vastness of its foreign trade is suddenly told that it may part with as much of the trade as can find other channels, and suffer comparatively no inconvenience in consequence. When one comes to read between the lines, he may see that the fallacy of the argument lies in the fact that it presupposes more or less a community of ownership. If the thirty-two millions of people who inhabit this country drew each a proportionate share of the total income, the loss arising from the loss of foreign trade might, by a like equal division, be little felt. But there is no such equality. You cannot equally divide the consequences. You have first a number who primarily suffer, and to whom the loss means ruin. You have then around the principal group a widening circle of suffering, which becomes less severe as it enlarges in extent, till in the far background you have those who are only remotely affected. If this be well considered, it will be seen that the loss of a portion of the extensive trade of the country may mean a calamity which cannot be measured in its effects by dividing its extent into the total means of the nation.

The nation is awakening from a sense of false security. Until quite lately the general idea was that free trade was a sort of patent medicine to the body politic, calculated to cure all diseases which could possibly overtake it. The impression was that strikes and high rates of wages, adulteration, imperfect skill, deficient energy, fraudulent commissions, deteriorations in quality, foreign competition, all meant nothing so long as free trade remained: had not free trade made the nation what it was, and was it not capable of remedying every evil? Lately the question has been raised as to the policy of giving too freely without exacting a return, and then the upholders of free trade who really understood its meaning spoke out. The theory of free trade did not depend on reciprocity. It suits, they say, Great Britain to release importations from all restrictions, to make all commodities as cheap as natural causes will allow, and not to mix up the scheme of revenue with ulterior objects. But they disclaim for free trade the character of a universal panacea. Professor Fawcett, in the first of a series of lectures on free trade, warned his hearers not to suppose that free trade would do more than aid the progress of a country, or its absence do more than make progress less rapid than it otherwise would be.[2] He protested against the idea that all the progress of the late years was due to free trade. The Marquis of Hartington recently ascribed the progress of the country almost entirely to the development of its railway system.[3] Mr.

[2] 'We in England are much too prone to overrate the advantages of free trade. Scarcely a week elapses without its being said, as if it were a triumphant rejoinder to all that is urged by the American, the Continental and Colonial Protectionists, "English exports and imports have more than quadrupled since protection was abolished, the income of the country, as shown by the yield of the income tax, has more than doubled, wages have advanced, and population has increased;" but a moment's consideration would show that other causes have been in operation besides free trade to promote this wonderful growth of prosperity.'

[3] It may be said – I think it is no exaggeration to say it – that almost all the progress this country has made in the last half-century is mainly due to the development of the railway system.' – The Marquis of Hartington at Chesterfield, Oct. 17, 1877.

Bright told his audience at Manchester that they must not suppose they were to be proof against the ills that history taught them had overtaken former marts of the world, and he drew an image of Manchester as an unpicturesque ruin. Mr. Goldwin Smith, the uncompromising advocate of breaking up the Empire, recently intimated that in his opinion this country could not hope to retain more than a small portion of its foreign trade. As, on the one hand, the advocates for disintegration do not pretend it will do more than preserve from some risk the wealth that has been made, so those who understand free trade do not pretend for it more than that it is an enlightened and logical fiscal policy.

The causes that affect the retention or loss of the trade of the country lie much deeper than the mere question of the extent to which it is advisable the Customs should be used to obtain the revenue requisite to provide for the government of the kingdom. It is necessary to look into these causes to decide whether or not it is wise of this country to seek to cut itself off from the dependencies till lately regarded as its strength, but which the new school has discovered to be its weakness. It is evident that *primâ facie* a country which has to import a great part of the two main necessaries of life, food and clothing, is heavily handicapped in the race with other countries. Given two countries with otherwise equal resources, it is clear that the one in which the people have to pay highest for food and clothing must be at a disadvantage. Let us now consider some of the particulars which have hitherto more than counterbalanced to this country its want of land; let us see how far these features are lasting, what causes may be at work in an opposite direction, and incidentally we shall gather whether Great Britain has better prospects from gradually approaching to a condition of isolation or from more largely than ever developing her exterior possessions.

With the exception of the very few products the sea renders up, everything that man uses is obtained, arises from, or owes its continued existence to the land. Great Britain is so crowded that its land does not suffice for its people's wants. It is wonderful how much of all that is used or consumed in the country is obtained elsewhere. Nevertheless it has been exceptionally prosperous because foreign countries have been so willing to take its manufactures. There now appears less willingness. Why is this? The answer is manifold. Many other countries have learned the arts that enable them to supply themselves. Capital, although not so plentiful as in Great Britain, is not wanting to them. With the means of furnishing themselves cheaper with food and clothing, their labourers start with an advantage. Under the influence of past success the labourers in this country have grown to want many things, to gain which they require higher wages; they have learned also to think that life cannot be sufficiently enjoyed if too long a portion of it is devoted to manual labour. The effects of the crowded condition of the country and its scanty space do not end with the necessity of importing from abroad the products of other lands. The want of room, and the consequent cost of such room as is to be procured, make themselves felt in every phase of industrial operations. Either space must be unduly limited, or the ruling value of the premises, or land, or dwellings required, raises the cost of manufactures. Not only does this apply to the actual premises a manufacturing concern occupies, but to the cost of the dwellings of every one from the highest to the lowest connected with the manufacture. The artificial conditions which surround trade do more to injure the demand for British manufactures than most people are aware. Persons in distant countries have grown so to believe in the dishonesty of agents that they send home orders with reluctance. The fraudulent charges which are attempted to be excused under the name of trade usages are exercising a most discouraging influence on the demand for British manufactures. Most unfortunately for the manufacturer, he in no way as a rule comes in contact with the consumer, or, in many cases, with those who directly supply the consumer. A vast amount of British productions before they pass into use by the consumer go through quite a number of hands. There is first the warehouseman in England, the merchant who buys from him, the merchant abroad who receives the goods, sometimes a warehouseman abroad, and lastly the retailer. More or less the manufacturer trusts his reputation to each and all of these intermediate hands. Exorbitant profits can be put on his manufacturers, his third and fourth-rate articles can be represented as his best. So reckless are manufacturers of the representations that may be made on their behalf, that it is to be presumed they many of them lay themselves out for making rapid fortunes rather than for establishing lasting businesses. The manufacturer does not do all he might to make fraud difficult. Occasionally it is to be feared he winks at it. It was a short while since stated that some manufacturers prepare two price-lists – the one showing the real price to the agents here, the other showing advanced prices to justify the agents in making additional charges to their principals. The want of connection between manufacturers and consumers places the former at a disadvantage in respect to meeting progressive requirements. The American manufacturer is alive to every invention, and is always on the look-out for improvements. So would be the British manufacturer if he was sufficiently alive to what was required. But he is unable to know what his customers take from him merely to resell, regardless of more than the showy qualities calculated to attract sale. The artificial conditions do not affect only export goods. The price to the consumer is so much in excess of that received by the manufacturer as to constitute a serious tax. Much of the reduction caused by abolishing import duties is replaced by the artificial nature of the trade system. For example, if consumers during the last twenty years could have purchased at what are known as cooperative prices, they might have endured without loss a fifteen or twenty per cent. *ad valorem* Customs duty on almost every article imported. They have submitted to excessive charges because they are unable to know to what extent improved facilities enable the manufacturer to cheapen his goods. It is a fact that manufacturers are in the habit of quoting from twenty to seventy per cent. discount on their wholesale catalogue rates. It is the business of the middle men as long as possible to keep consumers in ignorance of what manufacturers charge.

On the other side, England has the advantage of the vast multitudes requiring to be supplied. If the dense population has its evils, it also has this advantage, that it enables manufactures to be conducted on a giant scale with the minutest subdivision of labour that experience shows to be profitable. This, of course, places the manufacturer in a good position to supply foreign as well as home wants.

We now come to an influence more potent, perhaps, than any yet alluded to, the effects of which in the past and the future are rarely taken into account. The great stimulus to England's exterior trade during the last thirty years has not been free trade, but money-lending. Foreign countries have bought British goods with the money good British people have lent them. The remittances to foreign countries are not in gold, but in goods. What with the money lent to foreign Governments and invested in private foreign undertakings, the amount of capital supplied by Great Britain to exterior countries must have amounted to a prodigious sum. According to Dudley Baxter, the increase of national debts in the 21½ years ending 1870 amounted to 2,218,000,000*l.*, or 103,000,000*l.* a year. Seeing that these figures include a reduction of 20,000,000*l.* in the English National Debt between the two periods, it is evident the increase arises solely from the borrowing of foreign countries, India, and the Colonies. The two latter show an increase of 103,000,000*l.*, deducting which amount from the total, and adding the reduction on the debt of Great Britain, gives us 2,135,000,000*l.* as the increase of the national indebtedness of foreign countries during the 21½ years. We cannot accurately determine how much of this has been lent from Great Britain, but there can be no doubt a considerable part. But the money foreign countries have drawn from Great Britain for national debts does not represent all the indebtedness to this country. Private investments and investments in joint-stock companies have probably been quite as large in extent, and together the sums which have passed from Great Britain to foreign countries must be prodigious in extent.

Humiliating as the conclusion may be, there is little room to doubt that a great part of England's foreign trade has not arisen from inherent advantages, but from her having found the money to purchase her goods – or, in other words, having sent the goods abroad, and allowed the proceeds to remain there. The investing public have lent the money which has passed to the manufacturers. The clergyman and the maiden lady have assisted to build the tall chimneys and keep the machinery going.

The effects of lending money in this way are very peculiar. As long as the lending continues, there continues the flow of the exports to represent the loans. But stop the flow of money, and what follows is this: the borrowing country has to scrape together all sorts of productions to send abroad to pay the interest on the debt. The producers and manufacturers may not understand how the exchange affects them. All they require to know is that there is a demand for anything they can produce which can be exported. People ask, Why should the imports into Great Britain exceed the exports? If it be the case that England is lending less abroad than she is receiving for interest and investments, the difference is represented in one way by an excess of imports over exports. In lending its money to foreign countries and suddenly stopping fresh loans whilst exacting payment of interest, Great Britain has given a great stimulus to the producers of the rest of the world. The normal condition becomes that of Great Britain receiving supplies without exporting to pay for them. But there still remains to England the most powerful aid to its commerce – its shipping. The groove into which the conduct of England's shipping has fallen supplies one of the largest systems of trade protection and bounty that has ever been in operation. The whole principle on which the English shipping trade with other countries is conducted is to make the homeward freights supply the profits. On the outward route a bare return to cover expenses, and sometimes not even that, is submitted to; the homeward voyage is to make the whole trip a profitable one. A simple instance which is within the ordinary mark will suffice to show the operation of this shipping protection. A ship, carrying out a cargo of the value of 20,000*l.*, makes for her outward freight 2,500*l.* She will, under ordinary circumstances, make at least 5,000*l.* on the way home, or 7,500*l.* on the entire trip. If this were equally divided, there would be a return of 3,750*l.* each way; the difference on the outward route between that amount and the 2,500*l.* actually received is 1,250*l.*, and that 1,250*l.* is so much bounty to the 20,000*l.* of goods carried out by the trip. 1,250*l.* ought to be added to the outward freight; its omission is equal to a 6¼ per cent. bonus on the 20,000*l.* of goods, whilst the same amount may be added as an impost on the homeward freight. This system, be it observed, is not designed to help the country or its trade. It has accidentally or naturally arisen. Those who conduct the shipping trade look of course only to their own profit and advantage. Nevertheless the result is perceptible, and it is one of the consequences of England's control of the merchant marine.

Let us now put all these circumstances together: England, requiring to import a great deal of its food, clothing, and raw material, is at a disadvantage compared with more fortunate countries. She has to contend with high rents, with evil reputation earned by doubtful practices, with the misconceptions arising from the artificial system by which manufacturers and consumers are so widely separated, and with high rates for labour. On the other hand, she has the means of carrying on operations on the largest scale, and her shipping gives to her an immense advantage in supplying foreign countries. The greatest stimulus of all to her trade has been that she has lent the money to the countries which largely consume her productions, and she is now threatened not only with the withdrawal of this stimulus, but with its absolute reversal, in the manner in which foreign countries are stimulated to supply their productions to pay their liabilities.

Imperfect as has been the reference to these various points, about each of which a volume might be written, enough has been said to elicit three leading conclusions. First, England has no inherent right to trade supremacy; such supremacy as she possesses is to be ascribed to various causes which are liable to be weakened, and the arrogance is absurd which scarcely stops short of the belief that the rest of the world and its inhabitants have been created in order to absorb the manufactures of Great Britain. Secondly, that the system of shipping greatly aids England's exterior trade. Thirdly, that the demand for English goods largely follows the supply of English capital.

We have already seen that if England is to divest herself of her exterior possessions, she must reduce the magnitude of her shipping, and we find that that means she must relinquish a great aid to her foreign trade. We may now ask, Are not the Colonies expressly fitted to give that stimulus to trade which follows the supply of capital? No one who has any regard for the safety of the nation, or indeed for its continuing to own any national independence, can desire to see the stake of this country in foreign countries increased. Already Great Britain has become the mark for the cupidity of the rest of the world. It were better the foreign trade should go than that England should continue to lavish her wealth on foreign countries. And yet the whole question has come to this, What is she to do with her wealth? She cannot use it all within her own dominions unless for communistic purposes. Safe investments now return very low rates of interest. There must be a limit within the kingdom to the power of finding fairly profitable occupation for money. Should her surplus savings go to foreign countries or to her own dominions? If they go to foreign countries, they go where her own laws give her no redress. She will not fight to protect her subjects' foreign investments. The money sent by her subjects abroad passes out of their control, and may be subject to innumerable contingencies arising from the laws and necessities of the countries to which it finds its way. Need we seek a better warning than that supplied by the silver legislation which is now proceeding in the United States? British investments within British dominions are protected by British laws. In this short sentence lies the utter refutation of all the arguments by which it is attempted to be shown that England may regard with equanimity the loss of her exterior possessions. The case may be briefly stated: England has vast surplus wealth, surplus population, and immense territories which are capable of absorbing both the capital and labour. It is said by the advocates of disintegration that the capital and the labour will go to these territories whether or not they continue British. This is an assertion that may appeal to the Colonies to make them refuse federation, but it forcibly urges on the mother-country a retention of her dominions. The arguments which point to the Colonies as weaknesses assume for the Colonies a sort of divided existence. But if the Colonies are the every-day resource of the residents within Great Britain, it is not paradoxical to say that Great Britain will have larger interests wrapped up in them than the colonists themselves. In fact this result is rapidly coming to pass. The check upon foreign loans has led to an enormous increase in Colonial investments. During the last few years the market value of Colonial securities has largely increased, whilst immense amounts of capital are constantly sent from this country for investment in the Colonies.

At this moment England would be better off with five millions less people. Wherever these people go she has countless millions of money to send with them, to expend on productive investments. She has fair lands in abundance that only want capital and labour. How quickly or how leisurely the three – the land, the people, and the capital – should be brought together is a question depending for its solution on many causes; but it is not rash to suppose that the next generation within these islands will have as large a direct pecuniary interest in the Colonies as the present generation unhappily has in foreign countries. What a barbarous wrong to the future to convert these British into foreign dominions!

We are bound to admit there is much truth in the fears that are expressed that federation may not be agreeable to the

Colonies. Lord Blachford, having ruled the Colonies a great part of his life, is indignant at the idea of being ruled by the Colonies. 'Here', he says, 'I take my stand'. It is terrible to him that as the Colonies attain to mature proportions they should have a fair share in the control of federal questions. He feels as we may suppose the Southern planter might feel to whom it was suggested that his emancipated slaves should be allowed to exercise political power. Interference with local concerns, it need scarcely be said, has never been suggested. Each country province or dominion must manage its own concerns. The navy to belong to the whole Federation, powers to bring under one management the armies, and an approach as far as may be to a free interchange of goods – these are the aspirations of Federalists. They are met by the cold scorn that asks, Do the colonists presume to think they are fit to take a share in the government of the Empire? Sentiment plays more a part in the world's progress than Mr. Lowe is willing to allow. The Colonies have not been inclined to resent the manifest desire which has been shown to place foreign countries on an equal footing with them. Nor if the question of federation were raised on a broad basis, would they draw out a profit and loss account to test if each would more gain or lose by the transaction. But they will not be proof against the sneers that suppose they want a guarantee or some other sinister advantage; or against the contempt that sees in them inferior communities.

> Salamene's sister seeks not
> Reluctant love even from Assyria's lord!

There is something very appealing in Lord Blachford's excuses for the position in which the Constitutional Colonies have been placed. Would they, he contends, have been contented if any conditions had been attached to their control of the Crown lands or to their power of making tariffs? Was it not best to do the thing generously and let the Colonies have everything? One might give a harsh name to that generosity which is kindness at another's expense. The Colonial Office might readily see, or fancy it saw, the prospect of future peace and quietness arising from the gift to the Colonies of unrestrained powers. Lord Blachford, Mr. Lowe, and others, it must be recollected, assert that the inevitable result of the Constitutions which were given to the Colonies is their ultimate independence. They see, it is true, no loss to the Empire in consequence, but if for the sake of argument we suppose that that independence would be a great evil to the mother-country, it becomes very important to know if the nation and the sovereign were sufficiently aware of what was being done, or whether a bureaucracy took upon themselves to do that, the real purport of which was not sufficiently understood. We may remind Lord Blachford that neither nations nor people are in the habit of giving up that which is valuable to avoid merely urgent and covetous demands. If the Colonies were not entitled to the untrammelled use of the Crown lands and to unlimited discretion in respect to imposing tariffs, the Colonial Office policy of the past stands self-condemned in the excuses of its former chief. It is true the Colonies were greatly discontented with the Colonial Office before Constitutions were given to them. For many years the Colonial Office had appeared to see in the Colonies one single use, that of fields for patronage. Let us even admit that the patronage was not altogether injudicious, still it was felt and understood to be patronage; that is to say, the choice of persons to fill appointments was not dictated so much by regard to efficiency and suitableness as by the demands of party and personal government. The amount of self-government given to the Colonies was unreasonably small, and sufficient encouragement was not shown to those in the Colonies who proved themselves best fitted to discharge government functions. We may judge from what Lord Blachford says now that the feeling at the Colonial Office was, if we are to lose the patronage, what does the rest matter – give up everything. It is fair to say that a different spirit rules the Colonial Office now that Mr. Herbert replaces Lord Blachford, and that Lord Carnarvon has given quite another impulse to the policy of the department. Recently Sir Stafford Northcote expressed himself strongly in a sense entirely opposed to the disintegration theory. Indeed, if the action one might expect were to follow the utterance, what more could be asked than the legitimate outcome of these words? –

> At the present time, I need not say to you that England requires in every possible way to strengthen herself and to consolidate her power. I am not one of those who take a gloomy view of the possible future; at the same time it is impossible for any man who is in any way or degree charged

with the conduct of public affairs not to take a somewhat anxious view, and I believe myself that the true safety of England, the true line to follow for the preservation of the Empire which has been bequeathed to us, and for its strengthening and development, is not so much fear and jealousy of others as a determination to strengthen and consolidate within ourselves. I know well, and you know well, in the time we are able to look back upon, how many perils England has been threatened with, how many perils she has escaped. You know well, if you will look back over periods of years, and will take a candid view of the progress of our Empire, the sun of England is as yet far from setting – that the power of England is far from having attained its limits. I do not say that we are to extend the physical limits of our Empire to a great extent beyond the point at which they already stand, but I say this, that for the consolidation of our power, for the knitting together of our great colonial and Indian Empire with the mother-country at home, there is an enormous amount of work to be done, and it is to the doing of the work, and doing it fairly, that I look for the salvation of the greatness and continued prosperity of this Empire.

If we are right in our estimate of what will be the interest in the Colonies which the coming generation in Great Britain will possess, if we are right in thinking that it would be better if during the last twenty-five years much of the love given by her to the world at large had been given by Great Britain to her own people and possessions, it would seem impossible to justify the extent of the renunciation made to the Colonies of which Lord Blachford boasts.

The waste lands of the Colonies were essentially the property of the nation, and whilst it would have been a great mistake to have insisted on their being used, for any purpose injurious to the Colonies, it could not but have been fair to every interest concerned to have stipulated that part of their proceeds should continue to be available for the introduction of immigrants. So again with the tariffs. It would neither have been unwise nor unreasonable, to have made conditions respecting the nature of the Customs duties. Probably the Colonial Office is not to blame for this failure; it is most likely due to the unsuccessful attempt to obtain at all risks reciprocity from other nations. It cannot be too clearly understood that there is a wide distinction between that policy which dictates the abolition of import duties, to suit the interests of the nation itself, and which was really the so-called free trade, and the natural desire to see a similar policy adopted by other nations. Free trade, *i.e.* the abolition of import duties except for purely revenue purposes, has, it is admitted, worked well, but the attempt to lead other nations to adopt a like course has all but totally failed. It was to serve this part of the policy, that part which totally failed, that the Colonies were ostentatiously placed on the footing of foreign countries. If the past had to come over again, with the light of the knowledge since acquired, the remission of import duties would have been placed simply and solely on its own merits, whilst all arrangements with foreign countries would have been regarded as separate in their nature. It must be admitted, however advantageous to a country may be the abolition of import duties, that advantage is increased by a like course being followed by other countries. Of course, the more populous the country, the greater the advantage. Has it not been the case, that in the vain pursuit of reciprocity from foreign nations, there has been a renunciation of the reciprocity that might have been counted on from the nation's own dominions? In anxiety for the greater prize, the lesser one was overlooked. Wisely or unwisely, it does not matter which, foreign nations, without perhaps denying that they were submitting to present sacrifices, have obstinately refused to open their ports. They have not coveted the extended commerce Great Britain sought to thrust on them; we are further than ever from finding that foreign nations wish to obtain from us their supplies. The international feeling has grown only in England. In other countries there has rather been an increase of national as opposed to international sentiment. With the failure of the attempt to obtain the cooperation of other nations, the realisation should be stronger of the mistake which has been made in running after the foreign shadow and neglecting the home substance. Our international efforts have in no way increased foreign trade. Had we professed a most exclusive policy and merely abolished import duties to suit our own purposes, we should have had just as much foreign trade, but we might have done a great deal more to increase the trade between the different ports of the Empire. Free trade (properly so to be called) over so much of the habitable globe as is comprehended in the Queen's dominions, might surely be a sufficiently ambitious dream. The total neglect of all attempts to bring it about evidenced in the unfettered tariff power given to the Colonies with their Constitutions, was, to say the least, a mistake on the part of a nation that had so strong a feeling in favour of free trade. That which has followed is not to be wondered at. Left to themselves, the Colonies have regarded the tariff from a strictly local point of view. Denied the power to make reciprocal arrangements with Great Britain itself, they insisted on and obtained the right to make reciprocal arrangements with each other as well as with foreign countries. It would be rash to say that that which has been done can be altogether undone.

The Colonies, to the best of their abilities, consult their own interests. It is not their fault that they have been led to separate those interests from the interests of the mother country. Such a policy has literally been forced on them in the manner in which they have been placed on the footing of foreign nations. It is very hard to retrace, and the advocates of federation by no means pretend that it will necessarily carry with it a Customs union. The best they can urge is that it will facilitate a progress to one. If the dream of perfect freedom of trade over a large portion of the earth's surface cannot be realised, there may be an approach to it of momentous value to the Empire at large. It is difficult to say how much could be arranged. At present, for example, Colonial wines are placed at a positive disadvantage compared with French wines. The latter are in fact protected. Nor is the protection accidental. Such a system of charging the duty on wines is designedly adopted as will give French wines an advantage over Colonial and Spanish wines. If Australian wines were admitted to this country duty free, we are far from certain that the concession would not be regarded by some of the Colonies as sufficiently important to justify them in remitting the duties on all British articles. We mention this as merely an instance of what negotiation and federation may be able to effect.

Mr. Lowe asks if the mother-country gains any direct contribution from India or the Colonies. It has never been her policy to exact anything of the kind, as Holland does from her Colonies. Great Britain has considered the indirect benefits arising from the Colonies as sufficient. Mr. Lowe claims for those indirect advantages the character of direct ones. Certainly the prospective value of the Colonies to the mother-country has never been greater than now, when the fallacy of too large a pursuit of enterprise in foreign countries is recognised. Certainly also the Colonies are costing the mother-country less than they have hitherto done. But federation would bring with it direct contribution. No one, as a matter of principle, would deny that the Colonies should contribute to the maintenance of the navy. It is those who have thought that such a contribution might be looked upon as an obstacle to disintegration who have avoided asking for it. The necessity of contributing in proportion to property and population to the cost of the navy would be no bar to federation. Other obstacles the Colonies may see, this would not be one. So from Mr. Lowe's utilitarian point of view federation would not be barren. He would be spared the Barmecide banquet he dreads.

It is to be doubted if Mr. Lowe at all realises the extent to which the interests of the people of Great Britain extend beyond their own shores. His is the view of the politician, not that of the great multitude of citizens, who in one shape or another have interests beyond the seas. As fields for the labouring classes the Colonies possess irresistible fascination. They who do not go rejoice at least in the knowledge that they can do so, and there are few amongst them who have not friends there. The rest of the community other than the leisured few have interests more or less extensive beyond the seas. So much of that interest as is given to foreign countries it is certainly not desirable to increase, and if the Colonies are to become foreign countries the same objections would apply to the increase of British interests in them. If Great Britain can retain her dependencies for another fifty years, she must become powerful in the extreme. By that time her consolidated strength as compared with that of the rest of the civilised world would be nearly irresistible. As a mere matter of insurance, it would be better to maintain the connection, even at a heavy cost, than to have those dependencies added to the number of foreign nations. The boy who lends all his schoolfellows money is never popular. The sooner he draws in his loans the better for his pocket; he will never succeed in regaining good-will. Great Britain will vainly seek the love of foreign countries; she is far safer in trusting to the power of her own dominions. By courage, by wealth, and by enterprise she has lived through the great difficulties that beset her. A few years only are wanted to remove those that remain. Is she to falter at the last, and give up the fruit of so much past endurance and hardihood? Between England with world-wide interests and England shut up within herself it is hard to see how there can be any hesitation. Divested of her exterior dominions she would become the theatre of fierce war between the labouring, the moneyed, and the landed classes. Flooded with foreign goods to repay interest on past loans, sufficient occupation would be denied to the people; the moneyed classes would dread investments abroad, would see no room for investments at home, and would fight against the taxation they alone could pay. A fierce onslaught would be made on the land, and year by year the aggregate wealth of the nation would decrease. England is now one vast industrial concern. Deprive it of the means of making that industry profitable, and the loss of wealth will be as speedy as the previous gain. It is a fearful thing to deprive a people of the occupation and the objects which they have grown up to consider their own. There are three choices: one complete isolation; the second a further devotion to foreign interests, the leading principle of which is that England is to give everything, and not to receive even thanks in return; or the third, a return to the old healthy feeling that, recognising in Great Britain itself too narrow a field for the enterprise and industry of its people, sought and secured for them lands all over the globe, in the settlement and advancement of which the great characteristics of their race might have full scope. Is the mission to be given up because at the last moment before success is achieved a few who have been specially fortunate discover that their own particular goal is won? The consciousness of duties fulfilled is the truest human sense of happiness. In order to its attainment man must be occupied. Labour and work are in themselves as well as in their results the sources of enjoyment. If we could suppose that a people had so laboured as to leave nothing else to be effected, the happiest thing for it would be so much destruction of its labour as would leave it work to do over again. It cannot be for the happiness of the British race to shut it out from the labour and work for which, more perhaps than any other race, its restless energy craves. There is not work enough in Great Britain for those who have been born to the heritage on which the sun never sets. Lord Blachford may rest assured there is such an identity of thought in the British people as to make them feel wherever they are situated a sufficient unity of purpose to enable them to maintain one nationality, and Mr. Lowe may find an answer to the hard economic problems he propounds in the simple fact that the value of union to the British people is worth the indirect money risks he discovers. Still the result will probably be as they wish. Great Britain is not alive to her own interest, or rather her politicians do not keep pace with her industrial classes. These are multiplying their interests in the Colonies enormously. By the time that the governing class has discovered that the interests of the country demand federation, the Colonies will probably be so advanced on the road to independence on which Lord Blachford, Mr. Lowe, and others have bid them speed their way, that they may resolutely refuse all overtures to return. And so by the efforts of a few men, and the inaction of a great many, the most beneficent Empire that ever dawned on the world will be turned into a number of discordant States. If, however, federation is not to be, there is no gainsaying the truth of Mr. Lowe's contention, that it is a one-sided arrangement which makes the mother-country bound to the Colonies, and these free to depart whenever they please. Better at once to face the position than to continue to assist the growth of future aliens.

ENGLISH IMPERIALISM[*]
Anonymous

It is not easy to realise that such a policy as that of the
'Imperialists', as they are called on the Continent, should have,
we will not say any root, but even any possibility of root, in
these islands. Yet it is evident that Mr. Disraeli conceived very
early in his career the notion that such a policy, – a policy
which should magnify the Crown on the one hand, and the
wishes of the masses on the other, and should make light of
the constitutional limitations on either, – was still possible in
Europe, and might even have a chance in England. No doubt
the drift of 'Sybil, or the Two Nations', and the central idea
of 'Tancred' pointed in this direction; and even in 'Coningsby'
there were palpable hints that a monarch who should be able
to divine the thoughts of the people, who, more successfully
than Charles I. (that 'holocaust of direct taxation'), should
manage to find a voice for the nation, as distinguished from
the middle-classes, and to vindicate for the Throne the function
of personally representing the multitude, would soon be able
to supersede the clumsy machinery of Parliaments. Apparently
no policy could be more hopeless in this country. All the classes
shade so gradually into each other, that it is difficult to define
the political wishes of the unskilled artisan better than by
saying that they very nearly resemble those of the small shop-
keeper, those of the small shopkeeper better than by saying
that they very nearly resemble those of the wholesale dealer,
those of the wholesale dealer better than by saying that they
closely resemble those of the merchant or banker, those of the
merchant or banker better than by saying that they partake
very much of the wishes of the middle-class gentry, and those
of the middle-class gentry better than by saying that they are
fairly enough represented on the benches of the House of
Lords. Of course, these gradations, though slight at each step,

[*] From *Spectator*, 8 April 1876, pp. 457–8.

collectively amount to something substantial. The opinion of the House of Commons, which represents the nation, is not quite the same, either in drift or in its constituent elements, as the opinion of the House of Lords. Still, there is no wide gulf between any two classes. A monarch who tried to gain for himself popularity among the masses, and to play off that popularity against the middle-classes and the aristocracy, would be at a grievous loss what to begin with. He would be in great danger of repudiation by the masses, if he did anything of which the shopkeepers did not approve, and he would indeed stand in considerable danger of being repudiated by all for the mere attempt to play off one section of the people against another.

But the difficulty of carrying through such a policy with the slightest success in this country is no reason at all why Mr. Disraeli should not have looked upon it with favour. Though the head of the Conservative party, he was never a Conservative, and has no notion at all of the strength of Conservatism which penetrates the whole fabric of British society. Whether this last little experiment on the popularity of the attempt to raise the titular magnificence of the Crown is or is not likely to be a failure with the masses, is yet a question which nobody seems fully able to answer. Lord Shaftesbury says very strongly, – and we doubt whether any member of the Legislature has more access to the real opinions of the masses than Lord Shaftesbury, – that it is not a success. Our opinion has been a hesitating one on this point. Our impression was, not certainly that it had been a definite success, but that it had not definitely failed, – that there was none of the irritation and disgust towards the attempt 'to gild refined gold', as Lord Selborne put it, among the working-class which there is among the middle and upper classes. Lord Shaftesbury, however, tells us that he could produce plenty of letters and documents, 'even from Whitechapel', to show that the new title is not popular. They 'have their suspicions' of it, is the phrase which Lord Shaftesbury has found them using. In other words, their bias, like that of the middle-classes, is towards dislike of the innovation and towards a disposition to impute it to some arbitrary and unwholesome craving, rather than to any laudable and natural motive. If so, they have got no idea that it could do them any good to give the monarch additional dignity. They may believe that the Queen, as she is, has much more power to carry measures for their good than she really has. But even if they do believe this, supposing Lord Shaftesbury's information is correct, it has not yet occurred to them that if they could but increase the importance of the Throne, the Monarch might help them to put down the injustice of the rich. According to this view of the feeling of the multitude, though they may not always wish for the same things as the middle-classes, they would prefer to take their political cue from the middle-classes, whom they half understand, and towards whose position they aspire, to taking it from the Throne, whose motives of action they hardly understand, though they may have the blindest confidence in its traditional power and rights.

But whether it is true or false that this attempt to 'electro-plate' the Crown is differently looked upon by the different layers of English society, one thing is clear, that the progress of democracy, which the present Premier has done more to hasten than any public man of his day, opens the way for any statesman who is so disposed, to alliances with the prejudices and ignorance of the masses, such as constitutes the very essence of the Imperialist policy of France. Despotic decrees, such as are likely to be ratified by Plébiscites, are the favourite engines of French Imperialism; and though in England it will be impossible, for a great many generations to come, to excite any loyalty towards despotic decrees, even though they should be of a kind to receive the ratification of a popular vote, yet doubtless the temptation will too often be felt by the popular statesman who thinks he sees his way to the external support of the masses, to get legislative prudence and deliberation over-ruled by an appeal to popular prejudices and clamour. And this, whether it be done by magnifying the power of the Throne directly or not, is really of the essence of the Imperialist policy. It may be a mere accident that Mr. Disraeli has had the chance of proposing an addition to the Queen's style and title which was intended to enhance its grandeur, and probably was not originally at all meant to be labelled, as Lord Rosebery tells us, in his clever speech, that the present proposal is to be labelled, 'For external application only.' But it certainly was not a chance that Mr. Disraeli persuaded his party to have confidence in the Conservative tendencies of the Residuum, and proved by practical experiment that there is often less enlightenment in the masses than there is in the higher strata of a civilised society. That is a policy which, as the democratic organisation of government proceeds, must necessarily suggest itself to the rulers of any self-governing nation, and its failure or success must depend on the closeness of texture in the social fabric, – that is, the amount of sympathy or estrangement between the classes which come nearest to each other in numbers, wealth, and the character of their interests, and the consequent dislike for, or inclination to grasp at an alliance with some political extreme, for the purpose of getting the better of those intermediate sections of society which constitute the mean.

Whether such a policy is ever destined to succeed in England no one as yet can say. But it has already been tried on a small scale – not perhaps very successfully – by Mr. Disraeli, and may yet be tried on a larger scale. The true ground for hope – we will not say confidence – is that English Reform has been too steady and gradual, and that, as a consequence, the neighbouring sections of English society are too closely related to each other, to admit of success. English Conservatism is the Conservatism of a people without startling jealousies between neighbouring grades. If there be any possibility of the unnatural alliances of which Imperialism makes its boast, it would be of an alliance between the agricultural labourers, probably the most isolated, the least assimilated of all the elements of our society, and an adventurer on the Throne, or any other power whatever which chose to avail itself of the distrust felt by these labourers towards their employers. But an adventurer on our Throne is hardly possible, and there is, we think, no slight reason to hope that there are no gaps wide enough in the fabric of English society to render the union of extremes against the means, which is of the essence of Imperialism, a policy likely to prosper. The Conservatism which makes most play with such a policy as this, is not the Conservatism which has been, like ours, the shadow which follows on advancing Liberalism. It requires great chasms in social feeling between class and class to manoeuvre a policy of this kind with any brilliant success, and of such chasms there are but few, and we hope not very wide ones, in the fabric of our social system. If Lord Shaftesbury is right, as we trust he may be, if it should turn out that the hesitation which there has certainly been among the people ends in complete accord between the working and middle classes, and a cordial rejection of this policy of making advances towards the Throne, we shall have had the best proof which political events could afford of the advantages of a long-continued policy of gradual reform; – a reform which results in making the political wishes and tastes of the classes nearest to each other so much alike, that the more educated feeling guides the less educated, instead of exciting its jealousy and its opposition.

OUR ROUTE TO INDIA*
Edward Dicey

'Never to prophesy unless you know' is a wise rule for all
writers on subjects connected with the vicissitudes of war, but
especially for those whose vaticinations are liable to be falsified
by events during the interval between composition and publication. Still there is one forecast with reference to the war
now commenced in grim earnest which I can venture to make
confidently; and that is, that the war, whenever and however
it closes, will not leave things as they were previous to its
inception. Putting aside the passing speculations of the hour,
it seems to me as manifest as any unaccomplished fact can
well be, that we are on the eve of a fundamental revolution in
the affairs of Eastern Europe. We have come to the beginning
of the end. In saying this I am not expressing an opinion
whether the end is desirable or otherwise. Personally, I believe
it would have been better for the world if the settlement of
the Eastern Question could have been deferred for another
generation. The prospect of Turkish rule over the Balkan peninsula being replaced by a Russian Protectorate affords me no
satisfaction. But whether your sympathies are Turkophil or
Russophil, whether you deem Turkey to be the victim of the
most iniquitous of intrigues, or whether you hold Russia to be
engaged in the holiest of crusades, I fail to see how you can
shut your eyes to the patent fact that Ottoman rule in Europe
is doomed. That this should be so does not indeed prove that
it ought to be so. Good things as well as evil things have
their day. Bulwarks of civilisation are no more immortal than
remnants of barbarism. All I contend for is that, in Eastern
Europe at any rate, the 'manifest destiny' is with the Christian
as against the Moslem, with the Slav as against the Turk. It
may be, though it scarcely seems to me within the region of
probability, that Turkey may pull through the present crisis

* From *Nineteenth Century*, vol. 1 (June 1877), pp. 665–85.

without absolute dismemberment of her Empire. But even on this hypothesis she can only owe her safety to the mutual jealousies of the Western Powers. It does not lie within the scope of this article to discuss the possible or probable arrangements which may be made at the conclusion of the war. As a matter of fact, however, it may be taken for granted that, whenever peace is made, Russia, whether in Europe or in Asia, will have taken a considerable step towards the overthrow of Ottoman rule, while Turkey will be left less able than she has proved hitherto to present any formidable resistance to the advance of Russia. Even the most sanguine of believers in the regeneration of Turkey under constitutional government would admit that the proximate, if not the immediate, occupation of Constantinople by Russia lies within the domain of possibility. You do not insure your house against fire because you think it likely to be burnt down, but because you think it possible it may be burnt down. It is sufficient, therefore, for us, as a nation, to know that the command of the Bosphorus passing into the hands of Russia is a possibility, to make it incumbent upon us to consider in what mode we should insure ourselves against the dangers arising out of this possible contingency.

The first question, then, which suggests itself is what practical difference it would make to England if the Bosphorus passed, either nominally or virtually, from under the command of Turkey into that of Russia. I may say in passing that the conditions of the problem under consideration would be modified in degree rather than substance, if, as many persons imagine, the interests of Germany and Austria should compel them to preclude Russia from obtaining possession of Constantinople. If once a vigorous independent government, which the force of events might lead to cooperate with Russia, should be established on the Bosphorus, we should lose the protection afforded to our Indian possessions by the fact of the lands lying east and west of the channel dividing Europe and Asia being under the dominion of a friendly, inert, and unprogressive power. Mr. Bright asked triumphantly at Manchester why we should be affected by a war three thousand miles away. The obvious answer is that the most important possessions of the British Crown lie yet more than three thousand miles further to the East. Of course, if it is contended that our Indian

Empire is not worth preserving, *cadit quœstio*. It would be entirely foreign to my purpose to argue this point. I must ask my readers to take for granted, as the basis of my argument, that the preservation of our dominion in the East is a matter of paramount importance to us, only less important, indeed, than the preservation of our national independence. I may be wrong in this assumption; but it is one which, whether right or wrong, is shared by the vast majority of Englishmen. I say, then, unhesitatingly, that the chief, though not the sole, concern we have in the settlement of the Eastern Question lies in the effect that settlement must produce on the security of our Indian possessions. A mere glance at the map serves to show how the Ottoman Empire, together with the adjacent Mussulman kingdoms, lies like a huge breakwater between Russia and India. We are often told that the only solution of the Eastern Question is to drive the Turks back into Asia. It may be so. But the notion which the authors of this theory seem to hold, that the Sultan could transfer the seat of empire to Damascus, or Bagdad, or Smyrna, or Heaven knows where, is an utter delusion. Constantinople is the keystone of the arch which supports the crumbling edifice of the Ottoman Empire. Take that away, and the whole structure falls to pieces. To build up a new empire east of the Bosphorus is a task beyond the capabilities of the Turks. Whatever power holds Stamboul is, in virtue of all precedent, mistress of Asia Minor. No doubt Islam would be a force to be taken into account even if there were no caliph in existence; and there would still be Mohammedan States notwithstanding the fall of Turkey. But our own experience in India has shown us that isolated and disjointed Mohammedan communities cannot hold their own against a dominant European Power. Thus, if the Cross should ever replace the Crescent on St. Sophia, Russia, instead of being opposed in her advance towards India by the formidable strength of a great and united if decaying empire, would only be confronted by a number of isolated and disjointed States resembling those of Central Asia, which, from their want of cohesion as well as from their internal jealousies and divisions, must inevitably fall an easy prey to any civilised military Power. Of course I may be told, as we are now daily told by our public instructors, that Russia has no idea of attacking Constantinople, and would be guilty of absolute insanity if she were to entertain any such idea. For my purpose, however, it

is sufficient to show that a Russian advance on the Bosphorus is within the domain of possibility, and that the almost
certain result of the present war will be to remove some at
least of the more serious obstacles which have hitherto barred
the advance of Russia Stamboul-wards, whether on land or
sea. Supposing the war should at its close leave the frontiers
of Roumania extended to the Balkan under a Russian Protectorate, Russian territory increased in Asia Minor by the
annexation of Armenia, and the free passage of the Bosphorus
thrown open to Russian men-of-war, it would be impossible
to dispute the fact that Russia had made a long step towards
the dismemberment of Turkey and the seizure of Constantinople. And yet, in the event of Turkey being worsted in the
coming campaign, such terms of peace as those I have indicated
are the least that Russia is likely to demand. Thus, whether
we like it or not, we are bound in common prudence to face
the contingency that at no distant period Russia may
command the head of the Euphrates valley by land, and the
Bosphorus by sea. If once Constantinople passes directly or
indirectly into the hands of an active maritime State, the chain
of inland seas leading from the Mediterranean to the Sea of
Azof must become home waters, so to speak, of the Power
holding the Bosphorus. It is only the utter apathy and want of
enterprise, especially on sea, characterising Ottoman rule,
which has hindered Turkey from becoming the chief maritime
Power of the Levant. Given the possession of the Bosphorus,
and Russia would soon have an ironclad fleet in the Sea of
Marmora, which could sail out at any moment and reach Port
Said long before reinforcements could arrive from Malta. It is
said that in the case of Russia obtaining the passage of the
Bosphorus, we could neutralise the danger by keeping a fleet
stationed at Besika Bay, or by seizing the mouth of the Dardanelles and holding it as we do Gibraltar. But the former
safeguard could only be temporary in its nature; the latter,
even if feasible – which I doubt – would involve a heavy
constant outlay and a state of permanent antagonism not only
to Russia, but to all Powers interested in the freedom of access
between the Euxine and the Mediterranean.

Thus, if I have made my meaning clear, the state of things
with which we have to deal is this. A war has begun which,
as I deem, may probably, and, as all must admit, may possibly,
end in the over-throw of the Ottoman Empire. This overthrow

would weaken if not imperil our hold on India. How then are we to protect ourselves against the peril involved in the possible success of Russia? That is the question. Now, in the first place, I must state my conviction that no precaution within our power to take can place us in as strong a position as that we now occupy. Nothing could be as good for us as that the Bosphorus and the provinces west and east of it should remain under the rule of an unaggressive Power, friendlily disposed towards us by virtue of the instinct of self-preservation. But even waiving the question whether we should be justified in upholding a vicious system of government in European Turkey in order to promote our own advantage, it is obvious that we are utterly unable to uphold Turkish rule unless we are prepared to fight for Turkey whenever she is assailed, which, wisely or unwisely, we are not. Now the very fact that, according to my view, we should be manifestly weaker, in the sense of being more liable to attack in our Eastern possessions, than we are at present, in the event of Ottoman rule in Europe receiving a death-blow, renders it all the more essential that we should guard against the impending danger by such means as lie within our power. In plainer words, the mere possibility that Russia may obtain the command of the Bosphorus renders it a matter of urgent necessity to us to secure the command of the Isthmus route to India. In order to effect this, we must have the power of keeping the Suez Canal open to our ships at all times and under all circumstances; and, to secure this, we must acquire a recognised footing in the Delta of Egypt of a far more decided character than any we can claim at present.

No doubt, by the original firman issued by the Porte for the construction of the canal, its waters are declared to be neutral, and we often hear suggestions that this declaration of neutrality – which at present is a simple agreement between the Porte and the company – should be confirmed by an international guarantee of all the European Powers. But recent experience must have led the most simple-hearted believer in the authority of international declarations to doubt their practical efficacy. If the treaty of Paris guaranteeing the independence of Turkey, entered into within the lifetime of the present generation, and solemnly reaffirmed only six years ago, is now treated as so much waste paper by all the Powers concerned, what possible security can we have that twenty years, ten years, or twelve months hence, the European Powers could be relied upon to make war upon any State which infringed the neutrality of the canal, even if it were guaranteed by the most solemn and formal of international compacts? Moreover, as Sir Stafford Northcote pointed out the other day, the neutralisation of the canal, even if it could be secured, would be fatal to our interests as a belligerent.

Supposing the canal to be really neutralised, it is obvious that if two European Powers were at war they could not be allowed to traverse its waters with ships of war or transports, or even with merchant vessels carrying supplies to the rival armies. In the event of a war between England and Russia in the East, such a prohibition would be no practical disadvantage to the latter Power; for as long as we hold Aden and Perim we can close the mouth of the Red Sea against all comers. But to us any obstacle in the way of our sending troops and ships to and fro between the Mediterranean and the Red Sea at our pleasure would prove the most serious of disadvantages in the case of war, even if our Indian Empire were not the direct object of attack. If the Euphrates Valley route lay open to the Russian armies, while we could only convey troops to and from India by the long sea route round the Cape, the difficulty of defending ourselves against attack, both in Europe and Asia, would be more than doubled. Again, in the contingency to which I allude, it would be a matter of vital necessity to us, not only to have free right of passage for our own ships of war, but to have the power of excluding all others, during war time, from its waters. A hostile ironclad which once made its way as far as Ismailia or into the Bitter Lakes would prevent the passage of our ships by the mere fact of its presence. Then, too, it should be borne in mind that the canal, owing to the peculiarity of its structure, could very easily be rendered useless. Given four-and-twenty hours' time, and a company of sappers and miners in undisturbed possession of any portion of its sandbanks; and an amount of damage might be inflicted which would not only render the canal impassable for the moment, but which could not be repaired for weeks or months. In order, therefore, to secure our freedom of uninterrupted access to India across the Isthmus, it is essential that we should not only have an unrestricted right of employing its waters for war purposes, but that its course from sea to sea, as well as its ports of ingress and egress, should be under our protection. No strategical knowledge is required to appreciate the importance of the control of the canal to England. With the exception of that small school of politicians who hold that the British Empire should be restricted within the four seas, everybody would, I think, admit that the command of the canal – or, in other words, the occupation of the Delta – would be a gain to England, supposing it to lie within our power to obtain such a control, and supposing also that we could obtain it without any violation of duty, or without assuming responsibilities too heavy for our due performance.

I take the question as to our power to obtain control of the canal first, not because I deem it the more important, but because, if it cannot be answered in the affirmative, the further question whether we should act rightly in making the attempt ceases to be of any practical importance. Now, as a matter of fact, we could at the present moment, and in all likelihood for some months to come, obtain possession of the canal without difficulty and without opposition. I am not recommending a *coup de main*. All I need remark on this subject is that if a couple of ironclads were stationed at Port Said, and a single British regiment was landed at Alexandria, we should at once have assured a position from which no power could dislodge us except by war. Indeed, the same object could practically be effected if we hoisted the union-jack at the entrance to the canal under the care of a corporal's guard, and announced that hence-forward the canal and the Delta would be placed under our protectorate. We have in fact only to hold out our hand in order to carry our point. Of course this is no justification for high-handed insolence, just as the fact of Alderney being without a garrison would be no excuse for a French fleet sailing from Cherbourg to annex the Channel Islands. But, in considering whether it is desirable to effect an occupation of Egypt, the fact that the enterprise presents no military difficulty of any kind is one that ought not to be over-looked. The next point worth considering is how far such a step would bring us into collision with the other Powers of Europe. Till within the last few years England could only have planted herself in Egypt at the cost of a war with France. Under the reign of Louis-Philippe, and even under the Second Empire, France would have resisted any extension of British power in the Levant by all means at her disposal. That Syria and Egypt were in some special sense under the protection of France was throughout the first seventy years of this century a tradition of French policy; and France would undoubtedly have viewed any scheme for the occupation of the Delta by England very much as our statesmen would still view any proposal for the seizure of the Scheldt by Germany. But questions of remote foreign policy never take much hold of the popular imagination in any country, and least of all in France. It is at once the strength and weakness of the French mind that its interests are pretty well circumscribed within the area of France. Now for the present the thoughts of Frenchmen of all classes who have time to think of anything beyond the cares or pleasures of their daily life, are absorbed in the dread of Germany, and in the desire to promote any influences which may hereafter facilitate the recovery of Alsace and Lorraine. To secure an interval of peace during which the French army may be placed on a footing to defend France against a second German invasion is the one paramount idea of every French politician. On the Continent it is believed, with or without reason, that, if Constantinople should be threatened, England must fight for Turkey, and if England intervened the war must become general. Any arrangement, therefore, by which England could be induced to regard the aggrandisement of Russia with comparative indifference would be welcome to France, even if it involved some sacrifice of French influence abroad. To put it shortly, if France were offered the alternative of a general war or of the annexation of Egypt by England, she would choose the latter without a moment's hesitation. Whenever France recovers her strength, and shakes off the incubus of her dread of Germany, she will recommence her traditional rivalry with England in the Levant. But at this moment we could do what we could not have done for the last seventy-five years, and what very possibly we could not do a couple of years hence – that is, take possession of Egypt without the risk of a war with France.

Russia, from the days of the Czar Nicholas and Sir Hamilton Seymour, has advocated the policy of a partition of the Turkish Empire in which Egypt should fall to the share of England; and I have reason to believe suggestions of such a scheme were made within the last few weeks. While there was a possibility of the war being averted, our Government were, I think, right in turning a deaf ear to any proposal whose acceptance might have seemed to sanction the dismemberment of Turkey. But now that the attack has been made, and that the Russian armies are marching towards the Bosphorus, the position is changed. At any rate, if, in view of the advance of Russia towards Constantinople, we should see cause to secure our route to India by the occupation of Egypt, Russia would certainly acquiesce in our action; though if she had once secured her own position on the Golden Horn, she would assuredly oppose any British occupation of the Delta with all her strength. Germany, from whatever motive, has more than once of late intimated to our Government that she would view with satisfaction the establishment of English supremacy on the Isthmus; and Austria would certainly not oppose any measure which tended to strengthen the power of England in the Levant. Italy, Spain, Portugal, and Holland could hardly be expected to entertain a favourable feeling towards a project by which the command of the Suez Canal would pass into the hands of Great Britain. Still, at the worst, they would be obliged to accept accomplished facts. Moreover, our Free Trade policy has removed much of the jealousy with which any extension of our rule used to be regarded by our commercial rivals. The mercantile communities throughout Europe would feel a well-merited confidence that under the union-jack the passage of the canal would be as free as the Straits of Dover to the trading vessels of all nations. Thus I may take, as the second step in my argument, that the step I suggest could be taken by England not only without any immediate military difficulty, but without any risk of involving ourselves in hostilities with any European Power.

It being shown, then, that there are no material obstacles to our taking possession of the canal, it remains next to be seen what, if any, are the moral objections to its execution. No great public improvement can be carried out without interfering with private rights, and therefore it does not seem to me a fatal obstacle to the plan advocate that we should have to interfere with certain vested interests. If possible, we should endeavour to obtain the consent of the parties interested; if not, we should be obliged to dispense with their sanction. For reasons I shall enter into more fully later on, the protectorate of the Suez Canal involves of necessity the virtual occupation of Lower Egypt. But, as a question of abstract right and expediency, the two measures stand on a completely different footing; and all I have to consider now is, who are the parties whose interests we should be honourably bound to consult, and whose opposition we ought fairly to take into account, if we made up our minds to take possession of the canal. Now the title to the canal may be said to rest with three different parties – first, the French company by whom it was constructed; secondly, the Government of Egypt, as represented by the Khedive, to whom the ownership of the canal reverts after the expiration of the concession; and, thirdly, the Sultan, to whose dominions as Suzerain the canal, in common with every other portion of Egypt, may be said to legally belong. To take the last first, we may fairly say that Turkey's interest in the canal is of an entirely technical character. The Porte would find it difficult to sell its potential title to the canal for a single sixpence. Owing to the utter absence of any maritime enterprise in Turkey, the canal is of less practical value to the Ottoman Empire than to the smallest of European States possessing a seaboard of its own; and, apart from the consideration of its general relations to Europe, the Porte would gladly surrender its rights to England for an almost nominal return. My whole argument is based on the probability that the Ottoman Empire is no longer able to hold its place in the world. Granted this assumption, and we cannot afford to shape our action in deference to the wishes of a moribund Power. But, as a matter of fact, even if Turkey survives the war as an European State, I believe it would gladly see England installed in a position on the Isthmus which might serve as a counterpoise to the increase of power and territory certain to be acquired by Russia at the close of a successful campaign. With regard to the Khedive, his pecuniary interest in the canal, now that he has sold his founder's shares, would fetch very little in the market. The objections he might raise to our compulsory purchase of the canal, and the price at which he might be disposed to withdraw his opposition, may be better considered when I come to the question of an occupation of Egypt. I may say here in passing that he would, I believe, raise no difficulty about parting with his rights in the canal for a very moderate amount, if this end could be effected without detriment to his position as ruler of Egypt. In as far, then, as the canal itself is concerned, I may say that the only title we should have seriously to consider would be that of the company. The moral strength of this title I for one am not disposed to underrate. The accomplishment of this great enterprise – for which England above all other nations has cause to be grateful, and but for whose effectuation English interests in

India would be placed, at this crisis, in the gravest peril – is due in the first instance to the genius and energy of M. de Lesseps, and in the second to the confidence with which the French investors supported with their subscriptions an enterprise declared from its outset up to its completion to be insane and impracticable.

Still, if we were prepared to pay liberally, I think we might acquire possession of the canal with the consent, if not the approval, of the parties directly or indirectly interested in the concern. As a mere speculation it would be well worth our while to repay the whole amount of the money laid out on the canal, which may roughly be put down at thirty millions, if we could obtain absolute and uncontrolled possession of it as the highway between England and India. Practically we might buy up all the various rights of proprietorship in the canal for under half that sum, and yet content everybody. But the real objection to the purchase of the canal is that it is comparatively valueless to us unless we have command of the adjacent country, or, in other words, unless we occupy Lower Egypt. As I have endeavoured to show, we require, in order to protect ourselves from the results of a possible, if not probable, occupation of Constantinople by Russia, to secure an unrestricted right of passage for ships of war and troops to and from India by the Isthmus route. Even if we were the lawful owners of the canal, the possession would be of no value to us in a military point of view unless we were also in possession of the surrounding country. In times of peace a mere handful of troops would be sufficient to protect our property; but in the event of a war, or even the prospect of a war, we must be at liberty to occupy the Delta, and to erect fortifications not only at Port Said, but at every point along the coast where a landing could be effected. Military authorities agree that Egypt (by which I may say here once for all I mean the Delta) could be defended with very little difficulty by any Power who had the command of the two seas between which it lies. But, as I have already pointed out, the fact that the canal could be rendered useless with very little difficulty by a very small force, coupled with the further fact that any stoppage in the water passage across the Isthmus might be disastrous for us in the event of a war for the possession of India, makes it absolutely incumbent upon us, if we want to hold the canal, to secure ourselves against any attack being made upon it throughout the whole of its course across the Isthmus. In other words, we must have the power to occupy the Isthmus when we choose and where we choose. Of course it may be urged that in the case of war we should infallibly occupy Egypt whether we had any legal right to do so or not. The truth of this statement is obvious. But with a Russian ironclad fleet stationed in the harbours of the Black Sea and able to sail out into the Mediterranean through the Straits whenever it thought fit, we should be liable to have Egypt occupied by a hostile army before our troops could reach it. What we require, therefore, is the permanent occupation of a number of points on the Isthmus under similar conditions to those under which we hold Gibraltar and Malta. It is difficult for anyone who has not been there quite to realise how very small a place Egypt is; but the smallness of its area makes it absolutely impossible for two rival governments to be within its limits, and any Power which has military possession of the canal must virtually rule the country.

Now, in order to obtain possession of Egypt, all we have to do is to deal with the Khedive. For all practical purposes the Khedive and Egypt are identical. The question how the Egyptian people would be affected by the annexation of the Isthmus to England is one which deserves the fullest consideration; but in any arrangement concluded between the Khedive and England, or, for that matter, with any other Power, the Egyptians themselves can have neither voice nor part. It would be almost as absurd, if you were purchasing a flock of sheep, to ask the grazier for an endorsement of the contract on the part of the flock as it would be to insist that the Egyptians should be a party to any transfer of their soil from one owner to another. To all intents and purposes Egypt is a conquered country, ruled from Turkey by a small number of Turkish pashas.

In as far as I could ever ascertain, the substantial hold which the Khedive has upon his dominions is of the weakest kind. Even if he were the best beloved of Eastern rulers, he could not rely on the attachment of his subjects, from the simple fact that they have no power to make their attachment felt. Why the reigning dynasty in Egypt has remained so long in possession of the throne is a question not easy to answer. Mehemet Ali was one of those born rulers of men who achieve power and hold it by their own force of will. His successors have retained the Pashaship of Egypt partly because, though not of the same calibre with the founder of their dynasty, they have been one and all men of greater energy and intelligence than the average pashas of Turkey; partly because they profited by the traditional rivalry between England and France in the Levant, which had caused the latter Power to take Mehemet Ali and his dynasty under its special protection; partly, and perhaps more than all, because of the intense apathetic conservatism of the East, which holds the fact of a thing's existing reason sufficient why it should go on to exist. Still, the position of the Khedives, to use their present and better known name, has been from the first a very insecure one. At any time since Mehemet Ali's death the Porte, if it had so thought fit, could probably have deposed the reigning Viceroy and given the Pashalik to another member of his family or to a stranger. The Porte, however, though it had no love for the Egyptian dynasty, was afraid of attempting any violent change, as for the last thirty years – ever since, in fact, the Overland Route was first established – England would not have tolerated any direct reestablishment of Turkish authority in the Isthmus, while up to 1870 the Khedive could always have appealed to France to protect him against any overt aggression on the part of the Sultan. Moreover, the Porte had till the other day the strongest motives for avoiding an interference in the affairs of Egypt, which must necessarily have led to a reopening of the whole Eastern Question. And – what is perhaps more important than all the other considerations on which I have dwelt – the acquiescence of the Porte in the Khedivate has been secured by a system of wholesale and constant bribery. If ever a true balance-sheet of Egyptian finance could be published, the world would be astonished to discover what a vast proportion of the Egyptian debt had been incurred in presents to the statesmen of Stamboul, the courtiers in good odour at the palace, and the reigning favourites of the harem. Possibly a more determined man than Ismail Pasha might have run the risk of refusing to submit to the wholesale system of black mail to which he has been subjected by the Turkish Government; but, rightly or wrongly, the Khedive has never felt secure enough of his own throne to hazard the consequences of a capture with Turkey, and, not being prepared for this, he has had no option except to counteract the intrigues of the Seraglio by lavish and persistent bribery. Anyone at all acquainted with the history of Levantine politics is aware that the Khedive, though constantly deploring the evils of his connection with Turkey, has always shrunk from any decisive attempt to sever this connection. The truth is, that though the authority of the Caliphate is probably weaker in Egypt than in any other Mussulman State, it is still a force to be taken into account, and even a very feeble force will carry all before it if it encounters no opposition. After all, the title under which the Viceroy of Egypt exercises his authority is that of nominee of the Commander of the Faithful, and this title he must of necessity forfeit if he throws off his allegiance. The notion of there being a distinct Egyptian nationality which could be relied on to support the reigning dynasty as against Turkey is an utter delusion, which Ismail Pasha is far too shrewd a man to share. The army, indeed, is amply sufficient to suppress any popular rising against the Khedive's rule, even supposing such a thing were within the domain of possibility. But what the Khedive has to fear is not a popular but a palace revolution, and against this his army is utterly useless.

In no country is the maxim *Le Roi est mort, vive le Roi* more faithfully obeyed than in Egypt, and if any morning Cairo were to learn that Ismail Pasha's reign was over, and that Halim or Hassan, or any other Pasha, ruled in his stead, the army would obey the new *régime* with the same passive obedience as it displayed towards the old. So long as no Viceroy can govern without the consent of the Sultan, the Khedive has some security against sudden deposition by a rival. But independence once granted, and he is liable to be upset at any moment by any ambitious pasha who can secure the services of a handful of troops, or purchase the complicity of the harem, and who is not afraid to risk his life for the chance of a throne. In spite of all its varnish of European civilisation, Egypt is still an Eastern State, with all the ideas, traditions, and habits of the East; and the scene enacted the other day at Stamboul when Abdul Aziz was deposed might be re-enacted at Cairo, with far less danger or disturbance.

Nobody is better aware of all this than the Khedive himself, and I believe a sense of the insecurity of his own tenure of the throne has played a very important part in determining his foreign as well as his financial policy. Recent events have certainly not tended to lessen this sense of insecurity. The disasters of France, and her consequent withdrawal from any active participation in Levantine affairs, have deprived the dynasty

of Mehemet Ali of a most powerful though onerous protector-
ship. The financial embarrassments of Egypt have alienated the
not unimportant support which the Khedive received during
his solvent days from the moneyed interests of Europe; and
the example of Tunis, where the administration of the finances
has been taken possession of by an International Commission,
and the Bey reduced to a position of complete insignificance,
is of evil omen for Egypt. Throughout the discussions which
took place at the palace of Abdin during Mr. Cave's mission,
the Khedive used constantly to remark, 'On veut me mettre en
syndicat, et moi je ne le veux pas;' and this remark showed
clearly enough his appreciation of the danger with which he is
threatened, not so much by his indebtedness as by the international character of his liabilities. Then, again, the prospect
of the dissolution of the Ottoman Empire cannot but fill him
with alarm. If Turkey falls to pieces, Egypt indeed may recover
her independence, but the Khedive's personal position, as the
Viceroy of the Sultan, would be materially weakened. Moreover, the Khedive cannot but be aware of the growing
dissatisfaction felt against his rule by the population of Egypt.
The burden of an excessive, and still more of a capricious,
taxation has become well-nigh unbearable even by the long-
suffering Fellaheen. In itself this discontent is of little importance. The inhabitants of Egypt have been set to make bricks
without straw from the days of the Pharaohs, and even if their
discontent should ever take an active form, the Turkish colony
in Egypt, which has the command of the army, is strong enough
to suppress any native revolt. But there is in Alexandria and
Cairo a large, turbulent, and unscrupulous European element,
and if this foreign element were to take advantage of popular
resentment against unwonted oppression to organise an insur-
rection against the dynasty, the danger would assume a very
different character. It is a fact worth noting that, when the
Viceroy ordered the suspension of payment on the debt, there
were demonstrations at Alexandria at which shouts were raised
of 'Down with the Khedive!' Of course the demonstration was
made by foreigners, not by natives; but this circumstance does
not diminish its intrinsic gravity.

Now, by the firman which Ismail Pasha purchased from the
Porte, the rule of succession has been altered in favour of his
eldest son, in lieu of his uncle. The reform is a very good one
in the ultimate interests of Egypt, but it has alienated the

Khedive's family, and has given a shock to the conservative prejudices of a Mussulman population. By the usage of Islam, Halim Pasha, the youngest son of Mehemet Ali, is the natural and legal successor to the throne in the event of the Khedive's death or deposition. Not much is known about Halim, but he is believed at Cairo to be ambitious and unscrupulous, and is understood to resent bitterly his exclusion from the succession in favour of his nephew. He lives, too, at Stamboul, and is a favourite with the Divan, and was one of the last ministers of Abdul Aziz. In the event of any attempt to overthrow the authority of the Khedive, Halim Pasha would probably be the prince in whose behalf the rising would be made. The Khedive is keenly alive to this danger, and his perception of his own insecurity is likely to make him look more favourably than might be the case otherwise on the prospect of Egypt being placed under British protection. No doubt His Highness would prefer an arrangement under which we guaranteed his dynasty from attack both at home and abroad, and yet left him in undisturbed possession of his sovereignty. But he is too shrewd a man not to see that such an arrangement is out of the question. Surrounded as he is with dangers arising out of the impending collapse of Turkey, the ambition of foreign powers, the gravity of his financial embarrassments, the claims of his foreign creditors, the disaffection of his subjects, and last, though not least, the intrigues of his own kinsfolk, he would probably be not unwilling to allow Lower Egypt to pass virtually under the dominion of Great Britain in return for the security which he would have as a protected prince, enjoying all the honour and emoluments of sovereignty, and still exercising a qualified amount of sovereign power in the Delta together with supreme authority in Upper Egypt. The Khedive has many high and noble qualities. Judging him, as it is only fair to do, by an Oriental, not an European standard, you cannot avoid admiring his indefatigable energy, his desire to develope the resources of his country, his ambition to stand well in the opinion of the world, and to associate his name with great undertakings and grand achievements. His ambition may be perverted, his policy may be erroneous, his mode of carrying out his objects may be utterly unjustifiable; still, with all that, it must fairly be said of Ismail Pasha that he has higher ends and aims in life than sensual self-indulgence; and to say this is to say a good deal for a prince born and bred in the harem. But, unless my own estimate, and that of those who know the Viceroy far more intimately, is entirely erroneous. His Highness is not the man to fight a battle when the odds are heavily against him. In other words, if our Government should show that they are resolved on obtaining a dominant position in Egypt, the Khedive's instinct would be to make the best bargain he could for himself and his dynasty, not to offer a well-nigh forlorn resistance. It lies in his power to transfer supreme authority to us over the Isthmus by the mere exercise of his will, and therefore, as a matter of policy as well as equity, we should be liberal, if not lavish, in the terms we might offer to secure his cooperation. But at the best it does not lie within his power to hinder us from occupying the Isthmus at our own free will and pleasure; and if, on other grounds, we should deem it right to act, we should not be deterred from action by the impossibility of obtaining the Khedive's consent.

Nor, I think, need we fear any opposition from the creditors of Egypt. Morally speaking, there are few interests in the world less deserving of consideration than that of the Levantine holders of Egyptian bonds. It would be difficult to find a more worthless community than that of the Alexandrine financing money-lenders who tempted the Khedive to reckless extravagance by the proffer of loans at exorbitant rates, who have made enormous profits out of the necessities of their patron, and who now turn against him because he has declined to give them preferential advantages over his *bonâ-fide* creditors. Nor, I own, have I much more sympathy for the wrongs of the foreign bondholders. It was with no desire of promoting the development of Egypt, but simply from the hope of getting a large return on their investment, that they lent their money to the Khedive, and they never troubled themselves to inquire by what means or what exactions their interest was to be paid. Still, in order to avoid future complications with foreign Powers, it would be well for us to secure the sanction of the Egyptian bondholders, and this we should have little difficulty in doing. I have not the space, nor is it needful for my purpose, to enter on a disquisition as to Egyptian finance. But I may say in passing that no one of the various schemes hitherto proposed, neither that of Mr. Cave nor Sir George Elliot nor Mr. Rivers Wilson, neither the State Bank project of Messrs. Pastré and Sinadino, nor the arrangement devised by Mr.

Goschen and M. Joubert, provides anything approaching to security for the liquidation of the debt. 'Qui a bu boira' is true in public as well as in private life, and from the necessities of his position the Khedive cannot control his expenditure even if he were disposed to do so. So long as his sovereign authority is uncontrolled, he has the power of borrowing money, all pledges and agreements to the contrary notwithstanding; so long as he can borrow there will be plenty of people ready to lend him money – for a price; and so long as money is offered to him he will take it. From this vicious circle there is no escape, and the chief practical effect, to my mind, of any settlement which, like Mr. Goschen's, affects to put the Khedive's affairs in order, is to restore his credit for the time, and to renew, in consequence, his power of contracting fresh and more onerous liabilities. But in the event of our occupying the Delta, the main source of all the revenues of Egypt, the Khedive would lose the security on the strength of which alone his loans have been contracted. In all likelihood it would be to our advantage to guarantee the payment of the Egyptian debt. But, even if we did not, the indirect guarantee afforded by our presence that the revenues hypothecated to the service of the debt would be applied to their avowed object, would revive the value of Egyptian securities to an extent which would more than satisfy the *bonâ-fide* bondholders.

This leads me to the question how occupation of the Delta by England would affect the population of the soil. Occupation does not necessarily involve annexation – a point on which I may have something to say further on – but we have no business to occupy Egypt unless we are prepared also to face the contingency of our being ultimately compelled to annex it to our dominions. Now I have a strong personal opinion that, as a rule, Oriental nations are happier under native rule, arbitrary and capricious as it may be, than under the strict and methodical sway of Europeans. Between East and West there is a moral gulf not easily to be bridged over. Their ways are not as our ways, their thoughts are not as our thoughts; and if the Egyptians had nothing more to complain of than the common lot of nations ruled by Islam, I should hesitate, even though I might still deem annexation necessary in our own interest, in advocating it on the plea that it would contribute to the happiness of the population But the position of Egypt is an exceptional one morally as it is physically. From time immemorial the Egyptians have been bondsmen, hewers of wood and drawers of water. Their history, if written by themselves, would be that of a succession of task-masters. No knowledge of ethnology is required to see that the Fellaheen belong to a completely different race from the Turkish landowners, and yet they have neither faith, nor language, nor individuality of their own. They are a hard-working, long-suffering, simple-minded people, crushed in spirit by long ages of servitude, regarding it as the natural order of the universe that they should not reap the fruit of their own labour, and accepting hard usage and ill-treatment as all in the day's work. Bondage is the normal condition of the Egyptians, and, by the peculiar configuration of the country, they are bondsmen with no possibility of escaping from their bonds. Egypt is a narrow tract of country occupied by a dense population, and surrounded on every side by the sea or by the desert. Thus there is no escape for the Fellah from his task-masters. It is only by a series of miracles that the exodus can be represented as possible, and the days of miracles are past. The climate of Egypt is so beautiful, the soil so fertile, the ways of life so simple, that even grinding oppression does not suffice to stop the increase of the population. It is difficult to conceive of anything more wretched than the mud huts in which the tillers of the soil live huddled together, more like rabbits burrowing in a warren than human beings. Half clad, underfed, and overworked, afflicted with every malady due to want of proper food and common cleanliness, they toil on, winter and summer alike, without complaint, or even, I should say, without any deep sense of wrong. To be subject to every kind of exaction, to be forced to leave their own fields to work for others, to have their water supply cut off to suit the wants of the pasha, to labour on the canals and roads under the lash, to be defrauded of their wages, to be taxed, bullied, and cheated by every official, seems to them natural if not right. I remember once seeing a public road not half an hour out of Cairo being repaired by forced labour. The labourers were men, women, and children. To each batch of ten labourers there was attached a ganger with a stick, who kept striking the labourers when they loitered in their work. The foreman, whip in hand, went about cutting at the gangers, and the engineer had a kurbash wherewith to chastise the foreman. The scene was typical of the whole social fabric of Egypt, and what was more typical still was that everybody concerned took it as a matter of course. It is necessary to bear in mind the normal condition of the Fellaheen in order to realise the significance of the fact that of late their lot has been felt to be unbearable even by themselves. I do not accuse, or even suspect, the Khedive of wanton oppression. On the contrary, I believe him to be a man of kindly disposition, who would sooner see other people happy, if it did not interfere with his own comfort or convenience, and who has a certain dim consciousness of the truth, ignored by most Eastern rulers, that the prosperity of his people is an element of his own greatness.

But necessity knows no law; and of late years the Khedive has been so pressed by the exigencies of his financial position and by the never-ending demands arising from his schemes of conquest and aggrandisement, that he has stuck at nothing to supply his need of men and money. The Delta was the milch cow, and has been squeezed accordingly. The fields have been deprived of their labourers to fill the ranks of the army, and the peasantry have had money wrung from them by every kind of coercion and fraud and cruelty. The hold that the late Minister of Finance had upon his master was that he knew the secret of screwing the utmost farthing out of the cultivators of the soil, and that he hesitated at nothing to supply the constantly recurring wants of the Treasury. The Moufettish has been sacrificed to European opinion, as represented by Mr. Goschen, but the system of extortion goes on the same. The country is being ruined by oppression and arbitrary taxation. To improve your land or to make money is to expose yourself to immediate extortion on the part of the tax-collectors. What little money is made is hoarded out of sight by its owners; the mere fact that a man has paid his taxes one day is made a reason for squeezing more out of him the next. The Khedive levies black mail on the pashas, the pashas on the head men of the villages, the head men on the Fellah, and so on through an endless system of extortion. Under such a system corruption prevails everywhere. The officials take bribes, the Government is defrauded, and the condition of the Egyptian people is worse than it has been within living memory. In the old days the difficulties of communication hindered any elaborate system of extortion from being universally applied; but now, with railroads, telegraphs, and all the outward appliances of modern civilisation, the whole of Egypt is brought, so to speak, under the operation of a thumb-screw which is applied with unsparing and relentless severity.

Nor is there any remedy for this state of things so long as no power stands between the Khedive and his subjects. By Mr. Goschen's scheme the taxation of Egypt must be kept up at the highest point possible in order to meet the interest on the debt. By this scheme, too, the margin of funds at the disposal of the Khedive after providing for necessary outlays is quite inadequate to his requirements. The result will inevitably be that the Fellaheen, besides being taxed to the utmost for the regular taxes, will have fresh imposts placed upon them irregularly in order to provide funds for the privy purse of the Viceroy. To anyone acquainted with Egypt nothing is more significant than the fact that the one point on which the Khedive refused to listen to any representations in his discussions with Mr. Goschen was, if I am rightly informed, as to the nomination of the tax-collectors. Whatever other arrangements might be made, His Highness laid it down as a *sine quâ non* that the revenue should be actually collected by officials appointed by him and holding their posts at his pleasure. Under these circumstances it is not wonderful the tillers of the soil in Egypt should find their burdens harder than they can bear, and should be ready to welcome any change. I am told by recent travellers in Egypt that whenever they got into conversation with the villagers along the Nile, the invariable question asked was when the English were coming to take the country. To suppose that the Fellahs have any intelligent or independent preference for English rule would be to credit them with a far higher degree of education than they possess. But, in the strange way in which reports spread in the East, stories have of late been current amidst the Fellahs of a change to be brought about in their condition by the English, and they feel that any change must be one for the better. What the Egyptians, as I believe, would like would be the rule of a Pharaoh placed under such control as to protect them from gross oppression and excessive extortion. In other words, the best thing for Egypt, in as far as the people are concerned, would not be its annexation to England, but the transfer to England of the authority exercised, or rather supposed to be exercised, over the Khedive by the Porte. If there were a British Resident at Cairo supported by the very small naval and military force required to protect the canal, we should confer the utmost benefit on the Egyptian people, and inflict the least detriment on the authority of the Khedive consistent with providing adequate security for our own interests. The Khedive would be compelled to govern with decent regard to justice and humanity by the consciousness that any gross outrage would be brought to the knowledge of the British Resident, and that continued misgovernment would entail his deposition, while on the other hand the country would still be administered in the way best suited to the character of the people.

It would be mere hypocrisy to contend that the primary motive with which I, and those who think with me, advocate the occupation of Egypt is a desire to benefit the condition of the people. If this were our motive, it would be our duty to recommend the annexation of Upper as well as Lower Egypt. The reason why I advocate the measure is because I regard it as one demanded by our Imperial interests under the changes now impending in the East. Still it is not unimportant to show that, in thus protecting our route to India, we should at the same time, as I believe, confer a great boon upon the people of Egypt. In the same way – though I regard this also as a matter of subsidiary importance – it is worth while to point out that this extension of our responsibilities, if not of our dominions, would involve little or no outlay on our part. Every financial authority who has examined the condition of Egypt is agreed that its revenue may fairly be calculated at close upon 10,000,000*l.* a year. Now, if the Khedive were relieved from the necessity of keeping up an army out of all proportion to the real need of the country, as well as from the obligation of paying tribute both directly and indirectly to the Porte; if he were further restrained from costly schemes of annexation, from insane outlay on unremunerative works, and from reckless personal extravagance, the cost of the administration and the court might be well defrayed for some two millions. Moreover, given the protection that would be secured by British control, and we might reckon safely on a rapid increase in the revenue, which is mainly derived from the land tax. The climate is so perfect, the soil so fertile, the population so industrious, that it is difficult to assign limits to the productiveness of Lower Egypt under decent government. If there were anything like security of tenure, if there were any reasonable probability that the tiller of the soil would reap the fruit of his own labour, and the profit of his own improvements, if there were any approach to certainty that when once the legal taxes, however onerous, had been paid, no more would be required of the tax-payer for a stated period, you would witness a perfectly marvellous development of native industry. Moreover, the area of cultivation might be almost indefinitely enlarged by the extension of irrigation works. If once you had security for property, foreign capital would find few more lucrative employments than the reclamation of the desert fringe adjacent to the Delta, which only requires water, as may be seen along the banks of the canal, to render it the most fertile of soils. It is not an exaggeration to say that under British control Egypt could liquidate her debt in half a century, without laying any greater burden on the tax-payers than they would gladly and cheerfully pay in return for protection to life and security to property. Never was there a country which from its natural configuration and the character of its inhabitants could be more easily or economically governed than Egypt. Questions of hostile nationalities or rival creeds hardly enter into the consideration of an Egyptian ruler.

Moreover, if we had once a *locus standi* in Egypt as the dominant power, we should occupy a commanding position over the whole region lying between the Red Sea and the frontiers of India. It is no mere accident that the dominion of Syria and Arabia has, with rare intervals, belonged to the Power which held the Isthmus. Given a strong military position in Egypt, and we could afford to be indifferent to any attack on India along the Euphrates valley. The Egyptian troops, when well led, are excellent; and the services of the Bedouins, which would be at the disposal of any Power exercising a protectorate over Egypt, would supply us with the means of conducting desert warfare. All these, however, are collateral and subsidiary advantages to which I attach little value. The one thing needful for us is to secure the free passage of the canal. I see it often stated that, in the event of our holding the canal, we ought to hold Candia also, in order to keep a fleet stationed in its harbours. How far this is necessary for our safety is a strategical point on which I need express no opinion. But, unless it is absolutely necessary, I should deprecate our encumbering the question of an occupation of Egypt with that of the annexation of Candia.

If, however, competent authorities should declare that the possession of Candia is essential to the protection of the Suez

Canal, then all other considerations must give way to this. For, if I have made my meaning clear, it has become to us, under the existing, and still more under the impending, conditions of Eastern Europe, a matter of absolute imperative necessity to secure a permanent free right of way through the canal in times of war as well as in times of peace. No scheme of neutralisation can meet our wants. Indeed, neutralisation, in any intelligible sense of the word, would place us in a worse position than that which we at present occupy. International guarantees, whatever their intrinsic value may be, are not securities on which we can afford to stake our free communication with India, or, in other words, the security of our Empire. A conviction of the absolute necessity of our securing command of the canal is shown in the demand recently raised for its purchase. But even if by arrangements with the shareholders we could place ourselves in the shoes of the Suez Canal Company, we should only have advanced one step towards the attainment of our object. As our route to India, thanks to the canal, lies across the Isthmus, and as the holder of the Isthmus commands the canal, we ourselves must, for our own safety's sake, be the holders of the Isthmus. Either we must be prepared to see our highway to India barred or interrupted in the event of war, or we must occupy Lower Egypt. From this dilemma I can see no escape.

To recapitulate – I have shown, or at any rate endeavoured to show, that the reopening of the Eastern Question renders our trans-isthmus route to India of more vital importance to us than it has been hitherto; that it lies within our power to make ourselves masters of the canal and the Delta without any immediate difficulty; that, owing to the existing relations of the European Powers, we could now, for the first, and possibly the only, time in our history, become masters of Egypt without exposing ourselves to the risk of an European war, and without giving mortal umbrage to any other nation; that the various rights of ownership in the canal might be purchased by us at no very heavy cost; that the Khedive himself could, with no great amount of pressure, be induced to accept our protectorate as an escape from more urgent and formidable perils; and that the protectorate thus established would be a positive advantage not only to ourselves, but to the people of Egypt. In plainer words, an unparalleled opportunity is afforded us for obtaining possession of the canal and the

Isthmus with little cost or risk; and this opportunity comes, too, at a time when the possession of the canal is exceptionally important to us. Shall we avail ourselves of this opportunity or let it pass by? That is the question. I am not blind, no thinking man can be blind, to the ulterior consequences of such a step. If we take it we must be prepared to run the risk of an extension of our Imperial responsibilities, of possible complications in the future, of not improbable entanglement in the issues which are sure to ensue upon the settlement of the Eastern Question. My answer is, or would be if I were called to decide, It is too late for us to shrink from responsibility. If it were given to any Englishman to say now whether, if the past could be undone, it would be wise for us to enter on the career which has made these small and remote islands the centre of a world-wide Empire, I can understand how the most patriotic and fearless of our fellow-countrymen might shrink appalled from the magnitude of the task we should be called on to undertake. But the time has gone by when we could enter on any such speculation. For evil or for good the burden of an Empire has been placed upon our shoulders. We would not, I believe, lay it down if we could; we could not if we would. We, too, have our manifest destiny, which we have no choice save to follow. The same causes which compelled us the other day to annex the Transvaal Republic in the south of Africa compel us also to occupy the Isthmus. And if a want of resolution, a shirking of responsibility, from an irresolution of purpose or a dread of incurring reproach, should cause us at this crisis of our fate to hesitate about establishing our right of way across the Isthmus, then I can only say that as a nation we have lost those imperial qualities by which our forefathers created the England of to-day.

AGGRESSION ON EGYPT AND FREEDOM IN THE EAST*
William Ewart Gladstone

Any one whose thought and action have been engaged, like my own, for a twelvemonth past, with the Eastern Question in its very sorest place, namely, the point of contact between the race dominant while inferior, and the races superior yet subject, may well experience a sense of relief when the scene is shifted from Bulgaria, or from Constantinople to Egypt. He passes at once from a tainted and stifling atmosphere to one which allows of respiration, and which is by comparison free and almost fragrant. It was therefore not without a qualified and relative pleasure that I found a writer eminently competent for the task was about to raise, in this Review, the Egyptian question. This phrase does not signify, as the uninstructed in modern diction might suppose, the question how Egypt should be handled for her own interests and the welfare of her people, but the question whether, and how, her and their political condition is henceforward to be determined by our interests, and for the welfare of our people. An investigation this, not particularly inviting from a moral point of view; but one which Mr. Dicey has twice approached[1] with a candour and a courage equal to the desire he shows to accommodate conflicting interests and claims, so far – and it is not very far – as the necessities of his case will permit.

Mr. Dicey is confident in the support of his countrymen. The occupation of Egypt by England, he thinks, is generally acknowledged both at home and abroad to be only a question of time.[2] He lifts the subject out of the wide whirlpool of the general controversy. He does not join in the wild, irrational

---

* From *Nineteenth Century*, vol. 2 (August 1877), pp. 149–66.

[1] *Nineteenth Century*, June, 1877, Art. X [pp. 163ff. in this volume] and August, 1877, Art. I.

[2] P. 1.

denunciations of Russia, so dear not to the people but to the clubs; and he appears to think we could not be justified in upholding a vicious government of European Turkey by any considerations of our own advantage.

It may be that he is correct in his estimate of the tendency and probable verdict of public opinion. It is not to be denied, that the territorial appetite has within the last quarter of a century revived among us with an abnormal vigour. The race of statesmen who authoritatively reproved it are gone, or have passed into the shade; and a new race have succeeded, of whom a very large part either administer strong incentives, or look on with indifference. The newspaper press, developed in gigantic proportions, and, in its action on domestic subjects, absolutely invaluable, is to a great extent wanting in checks and safeguards to guide its action on our foreign affairs, where all the weights are in one scale, and we are, as it were, counsel, judge, and jury for ourselves. Nations are quite as much subject as individuals to mental intemperance; and the sudden flush of wealth and pride, which engenders in the man arrogant vulgarity, works by an analogous and subtler process upon numbers who have undergone the same exciting experience. Indeed, they are the more easily misled, because conscience has not to reproach each unit of a mass with a separate and personal selfishness. With respect to the Slav provinces, the 'strong man' of British interests, of traditional policy, and of hectoring display, has been to a great degree kept down by a 'stronger man'; by the sheer stern sense of right and wrong, justice and injustice, roused in the body of the people by manifestations of unbounded crime. But it may be very doubtful whether, in questions where ethical laws do not so palpably repress the solicitations of appetite, the balance of forces will be so cast among us as to insure the continuance of that wonderful self-command, with which the nation has now for so long a time resisted temptation, detected imposture, encouraged the feeble virtues, and neutralised the inveterate errors of its rulers.

I am sensible, then, of the good which a discussion about Egypt may effect, as a counter-irritant, in abating inflammatory action nearer to a vital organ. I nevertheless incline to believe that every scheme for the acquisition of territorial power in Egypt, even in the refined form with which it has here been invested, is but a new snare laid in the path of our policy. I will then endeavour succinctly, and I hope temperately, to test the proposal upon the several particulars of Mr. Dicey's argument, to which I must now briefly refer.

His first and fundamental proposition is that the preservation of our dominion in the East is only less important to us than the preservation of our national independence.[3] His next, that the bare possibility of Russia's obtaining the command of the Bosphorus makes it matter of urgent necessity (or again of 'absolute imperative necessity'[4]) that we should secure our route to India. The third step in the argument is joined with the second: the route, of which we must thus be masters, is the route of the Suez Canal.[5] Fourthly, it is held that the Canal 'must be kept open to our ships at all times and under all circumstances'.[6] And fifthly, the 'command of the Canal' involves 'the occupation of the Delta' of the Nile. This is called, in some passages, the occupation of Egypt; and I believe there is a closer connection between the two than Mr. Dicey seems to imagine. But, in strictness, he scarcely means more than the Delta. And, for the benefit of those among us who are nervous at the visions of responsibility and charge thus evoked from the mist of the years to come, he holds that nothing will be required of us 'for the future' but – [7]

1. The erection of a few forts on the Syrian side of the Isthmus (query, with nobody in them?).

2. The presence of a small British garrison at Alexandria (query, in the presence of the rather large and very respectable army of the country?).

3. An ironclad at Port Said. (But why nothing at the other end, when our dangers from Russia through the valley of the Euphrates and the Persian Gulf are about to be so formidable?)

4. A Resident at Cairo; or the transfer of the governing power to an Administrator appointed with our consent.[8]

---

[3] *Nineteenth Century*, vol. i. p. 666 [p. 165 in this volume].

[4] Ibid. p. 684 [p. 186 in this volume].

[5] Ibid. p. 668 [p. 167 in this volume].

[6] Ibid.; also p. 669 [p. 167 in this volume].

[7] *Supra*, p. 10.

[8] Vol. i, p. 682 [p. 183 in this volume], and *supra*, pp. 10, 11.

Now I must, in fairness, at once tender some admissions.

First, that there are foreign Powers, and Russia in all likelihood among them, who would with pleasure see us engaged in this operation.

Secondly, it is recommended by the benevolent consideration that the government of Egypt is bad, and that if we were its masters we ought to be able to seal more speedily the doom of slavery, and to relieve the people from much of severe and grinding oppression.

Lastly, that I myself approach the question under adverse prepossessions. It is my firm conviction, derived, I think, from my political 'pastors and masters,' and confirmed by the facts of much experience, that, as a general rule, enlargements of the Empire are for us an evil fraught with serious, though possibly not with immediate danger. I do not affirm that they can always be avoided; but, that they should never be accepted except under circumstances of a strict and jealously examined necessity. I object to them because they are rarely effected except by means that are more or less questionable, and that tend to compromise British character in the judgment of the impartial world; a judgment, which I hope will grow from age to age more and more operative in imposing moral restraint on the proceedings of each particular State. I object to them, because we already have our hands too full. We have undertaken responsibilities of government, such as never were assumed before in the whole history of the world. The cares of the governing body in the Roman Empire, with its compact continuity of ground, were light in comparison with the demands now made upon the Parliament and Executive of the United Kingdom. Claims made, and gallantly, or confidently at least, confronted; yet not adequately met. We, who hail with more than readiness annexations and other transactions which extend and complicate our responsibilities abroad, who are always ready for a new task, yet leave many of the old tasks undone. Forty years have passed since it was thought right to reform fundamentally our municipal corporations; but the Corporation of London, whose case called out for change much more loudly than any other, we have not yet had time or strength to touch. Our currency, our local government, our liquor laws, portions even of our taxation, remain in a state either positively discreditable, or at the least inviting and demanding great improvement; but, for want of time and strength, we cannot handle them. For the romance of political travel we are ready to scour the world, and yet of capital defect in duties lying at our door we are not ashamed.

I protest upon another ground, which, if not more broad and solid than the two foregoing grounds, is yet at least more palpable. The most pacific of prudent men must keep in his view the leading outlines of the condition which we shall have to accept in future wars. As regards the strength, the spirit, the resources of the country, we have nothing to fear. Largely dependent at other times on timber, hemp, and metal of foreign origin for the construction of our navy, we now find ourselves constituted, by the great transition from wooden to iron ships, the principal producers of the one indispensable raw material, and the first ship-manufacturers of the world. But one subject remains, which fills me with a real alarm. It is the fewness of our men. Ample in numbers to defend our island-home, they are, with reference to the boundless calls of our world-wide dominion, but as a few grains of sand scattered thinly on a floor. Men talk of humiliation: may we never be subjected to the humiliation of dependence upon vicarious valour, bought dear and sold cheap in the open market. Public extravagance does not with us take the humour of overpay to our soldiers and our sailors. In war time, we must ungrudgingly add (and it is no easy matter) to the emoluments of the services. But after we have done all that is possible, we shall not have done enough. It will still remain an effort beyond, and almost against, nature, for some thirty millions of men to bear in chief the burden of defending the countries inhabited by near three hundred millions. We must not flinch from the performance of our duty to those countries. But neither let us, by puerile expedients, try to hide from ourselves what it involves. To divest ourselves of territory once acquired is very difficult. Where it is dishonourable, it cannot be thought of. Even where it is not, it is likely to set in action some reasonable as well as many unreasonable susceptibilities. If then we commit an error in adding to territory, it is an error impossible or difficult to cure. It fills me with surprise that the disproportion between our population and our probable duties in war is so little felt, especially (so far as I know) by professional men, as a pruden-tial restraint upon the thirst for more territory. The surrender of the Ionian Protectorate was not founded on a desire to husband our military means; but, even as estimated by that result, it was one of the very best measures of our time.

I must now frankly demur to each and all, in succession, of the arguments, which are supposed to render some kind of occupation in Egypt expedient, and even imperative.

The first of them is, that the retention of our Indian dominion is a matter comparable in some sense with, and next in importance to, our national independence. Now I do not wish to stimulate our national pride. Ministrations at that altar are already far too much in request. But I confess my belief that a high doctrine of the dependence of England upon India is humiliating, and even degrading. I admit, in whole or in part, no such dependence. I hold, firmly and unconditionally, that we have indeed a great duty towards India, but that we have no interest in India, except the wellbeing of India itself, and what that wellbeing will bring with it in the way of consequence. If, in a certain sense and through indirect channels, India is politically tributary to England, the tribute is one utterly insignificant: it is probably not near a hundredth part of the sheer annual profits of the nation, nor near a fourth part of the unforced gains of our commercial intercourse with that country. India does not add to, but takes from, our military strength. The root and pith and substance of the material greatness of our nation lies within the compass of these islands; and is, except in trifling particulars, independent of all and every sort of political dominion beyond them. This dominion adds to our fame, partly because of its moral and social grandeur, partly because foreigners partake the superstitions, which still to no small extent prevail among us, and think that in the vast aggregate of our scattered territories lies the main secret of our strength. Further, it imposes upon us the most weighty and solemn duties; duties, nowhere so weighty and solemn as in India. We have of our own motion wedded the fortunes of that country, and we never can in honour solicit a divorce. Protesting, then, against the sore disparagement which attaches to this doctrine of dependence, I am so far in practical agreement with the argument on the other side, that I fully aver we are bound to study the maintenance of our power in India, under the present and all proximate circumstances, as a capital demand upon the national honour.

But, alas! this agreement is but for a moment; and it 'starts aside like a broken bow' when we observe an assumption which underlies all the arguments for an occupation in Egypt, namely, the assumption that the maintenance of our power in India is after all, in its Alpha and its Omega, a military question; though subject, we may hope, to the condition, that it is to be maintained without violation of the moral laws. Now this appears to me to be an inversion of the due order of ideas; an inversion dangerous to us and most degrading to India. I hold that the capital agent in determining finally the question whether our power in India is or is not to continue, will be the will of the two hundred and forty millions of people who inhabit India, their positive or their negative will, their anxiety, or at least their willingness, to be in connection with us rather than encounter the mischiefs or the risks of change. The question who shall have supreme rule in India is, by the laws of right, an Indian question; and those laws of right are from day to day growing into laws of fact. Our title to be there depends on a first condition, that our being there is profitable to the Indian nations; and on a second condition, that we can make them see and understand it to be profitable. It is the moral, and not the military, question which stands first in the order of ideas, with reference to the power of England in India, as much as with reference to the power, in England itself, of the State over the people.

Moreover, these truths are no longer to be regarded as truths of the study only. It is high time that they pass from the chill elevation of political philosophy into the warmth of contact with daily life; that they take their place in the working rules, and that they limit the daily practice, of the agents of our power; that they not only obtain recognition, but likewise acquire familiarity with the thought and the habitual temper of the British people: for unless they do, we shall not be prepared to meet an inevitable future, we shall not be able to confront the growth of the Indian mind under the very active processes of education which we ourselves have introduced, or to develope the copious resource, and the powers of elastic adaptation, which the tide of on-coming needs is certain to require.

Again, however, my line of march approximates to that of the opponent. As I admit army administration to be a great question at home, while denying that it is the prime vital function of the State, so I must allow, the military question to be great, and even relatively somewhat greater, for India, as a vital condition of our power and standing there. But again, approximation is to be followed by early and wide divergence. The possibility, I am told, of Russian power on the Bosphorus requires us, as matter of absolute necessity,[9] at once to secure our route to India. Why? And first, is Russian power on the Bosphorus a practical possibility? As far as I can judge, in the belief of nineteen-twentieths of Europe, it is not. We have indeed, by incredible folly, brought about a state of things which has greatly weakened the admirable barrier some years ago erected in Roumania; and the same perversity and blindness have given to the Russians a separate foot-hold in Bulgaria, which we have compelled to hail the Czar as her sole deliverer. But that man must estimate strangely first the prudence of Russia, secondly the force of Russia, thirdly the disposition and the power of Europe at large, who can think that our errors have even now made probable what I grant they have brought within the verge of abstract possibility.

We do not, however, because it is possible our house may be broken into, sit up all night and every night. We seem, many of us, to have, with all our bold assumptions, but a small stock of self-respect; and too readily to let our fears befool us. One moment we describe Russia with contempt as bankrupt, the next we enthrone her as omnipotent in Constantinople, and having placed her there we next gratuitously supply her, who cannot at sea look even Turkey in the face, with an unbounded store of fleets and armies, which she is at once to use, seemingly out of sheer depravity, in stopping the Suez Canal, while the fleets of England, France, Italy, and Austria are to look on in stupefied dismay. Anticipations of this kind have their explanation, not in any state of facts rationally examined, but in what Dr. Carpenter calls unconscious cerebration: they are the products of an over-heated brain. The grisly phantom rises from the deep, now a little nearer, and now a little farther off; sometimes at one point of the compass, and sometimes at another. In 1859 and the following year, it was from France. About 1862, he migrated to the American shore, and glared on us from that horizon. In 1870, he recrossed the Atlantic, and inspired the notorious 'Battle of Dorking'. He loves travel and variety of costume, and he now wears a

---

[9] Vol. i. p. 666 [p. 164 in this volume].

Russian dress. Alas! and must it thus ever be with this nation, once so manly and so self-possessed? Is perpetual panic to wait as a scourge upon the grossness of our prosperity, like gout and its impish train of mischiefs on the intemperance of the proverbial alderman?

But let us take all these dreams already to have become realities. Still it will perhaps be admitted that this all-conquering, all-devouring Russia will have to make at any rate a portentous effort, when she is to leap from Constantinople to Calcutta, and when, in order to do it with more security, she stops the Suez Canal, to cripple our power, and secure her own safety there. She will surely not put herself under such a strain, except for an adequate result. Suppose the very worst. The Canal is stopped. And what then?

A heavy blow will have been inflicted on the commerce, the prosperity, the comfort of the world. We, as the great carriers, and as the first commercial nation of Christendom, shall be the greatest losers. But it is a question of loss and of loss only. It is a tax and a tax only. What came and went quick and cheaply must come and go slow and dearer; and less will come and go accordingly. We have, however, in full proportion to other countries the ability to bear loss, for we have much more to draw upon. But it is wearisome to pursue in detail a preposterous hypothesis. I turn then to the military question, and ask how much will Russia have gained, after she has brought into the hard form of fact the impossible and the incredible?

The answer is, that she will have introduced an average delay of about three weeks into our military communications with Bombay, and less with Calcutta. It seems to be forgotten by many, that there is a route to India round the Cape of Good Hope, as completely as if that route lay by the North-west Passage. Yet the discovery of the new water-path, when it was achieved, was an event greater in relation to the contemporary condition of the world, than the *percement* of the Isthmus of Suez has been for the nineteenth century; and the name of Ferdinand de Lesseps will not be brighter in history than that of Vasco de Gama. I need not say that the Cape route to India is still largely used, though the Canal draws the picked portion of the trade. But no through service to India for mails and passengers has been organised or could live. The Cape itself lies halfway; and it may be termed also equidistant from

Calcutta and from Bombay. The important and growing settlements of that region have not, however, escaped the eye of
British enterprise. Two services of large vessels carry the mails
weekly from England; and the energy of Mr. Donald Currie,
who conducts one of these services, has reduced the passage
to twenty-three, twenty-two, and even twenty-one days. Supposing that in time of war we were compelled to resort to this
route, we must double the period just named to cover the
entire distance to India; and the result is a loss of three weeks
to Bombay, and less to Calcutta, as compared with the present
route by Brindisi. But, as the Continent cannot be counted on
for war time, we must make the comparison with the voyage
from Southampton, which lengthens the present passage by
some days, and thus reduces the loss below three weeks. This
will hardly make the difference to us between life and death
in the maintenance of our Indian Empire. The grim Autocrat
of the Russias (such we must paint him) will be disappointed,
when we escape his clutches after all.

Indeed, Russia or no Russia, it seems to be very doubtful
whether confident reliance can be placed upon the Canal for
our military communications with India, under the varied and
shifting contingencies of war. I make no doubt whatever that
we shall secure and firmly hold whatever can be attained by
maritime supremacy at both extremities of the Canal. But
neither maritime supremacy nor the promised forts on the
Syrian side will secure unbroken freedom of passage along a
water-way where there is only a depth of twenty-four to
twenty-eight feet, with a general width sufficient for one vessel,
to be obstructed. 'Given four-and-twenty hours' time', says Mr.
Dicey,[10] 'and a company of sappers and miners in undisturbed
possession of any portion' of its sandy banks, and damage
might be done 'which would not only render the Canal impassable for the moment, but which could not be repaired for
weeks or months'. Even if it were possible to hold the line,
approaching a hundred miles, as a continuous fortification, it
does not at once appear how the Canal could be secured
against the furtive scuttling of ships. If it cannot, what becomes
of all the costly care for the military custody of the banks?
And in what position would England be placed before the

---

[10] Vol. i. p. 669 [p. 168 in this volume].

world, if, for the sake of convenience on our military road to India, we insist on bringing about dangers to the Canal, from which, as the commercial and pacific highway of the world, it might but for us be free? Upon the whole it would not surprise me to learn that the authorities of our War Department, aware of all the difficulties of the case, have already discounted them by laying their account with a return to the old route of the Cape for times of war.

But I have not yet exhausted the topics of scruple and objection. And I next ask, why is the territorial occupation of Egypt needful or useful for the military command of the Canal in time of war? Why will it not suffice, supposing this command to be necessary and to be practicable, to secure it by the proper measures at sea, and if needful by land, at the proper time? They would then be free, as I shall show, from the unlimited embarrassments, with which any permanent scheme seems to be begirt; and they would carry with them their only possible warrant in the overruling necessities of the moment. Shall we be told that prevention is better than cure, and that we might have to wrench the country out of other hands? I ask out of what hands? Even the fabulous energies of Russia are not credited with including such a measure in her plans. It is, on the contrary, traditional with her to make over Egypt to our mercies. It will be remembered, with what patience or even favour our ill-contrived and useless purchase of an interest in the Canal was regarded by great part of Europe: a measure which might have given rise to serious complications, had there been a disposition elsewhere to view it in the same spirit of implacable suspicion as that which we ourselves are too apt to indulge. Nor is there a single Power, which even the most inflamed imagination can at present conceive to cherish plans for anticipating us in the military occupation of Egypt. So that, if we raze out all our earlier protests, and admit all the propositions that have been (I think) confuted, there is not a shadow of a case for these fussy schemes, as I must call them, for involving us in difficulties at which I will now further glance.

Some of the less temperate of our adventurers (I must not call them buccaneers) in the South-east Mediterranean, unlike Mr. Dicey, include in their annexations the Island of Crete. This proposal would be indeed formidable, were it likely, as it is not, to be seriously entertained. If Austria and Russia, or either of them, should be tempted to extend their dominions by the incorporation of neighbouring Slav provinces, whose desire it is not to change masters but to be free, they will do it, as I believe, under the strong disapproval of the British nation, a disapproval which might some day find a vent. Yet even they would have some apologies, in consideration of religion, race, and neighbourhood, for such a proceeding, which we could not plead. Mr. Dicey seems to think, and it is quite possible, that an intervention of British power in Egypt might not be wholly disagreeable to the people of the country. But who has made this assertion respecting Crete? Has she not fought, and fought right well, for freedom? Although indeed she obtained, in doing it, but niggard measures either of aid or justice from the Powers of Europe. What Greek is there so debased, so grovelling, that he would consent to part on any terms from the bright inheritance of the name bequeathed him by his sires? In the case of subjects of the Porte, it may be that the sense of insult is lost in a more grinding sense of injury. But, in my view, nearly the most daring insult ever inflicted by man upon men is the proposal of Midhat Pasha in his Turkish 'Constitution' to Slavs, to Armenians, and above all to Hellenes, that they shall become 'Ottomans'. Crete is one of the oldest seats of European civilisation. It ought to have formed an original portion of free Greece. It is united with the Greek continent by every tie that can bind men, save the one still lacking of political organisation: by common race, history, feeling, language, and (for the large majority) religion. Differing from the Slav and yet more from the Armenian countries, it scarcely yet reckons two centuries of bondage. We found it well, on high grounds of principle and feeling, to allow Corfu and its sister islands to join themselves to Greece. I have a word to say, in this matter, even on what we owe to Turkey. But be that much or be it little, I trust and believe we shall never set the abominable precedent of reducing into a new political subordination an island which is a member of a recognised and partly free Christian family, and which has written in the best blood of its citizens, scarcely yet dry, its title to share that freedom.

Reverting to Egypt, I observe that Mr. Dicey dwells on the smallness of the territory. This smallness, he says, makes it absolutely impossible for two rival governments to be within its limits.[11] He proposes, however, all along, that we shall have, as far as it reaches locally, a supreme control in government; for we are to hold secure military possession, to keep down the taxes, and to check oppression.[12] Yet he also proposes that the sphere of our commanding influence is to be confined to the Delta. There appear to be here some inconsistencies. Of what use is military command within the Delta for the custody of the Canal? And is not the dualism of government, once renounced, also resumed? But I am not acting as a critic. What I seek to impress is, that territorial questions are not to be disposed of by arbitrary limits; that we cannot enjoy the luxury of taking Egyptian soil by pinches. We may seize an Aden and a Perim, where there is no already formed community of inhabitants, and circumscribe a tract at will. But our first site in Egypt, be it by larceny or be it by emption, will be the almost certain egg of a North African Empire, that will grow and grow until another Victoria and another Albert, titles of the Lake-sources of the White Nile, come within our borders; and till we finally join hands across the Equator with Natal and Cape Town, to say nothing of the Transvaal and the Orange River on the south, or of Abyssinia or Zanzibar to be swallowed by way of *viaticum* on our journey. And then, with a great empire in each of the four quarters of the world, and with the whole new or fifth quarter to ourselves, we may be territorially content, but less than ever at our ease; for if agitators and alarmists can now find at almost every spot 'British interests' to bewilder and disquiet us, their quest will then be all the wider, in proportion as the excepted points will be the fewer.

Egypt proper is indeed a small country. Our most recent and most comprehensive informant, Mr. M'Coan,[13] fixing its boundary at the First Cataract, points out that the French, in 1798, found a cultivable surface of only 9,600 square miles, since extended to 11,350. It cannot be allowable to suppose one portion of this tract under our supreme controlling authority, and another free from it. Moreover, it is vain to disguise that we shall have the entire responsibility of the

---

[11] Vol. i. p. 674 [p. 174 in this volume].

[12] *Supra*, p. 11.

[13] *Egypt as it is*. London, July, 1877, p. 19.

government, if we have any of it at all. Mr. Dicey says we must prevent intolerable oppression. I hold that we shall have to deal with all oppression, tolerable or not; and therefore and beyond all things with the entire taxation of the country, which is the fountain-head of the oppression, both tolerable and intolerable. In an Egypt controlled and developed by us, every detail of the popular life and state will be familiar to the English and the European eye. It will not be shielded by remoteness, as is even now the interior of our Indian communities; it is nowhere, so to speak, out of sight of the Nile. We cannot, as in our free colonies, divest ourselves of direct responsibility through the gift of self-government. If we could, the problem, simplified in one aspect, would be complicated in another; for who can say what would be the opinion of a self-governing Egypt on the question whether it would go to seek a master in the British Isles, or whether it would prefer an independent domesticated ruler, identified with its religion, not alien to its race, and rooted already by blood in the recent traditions of its resurrection and its growth? Be it the Foreign Secretary, or be it the Colonial Secretary, or be it an Egyptian Secretary of State, manufactured *ad hoc*, I cannot envy him his prospective charge: and though he would give certainty and finality (as the Russians everywhere do) to the abolition of slavery, and would import a multitude of improvements under the eye of our Parliament, and stimulated by its interpellations and debates, I am far from being entirely sure that the action of our popular system might not prove greatly too vivid and direct to please the sheiks and the fellaheen, even while it might profit them.

I fear, again, that we should be making a very dangerous experiment on the common susceptibilities of Islam. Not the absurd and wicked susceptibilities freely imputed to our Mohammedan fellow-subjects of India by many of the Turkish party in this country; who threaten us with the revolt of forty millions of men unless we are content to stand among the supporters of the most cruel and mischievous despotism upon earth. This threat we know how to appreciate. But the suscepti-bilities, which we might offend in Egypt, are rational and just. For very many centuries, she has been inhabited by a Mohammedan community. That community has always been governed by Mohammedan influences and powers. During a portion of the period, it had Sultans of its own. Of late, while politically attached to Constantinople, it has been practically governed from within: a happy incident in the condition of any country, and one which we should be slow to change. The grievances of the people are indeed great; but there is no proof whatever that they are incurable. Mohammedanism now appears, in the light of experience, to be radically incapable of establishing a good or tolerable government over civilised and Christian races; but what proof have we that in the case of a Mohammedan community, where there are no adverse complications of blood, or religion, or tradition, or speech, the ends of political society, as they understand them, may not be passably attained?

And it is worthy of remark that, at this very moment, Mohammedan sympathies appear to be operating in Egypt with great force. It is known with what powerful effect Egypt, though willing enough to make war on the Turk for her own advantage, yet was also ready to assist him in his quarrel against the subject Christian race in the Morea, and again in Crete. Even so at this juncture we have before our eyes the curious spectacle of a vassal who is doing much more than he has bound himself to do. At the outbreak of the present war, the Khedive proposed to support the Sultan by means of a force, which was to be raised and paid by voluntary contributions. But by quick degrees this cloud has been consolidated into a very real whale. Egyptian forces of sensible amount have already entered the field; further reinforcements are said to be in preparation; and it is also hinted that the Khedive, after having refused a short time back to share in the disgrace of the Turkish repudiation (by remitting his tribute to the Sultan, instead of sending it, as in good faith he ought, to Constantinople), is now ready, for the dear sake of his religion, to court shame and sacrifice morality.

> Te propter eundem
> Extinctus pudor, et quâ solâ sidera adibam
> Fama prior.[14]

Viewing all these facts, I for one am inclined, on prudential grounds, to say, 'Hands off.'

But if this be so with reference to the confined area of Egypt proper, much more must we be moved to abstain when we

---

[14] Æn. iv.321.

consider that Egypt proper is not alone in question. The rulers of a narrow country have striven hard to extend their authority over a space proportioned to its primeval dignity, and to the day when it contended with Assyria for the empire of the world. From the seat of their recognised dominion, they have directed the eye and stretched out the arm over all Nubia to Dongola, and beyond it into the Beled-es-Soudan, or country of the blacks, which reaches without a boundary away beyond Abyssinia, and as far as the frontier of Zanzibar. It is a territory, says M'Coan, five times larger than that ruled by the Pharaohs, the Ptolemies, and the Caliphs; for administrative purposes it already touches Gondokoro; and a glance at the map will show that from this point to the Mediterranean we have a reach of nearly two thousand miles, with an area, according to M'Coan, more than twice that of the Austrian Empire.[15] The population of Egypt proper approaches six millions, and that of Nubia and the Upper Nile is taken at ten to eleven millions.[16] Now, as relations of some kind have been contracted by the Khedive with this vast region and large population, the questions must press upon us with relentless force, first, whether, to protect a few score miles of canal, we are to take the charge of two thousand miles of territory; and, if not, then, secondly, at what point and by what process we are to quash the relations of superiority and subordination already formed, and to repudiate the obligations they entail?

It is urged with truth, that we receive from some quarters encouragement to enter upon these undertakings. For one I should attach more weight to this encouragement could I find sufficient proof that each and all the Powers of Europe are bent on consolidating the peace of Europe. But a suspicion has gone abroad that in some minds a disposition prevails to seek for safety, or to secure pre-eminence, in setting their neighbours by the ears. Nor can I entirely dismiss this suspicion with all the promptitude, nay, all the indignation, which might be desired. It is with quite a different sentiment that I turn to consider the probable attitude of one Power in particular, namely, France. In one part of his argument, Mr. Dicey seems

---

[15] *Egypt as it is*, ch. i. p. 19.

[16] *Ibid.* ch. ii. p. 22.

to rely upon her momentary weakness.[17] In its later development, he has arrived at the more comfortable conclusion that the statesmen of France 'are ready to acquiesce in any policy which might strengthen England's interests in the Isthmus of Suez'.[18] Without entering into details that could not be profitable, I must record an emphatic dissent. My belief is that the day, which witnesses our occupation of Egypt, will bid a long farewell to all cordiality of political relations between France and England. There might be no immediate quarrel, no exterior manifestation; but a silent rankling grudge there would be, like the now extinguished grudge of America during the civil war, which awaited the opportunity of some embarrassment on our side, and on hers of returning peace and leisure from weightier matters. Nations have good memories.

These remarks make no pretension to exhaust the subject; yet I think they suffice to show how radically inexpedient are the vague schemes now more or less afloat for our occupation of Egypt. They are directed exclusively against its sole occupation. I am not aware of any cause or warrant for any occupation of it whatever. But a joint occupation would be in most respects an essentially different scheme, and would require a separate treatment.

There remains, however, one point yet to be touched. It is the aspect of these schemes as before the high tribunal of international law and right. It is but just a twelvemonth, since we were instructed from official quarters to regard the re-establishment of the *status quo ante* as the desirable and normal termination of the Eastern crisis, both then and now subsisting. For a few months longer, we still heard much of the maintenance of the independence and integrity of the Ottoman Empire, and of upholding the treaties of 1856. Of late these formulæ seem to have been worn threadbare: causes, like persons, may take the benefit of an *alias*, especially if it be euphonious; and the popular or less unpopular *alias* of the hour is the consecrated ensign of 'British interests'. *In hoc signo vinces*. Now it is most singular that the propagandism of Egyptian occupation seems to proceed principally from those who were always thought to be the fastest friends to

---

[17] *Nineteenth Century*, vol. i. p. 671 [p. 170 in this volume].

[18] *Supra*, p. 6.

the formula of independence and integrity, and on whom the unhappy Turk was encouraged to place a blindfold reliance. I have heard of men on board ship, thought to be moribund, whose clothes were sold by auction in their hearing by their shipmates. And thus, in the hearing of the Turk, we are now stimulated to divide his inheritance.

Now I am one of those who hold it inadmissible, nay monstrous, to plead the treaties of 1856 as guaranteeing a lengthened license to cruel oppression beyond all hope of remedy. But if I find the Turk incapable of establishing a good, just, and well-proportioned government over civilised and Christian races, it does not follow that he is under a similar incapacity when his task shall only be to hold empire over populations wholly or principally Oriental and Mohammedans. On this head, I do not know that any verdict of guilty has yet been found against him by a competent tribunal. Mr. Dicey, in his considerate way of approaching the question, proposes that we should purchase the Egyptian Tribute, and this nearly at the price of Consols. I admit that we thus provide the Sultan with abundant funds for splendid obsequies. But none the less would this plan sever at a stroke all African territory from an empire likely enough to be also shorn of its provinces in Europe. It seems to me, I own, inequitable, whether in dealing with the Turk or with any one else, to go beyond the just necessity of the case. I object to our making him or anybody else a victim to the insatiable maw of these stage-playing British interests. And I think we should decline to bid, during his lifetime, for this portion of his clothes. It is not sound doctrine that for our own purposes we are entitled to help him downwards to his doom.

And this brings me to conclude with a few sentences of reminiscence and of prospect on the general situation. From first to last, in my limited sphere, I have pleaded in favour of meeting the case of the East by the measures truly remedial, measures sufficient but not excessive. Fearful of unexplained motive and undefined change, I held, when the tempest was at its height, that we ought to maintain, if possible, the integrity of the Ottoman Empire. But I believed that the conscience of our age could not permit the re-establishment, after what had happened, of the certainly execrable administration in the Slav provinces, and that the official staff, civil and military, should therefore be utterly removed from Bulgaria.[19] I have, therefore, been systematically declared by the 'friends' of Turkey – and well may she, if any, cry, 'God save me from my friends!' – to have urged that the Empire and the race should be driven out of Europe. But as to expelling the race I had never said a word; and as to expelling the Empire, I had said it should, if possible, be retained in the fulness of its territorial possessions; only with the substitution of tribute and suzerainty, which had up to that time so admirably met the case in Roumania, for a direct administration which could only aggravate from year to year the embarrassments of the rulers, and the miseries of the ruled.

This recommendation was in accord with the sense of the nation, although some sections and classes described it as the offspring of sentiment clad in the garb of rhetoric. The emancipation of the Slav provinces was held by the men of practice, and men of affairs, as they are pleased to call themselves, to be a wild impracticable notion, hatched in the brain of a political suicide. That it might be the better denounced, it was radically and systematically misstated as a recommendation to drive the Turks from Europe; and a person in a very high situation has since publicly apologised for having been first the victim and then the propagator of this misrepresentation. But, in this country, if you will only begin with contemptuously denouncing sentiment and rhetoric, you may be as sentimental and rhetorical as you please; and if you have loudly proclaimed yourself as a practical man, a man of facts, you may deal in fiction wholesale without fear or shame. These are the men who for a twelvemonth, in a large part of the London press, in society, and to a certain extent even in Parliament, have laboured to delude England to her mischief, and have deluded Turkey to her seeming ruin. The confutation of arguments, the detection of misstatements, the explosion of prophecies, the breakdown of calculations, does not move them in the least; nor did the frenzy of journalism, under influences notoriously not English, whatever their origin may be, ever reach a higher point on the thermometer than in an article of Saturday, the 21st of July, which assured the British people that, if they did not undertake the defence of Constant-

[19] *Bulgarian Horrors*, 1876,

inople, it was matter of doubt whether it would be worth while to make any sacrifice of blood or treasure in order to sustain the British Empire. These incendiaries are not shocked either at the havoc of the war they have had the chief part in bringing about, or at the disasters it has brought upon the Turks whom they professed, and doubtless desired, to defend; and, as Mr. Burke described in the Carnatic the terrible competition between the eagerness of man to destroy and the bounty of Providence to repair, so here it is a match, for stakes of enormous value, between petrolean speech and writing such as might move the envy of a maniac, and the hitherto incombustible steadiness and patience of the British people.

The situation is indeed one charged with mixed and checquered elements. I do not mean merely for those who, like myself, can never escape from the smarting recollection that we have dishonourably abandoned our solemn obligations to the subject races of Turkey; obligations which nothing could satisfy short of a real and constant effort to organise an European concert, and, by this potent and resistless organ, to effect a clean removal of their grievances. I do not here, however, dwell on the repudiation of our duties, but on the loss of our opportunities. The task, which for many was both safe and easy, is arduous and perilous for one. I am jealous enough of Russia to grudge to her the unparalleled position, which has been secured to her by our thoroughly ignoble conduct. I am suspicious enough of Russia to be wholly uncertain – as uncertain as if I were speaking of the English Cabinet – whether the higher or the lower influences that act within and upon her will prevail. Who can say whether, with a sagacious forethought and a lofty self-denial, she will in the making of the peace be modest for herself and rigid only for the subject races, or whether she will mar the more than knightly mission she has taken in hand by diverting her prodigious efforts to selfish ends? If she does the second, we shall have to reflect with remorse, that we gave her the opportunity she abuses. If she has the moral force to work out the first, what coals of fire she will heap upon our head! We may turn over with pious care every leaf in our new 'gospel of selfishness', but we shall find there no anodyne for the pain.

Among secondary, but still very weighty, reasons why we ought not to have left to the sole charge of Russia an European responsibility, was the high likelihood, to say the least, that in

Bulgaria, at any rate, the operations of the war would be tainted with barbarity. It may have been observed that we have no trustworthy evidence to show that this contingency has been realised on the Russian side in the Armenian campaign; and, in that country, the war had not been preceded by any but the normal misconduct of the governing power. But, in the south bank of the Danube, the land bristled with stinging and exasperating recollections. The Bulgarians are men, as I believe, at any rate the average humanity of Christendom; but, had they foregone every opportunity of retaliation after the frightful massacres in 1876, they would have been angels. For weeks past the Porte has published official accounts of cruelties inflicted on the Mohammedan population; cruelties very far short of those which it had itself commanded and rewarded, but still utterly detestable. To these utterances, except by a few fanatics, little heed was given; for the world had learned, on conclusive evidence, that the arts of falsehood have received a portentous development in Turkey, and have become the very basis and mainspring, so to say, of Ottoman official speech. As late as on the 15th of July the Correspondent of the *Daily News*[20] – and the title is now one of just authority – declared his conviction that there had not then been a single case in Bulgaria of personal maltreatment of a Turkish civilian by a Russian soldier. I can hardly hope this is now the fact. While I have little fear that there has been, on the part of Russians, widely extended cruelty, there must be among them, at least here and there, ruffians whom discipline will ill restrain; and we have also to bear in mind the diversity of races and civilisations in their army. The subject is one that calls for the closest attention. We have first to wait, as we waited last year, for a full exhibition of the facts; and then, without respect of persons, to estimate them as they deserve. Above all, we shall then have to observe, and honestly to appreciate, the conduct of the Russian Government in reference to proved barbarity. I have shown at large[21] that the essence of the case of 1876 lies, not in the massacres themselves, but in the conduct of the Porte about the massacres: the falsehood, the chicane, the mockery and perversion of justice, the denial of redress, the neglect and

---

[20] *Daily News*, July 17.

[21] *Lessons in Massacre*. London, 1877, *passim*.

punishment of the good Mohammedans, and finally the rewards and promotions of the bad, in pretty close proportions to their badness. If the Russian Government descends to the same guilt, I heartily hope it will be covered with the same, or more than the same, infamy. But if it actively assists or boldly undertakes the detection of crime, if, above all, it inflicts prompt and condign punishment on the offenders, of whatever race or land they be, it will then have done all that such a woful case admits to clear its own character, and to vindicate the honour of Christian civilisation.

In the face of these great events, of the gigantic military movements on the surface, of the subtler and deeper changes that are apparently in preparation underneath, the daring of human speculation is abashed, and we seem to see how the hand of the Most High has lifted the vast human interests of the case far above the level of the vacillations of Cabinets, the confused and discordant utterances of a journalism reflecting bewildered opinion, the intrigues of the schemer, and the dreams of the enthusiast. More and more, however, does the great Emancipation, which, twelve months back, friends did but hope for and every adversary scoffed at, mount above the horizon in a form growing more defined from day to day, and promise to take its place in the region of accomplished facts. No such deliverance has for centuries blessed the earth. We of this country may feel, with grief and pain, that, after setting off our *plus* and *minus*, we have, on the whole, done nothing to promote it. Whatever happens, may nothing still worse than this lie at our door. Even now, after all the efforts of the country to instruct its Government, there seem to be, from time to time, flickerings[22] of a fitful purpose not to rest content with having defeated the project of a noble policy, but even to mar the good we had refused to make. Let us hope that they are flickerings only; and that to abdicated duty we may not have to add a chapter of perpetrated wrong.

---

[22] Such flickerings are to be discerned in the recent return of the fleet to Besika Bay, and in the ostentatious reinforcement of the garrison of Malta: perfect examples of the art of disquieting and annoying one side without conferring the smallest advantage on the other.

MR GLADSTONE AND OUR EMPIRE*
Edward Dicey

Mr. Gladstone is far too experienced as well as too high-minded a controversialist to attach any great value to the discovery of flaws in the argument of an opponent, so long as he is not able to overthrow the argument itself. The eminent statesman who has honoured me by an elaborate criticism of the reasons I have advanced in these columns in favour of an English occupation of the Isthmus would be the first to admit that the substantial force of my plea is not invalidated by a demonstration that in my pleadings I may have over-estimated some of the advantages of occupation, and under-estimated some of the difficulties. I do not indeed admit that any such demonstration has been made. But the main gist and purport of my argument that the authority of England ought to be made permanent in Egypt would not be affected by any disproof of the minor considerations on which I have dwelt in support of my thesis. In like fashion I see little to be gained by showing, or attempting to show, that Mr. Gladstone is, as I hold, in error with respect to the details of the scheme against which he has recorded his powerful dissent. If, on general grounds, it is unjust, unwise, and inexpedient for England to include within the limits of her Empire the region through which the Suez Canal passes, then it is idle to waste time on proving that the route round the Cape is not equally serviceable for military or commercial purposes with the route across the Isthmus. If the whole story of the siege of Troy be regarded as a myth, there is nothing gained by considering whether the site of the ruins discovered by Dr. Schliemann corresponds with the description of the Trojan capital contained in the *Iliad*. If you deny the possibility of revelation, it is futile to discuss the authenticity of the disputed gospels. And so, too, if you hold

* From *Nineteenth Century*, vol. 2 (September 1877), pp. 292–308.

the extension of our Empire over Egypt to be unjustifiable and undesirable, there is no good in showing that such an extension would strengthen our military position, or improve the condition of the fellaheen. Given Mr. Gladstone's stand-point, we who advocate the occupation of Egypt have to show, in the first place, that the extension of our Empire is not a positive sin and evil; and only when we have shown this can we argue with any advantage that this particular extension is recommended by special considerations. If the title to an estate is disputed, the claimant gains nothing by arguing that the possession of the land in question would secure his right of way to other fields, or would improve the condition of the tenants.

Thus, if I read aright the article on 'Aggression in Egypt', which appeared in the last number of this Review, its distinguished author has raised a far wider issue than those with which I have dealt in what I have hitherto written on this subject. The venue of the case, if I may be pardoned the metaphor, has been removed from the Courts of Nisi Prius to those of Equity. In order to hold my ground I am now called on to defend certain principles which lie at the foundation of our whole Imperial policy. The task is one which for its full accomplishment would require volumes and not pages. Nor, under ordinary circumstances, should I have ventured to take the initiative in expounding what I hold to be the true theory of our national life, especially in opposition to a statesman who speaks with the authority justly due to a world-wide fame. But as I have advocated certain views with regard to England in relation to Egypt, and as Mr. Gladstone has taxed these views as forming 'a new snare in the path of our policy', I trust I may be excused if I endeavour to explain as succinctly as I may what I hold to be the part, whether you call it mission, or policy, or destiny, that this England of ours has played, and has yet to play, on the stage of history. Mr. Gladstone has stated correctly that my 'first and fundamental proposition is that the preservation of our dominion in the East is only less important to us than the preservation of our national independence'. I accept the statement thankfully. The only qualification I should make would be to substitute the word Empire for 'our dominion in the East'. India is the greatest of our Imperial possessions; but what I contend for is that the maintenance of our Empire is to us as a nation a matter of vital import, only to be postponed to the maintenance of our independence. On the other hand, Mr. Gladstone, if I am right in my estimate of his position, regards our Empire in general, and India in particular, as mere accidents of our national greatness – as sources of weakness, not of strength – as liabilities to be diminished, rather than as assets to be enlarged and secured. It is possible that in defining thus crudely the position occupied by Mr. Gladstone, I may be assigning to him opinions somewhat in advance of those to which he has committed himself in his 'Aggression on Egypt'. If so, I trust it will be understood that I am protesting rather against a school than against the utterances of an individual teacher. I think, however, it will scarcely be questioned that the definition just given of Mr. Gladstone's opinions represents fairly enough the anti-imperialist theory of English statecraft. To this theory of statecraft Mr. Gladstone has, as I understand, given his adhesion in the article on which I comment. He would doubtless repudiate the extravagances to which some of its chief adherents have committed themselves. But Mr. Gladstone's authority as the foremost of British statesmen and as the sometime Prime Minister of the British Empire so far surpasses that of the professors and publicists who have hitherto been the champions of the anti-imperialist dogma, that he can hardly complain if his name should be identified with the dogma in question, to the exclusion of others to whom its parentage is perhaps more justly due.

It does not logically follow that because a politician objects to any further extension of our Empire he should therefore be in favour of its dismemberment. But if once this country comes to the conclusion that we have had enough of empire, and that we should do wisely to reduce our Imperial liabilities as soon as we can do so consistently with the moral obligations we have undertaken, then the days of our rule as a great Power beyond the four seas are clearly numbered. Englishmen who live out their lives in these small islands, who give the best of their labour to the questions, conflicts, issues of our insular existence, are apt to forget what England is in truth. Take up any gazetteer, and you will find there what every schoolboy is supposed to know, but what to scores of Englishmen out of every hundred will read like a new discovery, the dimensions of the Empire of Great Britain. The United Kingdom, with an area of 120,000 square miles and a population of thirty-three millions, rules over eight million square miles of the globe's surface and two hundred millions of the world's inhabitants. Open any map, and glance for one moment at the dominions in which the Union-jack is the standard of the ruling race! Canada stretching from the Atlantic to the Pacific, the peninsula of India, the continent of Australia, the South of Africa, are only the largest blotches, so to speak, in a world chart blurred and dotted over with the stamp marks of British rule. Spread-eagle declamation about the Empire over which the sun never sets is not in accordance with the taste of our day, or the tone of thought which prevails amidst our governing classes. Facts and not fancies are the cry of the age. But it is well to remember that, after all, the existence of the British Empire is a fact and not a fancy. It is true that the conditions under which we hold our Imperial possessions are of the most varied kind. But whether the tenure be that of an ill-defined partnership as in Canada, or of direct military dominion as in India, there is this in common to all our colonies. Wherever the Union-jack floats, there the English race rules; English laws prevail; English ideas are dominant; English speech holds the upper hand. Our Empire may or may not be a benefit to England or to the countries over which she holds dominion; but its reality is as certain as its magnitude. If, by any possibility, one of the chief countries of the world could suddenly be made to disappear from the world's surface just as the lost Pleiad vanished from the face of the heavens, and if the country doomed to annihilation were selected on the same principle as that upon which boys act when they pull down an anthill, it is certain that the United Kingdom would be chosen for obliteration, on the ground that its sudden disappearance would cause the maximum of disturbance to the denizens of this planet. No greater scurry of human ants looking for new nests, seeking in vain for their lost shelter, could well be devised for the amusement of some malicious Titan to whom the earth was a play-ball than would be produced by the sudden submersion of these islands. Indeed, in as far as we know of the world's annals, no similar event could ever have produced so great a cataclysm throughout the inhabited globe, unless Italy had suddenly been swallowed up in the days when the Roman Empire was at the greatest of its power. In saying this, I am not asserting that England occupies, or ought to occupy, the foremost rank in the history of mankind. All I do assert is that

England, like Rome, is the corner-stone of an imperial fabric such as it has fallen to the lot of no other country to erect, or uphold when erected. This being so – and that it is so even the most fanatical of anti-imperialists will admit – the burden of proof surely rests with those who would pull down this Greater Britain, or allow it to fall to pieces, not with those who would consolidate or, if need be, extend the inheritance handed down to us by the labour, self-sacrifice, and courage of bygone generations of Englishmen.

The general issue of Empire or no Empire is not affected by considerations as to individual augmentations or cessions of territory. I may admit, as a matter of argument, that England gained, rather than lost, by the secession of her American colonies; that the cession of the Ionian Islands was a wise measure, and the annexation of Fiji an unwise one. I may even acknowledge that the secession of Canada from the mother country is an event to be looked forward to without regret. Personally I should dissent from most of these conclusions; but, even if I accepted them, I should see no cause to alter my view, that the maintenance of the Empire – that is, of British authority over a vast outlying territory – ought to be one of the chief, if not the chief, object of British statemanship. People, I think, are too apt to forget how it is that this Empire has come into being. In the strict sense of the word we have never been a conquering nation. Since the days when the Plantagenets essayed the conquest of France we have never deliberately undertaken the conquest of any foreign country; we have never made war with the set purpose of annexing any given territory. We have had no monarchs whose aim and ambition it has been to add fresh possessions to the crown, in order simply and solely to extend the area of their dominions. North and south, east and west, we have planted the British flag in every corner of the globe, but we have done so rather in obedience to real or fancied exigencies than to any lust of conquest. The definition which Topsy, in *Uncle Tom's Cabin*, gave of her being would be about the best that could be given of the origin of our Empire. ''Spects it growed', is the sum of what one can say about the subject. No individual name is associated with the foundation of our Imperial power. Indeed, it is curious that the men chiefly associated with the warlike glories of England – Marlborough, Nelson, Wellington – added little or nothing directly to our dominions beyond the seas. A motley

variety of causes, motives, accidents, have combined together
to create the Empire of England. In all the countless wars in
which we have been engaged from the time when England first
became a Power in Europe, we have fought by land and sea
to uphold or upset dynasties, to advance or suppress creeds, to
revenge injuries or to avert dangers, to protect our subjects
abroad or to secure the interests of our merchants at home.
But our conquests have come to us as the accidents of war,
not as the objects of our warfare. I do not deduce from this
that our annexations of territory have been obtained more
justly or more rightfully than those of Powers who have conquered for the sake of conquering. What I want to point out
is that our Empire is the result not so much of any military
spirit as of a certain instinct of development inherent in our
race. We have in us the blood of the Vikings; and the same
impulse which sent the Norsemen forth to seek new homes in
strange lands has, for century after century, impelled their
descendants to wander forth in search of wealth, power, or
adventure. 'To be fruitful, and multiply, and replenish the
earth', seems to be the mission entrusted to us, as it was to
the survivors of the deluge. The Wandering Jew of nations, it
is forbidden to us to rest. The history of all our conquests,
settlements, annexations, is, with rare exceptions, substantially
the same. Attracted by the hope of gain, the love of excitement,
or, more often still, by the mere migratory instinct, English
settlers pitch their tents in some foreign land, and obtain a
footing in the country. But, unlike the colonists of other races,
they carry England with them; they keep their own tongue,
marry amidst their own people, dwell after their own fashion,
and, though they may live and die in the land of their adoption,
look to the mother country as their home. As their footing
becomes established their interests clash with those of the
native population. Whether with or without due cause,
quarrels ensue; and then, sometimes by their own energy, sometimes by the aid of England, sometimes by both combined,
they establish their own supremacy, and become the ruling
race in the regions which they entered as traders. I neither say
nor think that the men who have founded the British Empire
were actuated consciously by any very high or unselfish
motives. I am not defending the morality of the process by
which the fabric of that Empire has been built up and bul-
warked. But the point I wish to have placed in a clear light is

that our Empire is due, not to the ambition of kings, not to the genius of generals, not even to the prevalence of one of those phases of military ardour through which most nations have to pass, but to the silent, constant operation of the instincts, laudable or otherwise, which have filled the world with the sound of the English tongue. If our Empire beyond the seas is to be undone of our own free will and consent, we shall have not only to rewrite our history, but to remodel our character as a nation. To say that our Empire is 'bone of our bone, and flesh of our flesh,' is not to express an opinion, but to assert a fact. So long as Englishmen retain at once their migratory instinct, their passion for independence, and their impatience of foreign rule, they are bound by a manifest destiny to found empires abroad, or, in other words, to make themselves the dominant race in the foreign countries to which they wander. If England were deprived to-morrow of all her colonies, and if her people still retained their independence and their energy, they would at once begin again to go through the process of empire-making; and this they would do not so much of intent and forethought as in compliance with a like instinct to that which leads ants, as soon as their scare is over, after the destruction of their nest, to set to work to build up a new shelter and abode.

I may perhaps as well say here that I do not regard the manifest destiny plea as a justification for the modes in which our Empire has been established. I have as little sympathy with the 'right of might' doctrine of Mr. Carlyle and his disciples as any one well can have who is not prepared to ignore the conditions under which mankind live and move and have their being. But when an argument is raised as to the expediency or inexpediency of extending our Empire, it is well to show that this Empire came into existence through the operation of natural causes associated with our national character, instincts, and propensities. If the retention of our Empire is regarded as a sin, then it is no defence to say that we are impelled to it by our English nature; but if all that can be said is that it is inexpedient, then the element of national proclivities becomes a most important item of consideration. I suppose, however, my opponents would retort that, even admitting the truth of my theory with regard to the process by which our Empire has been constructed, the influences to which I alluded have ceased to exist. They would argue that England has now reached a degree of civilisation or development under which a colonial empire is no longer a necessity of her existence. As I have said before, the *onus probandi* lies with the authors of this theory. At first sight a house is not strengthened by removing its foundations; a bank is not rendered more solvent by exhausting its resources. As a matter of fact, I believe the possession of a number of outlying dependencies scattered over every portion of the globe is an essential element of the commercial prosperity on which our greatness as a nation depends. Englishmen, as a rule, never seem to me to realise how accidental – I will not say how artificial – our insular greatness is in itself. We owe the fact that we are one of the great Powers of the world, not to the natural resources of our country, not to the military character of our people, not even to the advantages of our position, but to the circumstance of our having got the trade of the world into our hands, and thereby secured the preeminence due to the command of wealth. And the reasons why we have got the trade of the world into our hands are threefold. First and foremost, the possession of certain national qualities, which lead us to devote more energy, to run more risk, to undergo more inconvenience, in the pursuit of wealth abroad, than other nations are prepared to do; the second is the extent to which we are able to protect our commerce by our naval supremacy; and the third is the ownership of ports and stations all over the world in which our vessels can rest secure under our own flag. Without colonies we could not keep up our sovereignty of the seas, and when Britannia ceases to rule the waves, her commercial supremacy cannot be maintained. Moreover, our industrial greatness depends in no small measure upon the estimate formed of our power by foreign countries. Prestige is to a nation very much what credit is to an individual. It is not the fact that they are so wealthy, but the fact that they are believed to be so wealthy, which enables the house of Rothschild to command credit throughout the world. It is so with England. Our accumulated riches, our vast enterprises, our colossal trade would wither away to nothing, if we lost the repute of power which stands us in lieu of the reality. No thinking man can compare the immensity of our transactions with the smallness of the forces at our disposal without being conscious of how much we owe to prestige. I do not say that that prestige is baseless. On the contrary, I believe the world is not far wrong in the confidence it entertains in the potential strength of England, in the latent resources to be found, if need be, in her wealth, her energy, and her Empire. But if, with or without reason, that confidence were to be shaken, the effort we as a nation should be called upon to make in order to hold our own would be one from which we should find it hard to recover. And the confidence of which I speak, if not entirely owing to the magnitude of our Empire, depends upon it. If once we show a readiness to let the power our fathers won for us slip through our listless hands, our prestige is gone, and with it the credit which enables us to dispense with the sacrifices other nations are required to make in order to protect their independence. Our greatness, in short, is like that of Carthage rather than that of Rome, equally real while it lasts, but liable to be overthrown at far shorter notice. Of course it may be said that a greatness resting on so insecure a basis cannot last for ever. The statement cannot be gainsayed. Everything in this world, empires, races, creeds, is destined to pass away; and if the probable durability of the kingdoms of the earth could be estimated by any actuarial process, I doubt the first or even the second place in calculated longevity being assigned to Great Britain as she is known to us. But to say that on this account we should let the Empire fall to pieces is as unworthy as for a man to say he will take no part in the affairs of life because he has to die. Nation and men alike, we have all to play out our part during the span of time we occupy the stage. The proudest aristocrat in the world cannot seriously believe his house is likely to last for ever, and yet, if he is true to his faith, he labours none the less to hand down the family name and status unimpaired to another generation. And so even those who have no faith in the perpetuity of any State, and of England perhaps less than of others, may well toil and struggle to leave the inheritance of power and glory they have received from their fathers undiminished to their children.

Moreover, incidentally, our Empire is of priceless value to us as a nation. As a mere question of pounds, shillings, and pence, I believe we receive far more from our Empire by the extension of our trade than we expend on its maintenance. But, even if this were otherwise, unproductive possessions are not necessarily unremunerative. It would be easy, I suspect, to prove by figures to any owner of a moor that he lost money by not letting it out for sheep farms. But his answer would be that he gained more in the health, vigour, and energy he derived from shooting on his moors, than he could lose in money rental. In like manner it might be urged that even if we, as a nation, paid more for our Empire than it brought back to us, the bargain was still a cheap one. The energies of our race, the qualities which have made these islands what they are, find their scope, nutriment, and development in the work of colonising new lands, administering foreign governments, and ruling over less masterful races. Greater Britain serves as a safety-valve for Great Britain. At all times in our history we have had Drakes, Raleighs, Napiers, Cochranes, and Brookes, and so we should still have if England were confined within the four seas. But if the restless energies, the exuberant vitalities, the thirst for adventure, which found their vent and outlet in the far-away regions we have added to our dominions, had been locked up and immured within the narrow limits of our island home, our State would long ago have been torn to pieces by the turbulence of its component elements. When our English race was located within these small islands, it was bound to escape from its prison or to consume itself by the very excess of its own energy. It has been said that the parks are the lungs of London. It might be said, I think with greater truth, that Canada, India, and Australia are the lungs of England. Still, the world was not created for the benefit of Anglo-Saxondom; and I for one should be ashamed to plead the cause of our Empire beyond the seas, if all I could say of it was that it was good for England. For my own part, I cannot honestly put forward the plea so often urged of late, and to which Mr. Gladstone seems to have given the sanction of his high approval, that we rule India and the other portions of our Empire, in which we are masters and not settlers, on account of the benefits we confer, or hope to confer, upon the subject race. To my thinking it is a mere pretence to say that we went to India in the first instance, or stop there now, because we believe our presence to be a boon to the Hindoos. We have created an Empire beyond the seas for the reason described in the motto of the Kings of Savoy, 'Je suis mon aistre'. We too have followed our star, fulfilled our destiny, worked out the will implanted in us; and to say that we have been influenced in the main by any higher motive seems to me a self-deception. Still, though to assert that we have gone forth to foreign lands for the sake of doing good would be sheer hypocrisy, we may fairly say that we have done good by going, and are doing good by stopping. In the countries, such as Canada, Australia, and the Cape, where we have planted ourselves as settlers, the world at large has been the gainer by the substitution of civilisation for savagery. Indeed, it may be said of us, what can be said of few conquering races, that in no instance have we destroyed a superior civilisation, or left the world poorer in respect of culture by our conquests than we found it. And with respect to countries like India or Ceylon, where we rule as masters, not as settlers, as conquerors rather than as emigrants, we can make out a fair defence for our supremacy. We have substituted law and order for anarchy and oppression, settled peace for intestine warfare, a higher standard of government for a lower. I have no great belief in the theory that certain races cannot appreciate good government. After all, there is, as Sam Slick said, a good deal of human nature about men; and a desire for justice, a respect for honest dealing, are common to all mankind.

However keenly we may perceive the defects and short-comings of our Western civilisation, no man not given to paradox can question its superiority to that of the other quarters of the globe. Under it there is at any rate an opening for progress, an opportunity of change for the better, an escape from the dead suspension of moral and intellectual growth to which caste, and custom, and usage have condemned the East. Whatever else we may have failed to do, the mere existence of our Empire has brought new life into lands stagnant for ages, has stirred up dormant energies, has instilled the rudimental ideas of individual liberty, equality before the law, and public duty. Be our own future fortunes what they may, a new and, on the whole, a better era will date for no small portion of the globe from the days when Englishmen first extended their dominion beyond the narrow limits of their island seas; and the knowledge that this is so may fairly be counted against the many blots which stain our Imperial records.

There are, as far as I can see, only three arguments which can be brought to bear against the considerations briefly alluded to above. I may be told that we have no right to maintain an Empire abroad by force at all; that we have not the power to maintain this Empire without exhausting our strength; and that, finally, if we have both the right and the power, the gain is not commensurate to the cost.

Now, logically, I admit the difficulty of reconciling the existence of our Empire, or of any Empire supported by force, with the doctrines of the Sermon on the Mount. If the law of nations is to be regulated on the principle of doing unto others as ye would be done by, I do not see where the process of disintegration is to stop. The same principle which would call on us to surrender Gibraltar to the Spaniards, ought, in logic, to lead us to give back New Zealand to the Maories. It might be shown by an equally strong argument that America, if she is not in duty bound to restore their old hunting-grounds on the Potomac and the Hudson to the Red Indians, lies under a moral obligation to stop her advance towards the Pacific for fear of encroaching on the rights of the last of the Mohicans. As an abstract principle we are all prepared to agree with the truism contained in the Declaration of Independence, that governments derive their just power from the consent of the governed. But how this principle is to be applied to practical life neither the Old World nor the New has yet been able to discover. The Latin adage, *Quod fieri non debet factum valet,* cannot be made to square with any abstract rule of international morality. If we have no right to acquire Egypt, it follows that we have no right to hold India. If the consent of the governed is a *sine quâ non* of all just government, then we have no right to hold Gibraltar, or Malta, or Shanghai, or Singapore. Nor can we lay down any theory by which, though we are not at liberty to hold India against the wish of the Hindoos, we are at liberty to hold Ireland against the wish of the Irish. If it is said that the possession of Ireland is essential to us, while that of India is not, then the controversy is removed from the domain of principle to that of expediency, which is the very point I am contending. No sensible man argues that all annexations and all usurped dominions are good in themselves. All I desire to point out is that annexation and usurpation of authority are part of the recognised and legitimate weapons by which all nations hold their own in the struggle for existence.

As to the second plea, that we are wanting in the power to maintain the Empire as it exists, I should reply that this view is based upon assumptions which so far have not stood the tests of experience. One would have said beforehand that it was an utter impossibility for the small island home of the *penitus toto divisos orbe Britannos* to rule over an Empire far exceeding in magnitude that of Rome in the fulness of her glory. Still the thing has been done, and is being done, and it is idle to argue now that its accomplishment is an impossibility. Why, we may ask, in the nature of things, is the England of our day unequal to a task which she has performed for generation after generation? Our population is far larger than it has been at any previous period of our history; our wealth is greater; our command of the seas is as unquestioned as ever, while the discovery of steam and telegraphy has to a great extent removed the difficulty of communication between the seat of our power and our remote dependencies. There are positions in life in which it is safer to go forward than to retrace one's steps and England, as I hold, is in such a position. It is too late now to consider whether we were wise in burdening ourselves with an empire. We have got the burden on our backs, and we must either bear it or throw it aside together with the treasure it contains. If it ought to be our policy to get rid of the weight and cost of Empire, there is no good in dropping a province here and sacrificing a colony there. For the reduction of liabilities, whether financial or Imperial, retrenchment, to be of any service, must be wholesale and permanent, not retail and spasmodic. So long as we keep a bold front to the world, and show not only by word but by deed that we are resolved to hold our own, we run but slight risk of interference. But if once the belief should gain ground that our shoulders were becoming too weak to bear our burden, if once the British Empire should come to be regarded as the Sick Man, not of Europe, but of the world, we should be assailed on all sides, and should have to fight not only for our Empire, but for our national existence. And nothing would, in my judgment, tend so much to create a belief abroad in our national decadence as the discovery that we shrank from any step necessary to consolidate our Empire through fear of increasing the area of our dominions. We by custom and habit have got so used to the existence of our Empire that it seems to us to belong to the established order of things. To judge from the sort of language constantly used in the press and even in Parliament by the school of politicians who are opposed to any extension of our Imperial liabilities, one would suppose that the possession by England of India, Canada, Australia, and the Cape, the West Indies, and the rest, was regarded by the world at large as a natural and reasonable arrangement in which mankind has long ago agreed to acquiesce. To any one at all acquainted with the feelings with which England is regarded abroad by friends as well as by foes, there is something ludicrous in being seriously told, as we often are by our public instructors, that our policy is defence, not defiance. Why, the very existence of our Empire is a standing defiance to half the nations of the world. We acquired it because we were strong; we hold it only because we are believed – and as I deem with truth – to be strong still. And if we wish to keep what we have got in peace and quietness, we cannot well pay too dearly in order to perpetuate the belief which constitutes our security.

As to the third and last plea of my supposed objectors, I am sure it will not be raised by Mr. Gladstone. No statesman is likely to have less sympathy with the *cui bono* outcry raised in some quarters as an argument against the adoption of measures calculated to confirm our Empire. The question, 'What is the good of the Empire to Englishmen?' can best be answered by the further question, 'What is the good of anything which does not involve the satisfaction of some material want or the gratification of some sense or appetite?' When you once try to analyse the exact amount of advantage to be derived from any effort, or sacrifice, or labour, you soon find yourself out of your depth. If a man chooses to say, as many men think, that there is nothing in the world worth living for, except personal self-indulgence, then it is idle to argue with him as to the superiority of higher aims and objects. If I am asked to explain what good India is to me – speaking of myself as an unit in the mass of individuals which makes up the nation – I can only reply that I should find it equally hard to explain what good it is to me personally to belong to a country which enjoys national independence or political freedom. Patriotism, love of liberty, and even pride of race are all based upon the recognition of truths inconsistent with the *cui bono* theory of life. It would be difficult, if not impossible, to define philosophically what difference it makes to a man's personal comfort whether he is known or unknown, powerful or insignificant, celebrated or obscure. Still experience shows us that desire of fame, love of power, ambition of success for its own sake, are amongst the most powerful and permanent of the motives that influence mankind. As it is with individuals so it is with nations. There are races which seem devoid of the instinct of ambition; but to those nations which, happily or unhappily for themselves, have once known greatness, the sense of power, the exercise of mastery, the acknowledgment of strength, are as essential to the gratification of their mental wants as food and drink are to the support of material existence. The self-same instincts which created our Empire render its preservation a matter very near and dear to the hearts of Englishmen.

That the possession of our Empire does add materially to our power, greatness, and fame, it would indeed be idle to dispute. Nor is there any more need of arguing the point that to belong to a great, powerful, and famous nation, does in a very distinct, though not very easily definable way, add more or less to the satisfaction of all component members of the nation. That this satisfaction is not in itself ignoble or unworthy, Mr. Gladstone would, I am convinced, be the first to acknowledge. But, if I understand aright the train of thought which runs through Mr. Gladstone's article, he would urge that the satisfaction derived, and justly derived, from Empire is in the main confined to the governing classes, and that, in order to gratify the Imperial pride of the cultivated portion of the community, the interests of the working class are postponed to those of national aggrandisement. The force of this argument I should admit most fully, if it could be shown to me that the condition of the working class, that is of the great majority of Englishmen, would be improved by the reduction of our Empire within the compass of these islands. But so far I fail to see any proof that the evils of our social inequalities, great and unquestionable as they are, arise from the fact of England's possessing a large number of colonies and dependencies. No doubt men who live by manual labour derive less satisfaction from the sense of national greatness than men of fortune and culture. But in just the same way they derive less advantage from our national liberties and less delight from our national literature. To say this is only to assert that the rich have a greater share than the poor in all the possessions, moral as well as material, of England. I am not saying that this is right. All I say is that I fail to see how the unequal distribution of the good things of the world would be affected by the sacrifice of our Imperial power. It is obvious that any serious blow to our national prestige would immediately impair our national prosperity; and the loss entailed by the political decline of England would fall most heavily, in as far as material considerations are concerned, on the classes who live by their daily labour. Moreover, it seems to me a mistake to assume that there is any fundamental difference of view on questions of an Imperial character between the higher and lower classes of our society. Englishmen of all ranks have very much in common; and the John Bullism so universal amidst our artisans and labourers is only a somewhat coarser and more commonplace manifestation of the pride of empire which distinguishes our ruling castes. The instincts which year after year fill our emigrant vessels with English working men seeking new homes in the colonies of Greater Britain are almost identically the same as those to which the existence of our Indian Empire is due.

I have felt it necessary to dwell upon these considerations at perhaps undue length, because Mr. Gladstone's view of the relations between England and the Empire is utterly fatal to the policy I have been allowed to advocate in these pages with respect to Egypt. As I stated in my first article, my whole argument is based on the importance of upholding our rule in India. 'If,' I said, 'India is not worth preserving, then *cadit quœstio*'. With a courage which even those who dissent most strongly from his views must admire, Mr. Gladstone states distinctly that India is not worth preserving, in the sense, at any rate, which I attach to the word 'worth'. His view appears to me to be that our Indian Empire is a possession which we were unwise ever to acquire, which has not proved of any advantage to us, and which we should do well to get rid of at the first opportunity whenever we could do so without a breach of the obligations we have undertaken towards the people of that country. He admits, however, that there is no present possibility or immediate probability of our being relieved from our obligations, and that therefore, as a matter of honour, it is our duty 'to study the maintenance of our power in India'. I may remark here that this admission goes a long way towards establishing my plea for the occupation of the Isthmus. If you once admit that from whatever cause we are bound to maintain our power in India, it follows that we are bound to take the means requisite to the effectuation of this object. *Qui veut la fin veut les moyens*; and if, as I have attempted to show elsewhere, the command of the Suez Canal is essential to the safety of our Indian Empire, and if the command of the Canal can only be secured by the occupation of the Isthmus, then we cannot act up to our obligations towards India if we fail to occupy the Isthmus when it lies in our power to do so. I am well aware that Mr. Gladstone disputes the justice of my assertion that the control of the Canal is essential to the safety of India. Whether I am right or wrong in this opinion of mine is a question to be decided by practical, not moral considerations; and I am glad to think that Mr. Gladstone agrees so far with me as to admit that, under certain conceivable circumstances, it might be our duty to occupy Egypt for the protection of India.

For my own part, however, I must own that Mr. Gladstone's whole theory as to our rule in India seems to me untenable. He asserts that 'we have no interest in India except the well-being of India itself; and that we retain our rule of India, not for any profit or advantage of our own, but simply because, having 'of our own motion wedded the fortunes of that country, we could never in honour solicit a divorce'. I can understand such a theory being put forward to justify our Indian Empire. But it is certain that this theory is not one which Anglo-Indians on the one side, or the natives on the other, would be prepared to endorse. No doubt, in a certain vague and sentimental way, the eulogists of our dominion in the East are fond of talking of the mission we are performing in preparing India at some remote and undefined period to enjoy self-government and independence. To my mind, these professions always have a suspicious semblance to the statements sometimes made by men devoted to the pursuit of wealth, that their real object in accumulating riches is to devote them to works of charity at the close of their life. Professions of this kind are not consciously insincere; and I have no doubt that many of our Anglo-Indian officials do honestly cherish a belief that their labours in ruling India are ennobled, if I may use the word, by the fact that in some undefined way they are preparing India at some unknown date for freedom and independence. But this belief, however honestly entertained, did not hinder these self-same officials from putting down the mutiny with merciless severity, and would not hinder them from crushing with a hand of iron any practical attempt on the part of the natives to overthrow our rule. If it pleases anybody to imagine that the ultimate end and aim of our Empire in India is the creation of a free and self-governing Hindoo nationality, the belief may do good, and can certainly do no harm. But for any practical purpose it has as little influence on our administration of India as an abstract belief in the coming of the Millennium has upon our home legislation. I do not dispute for one moment that as a nation we do honestly wish to benefit the natives of India. I believe sincerely that our rule does benefit the natives. But, as a matter of fact, we rule India, not because we wish to benefit the natives, still less because the natives are conscious of the benefits we confer upon them, but because we deem the possession of India conducive to our interests and our reputation, because we have got it and intend to keep it, because to us has been given a mission like to that of ancient Rome, because we too might well be bidden to remember that *regere imperio populos* is the talent committed to us.

To my way of thinking, the theory that the greatness of England is, to quote Mr. Gladstone's words, 'except in trifling particulars, independent of all and every sort of political dominion beyond the area of the United Kingdom', involves consequences fraught with the utmost peril to our national welfare. When, therefore, I find this theory admitted by one whose individual opinion carries, and justly carries, more weight with the country at large than that of any other living statesman, I feel thankful at having the opportunity given me of raising my feeble protest against a view which, if carried to its logical results, must lead to the dismemberment of the Empire. At the same time, I own cordially there is little prospect of the anti-imperialist view finding favour with our own generation. The English nation has not yet been 'educated up' to the point at which the love of empire is regarded as an idle delusion. On the contrary, though I cannot agree with Mr. Gladstone in thinking 'that the territorial appetite has within the last quarter of a century revived among us with an abnormal vigour', yet I am convinced that the nation is firm in its conviction that the Empire of England must be upheld at all costs and all hazards. The conviction may be erroneous. That is another question. But so long as it exists the nation is bound in common sense and common prudence to neglect no steps necessary to the consolidation of our Empire.

Now I should be only repeating myself if I were to go through once more the arguments which I have urged in my foregoing articles to show that the command of the Suez Canal is daily becoming more and more important to us in order to secure our free communications with India, and that, in the event of the overthrow of the Ottoman Empire, it will become absolutely essential to our safety. I have, I think, shown further that, to secure the command of the Canal, we must hold the Isthmus. Those who doubt the accuracy of my assertions I would advise to open a chart of the world, and to inspect the position of the Isthmus of Suez, lying as it does as a sort of landlock in the very centre of our route to India; and if this inspection fails to convince them, nothing that I can add is likely to influence their opinion. As to the various minor objections Mr. Gladstone has raised to my proposals for direct intervention, I shall say nothing, not because I ignore their just weight, but because they hardly bear on the issue I have endeavoured to raise in this article. There is one of these objections, and one only, which seems to me to require special allusion. I had dwelt upon the smallness of the territory we should need in order to obtain full control of the Canal, and had urged this point in recommendation of my proposals. Mr. Gladstone retorts that, if we once occupy any portion of Egypt, however small, we shall be constrained to extend the area of our dominions. To cite his own eloquent words, 'Our first site in Egypt, be it by larceny or be it by emption, will be the almost certain egg of a North African Empire, that will grow and grow until another Victoria and another Albert, titles of the lake-sources of the White Nile, come within our borders, and till we finally join hands across the Equator with Natal and Cape Town.' The prospect thus raised is, as I think, as likely to be fulfilled as a mirage of the desert is to be converted into reality. Nor do I quite see why the occupation of the Isthmus should force us to seize the Upper Nile any more than the occupation of Gibraltar has compelled us to annex Spain. Still I cannot shut my eyes to the possibility that any intervention in Egypt, however limited in its immediate intent, might ultimately lead to an extension of our Empire in the Valley of the Nile. This need not be so; I do not think it would be so; but, even if it were to be so, I should see no cause for regret. There is no region in the world with which I am acquainted in which British energy, British capital, British honesty of administration, might be applied with greater advantage to England, with greater benefit to the subject race, and with less of the evils incident to all foreign rule, than the fertile Nile-watered lands ruled over for unknown ages by one endless series of taskmasters, of whom the reigning dynasty is well-nigh the hardest. Nowhere, indeed, on the world's surface could there be found a country better fitted than Egypt for the exercise of those ruling instincts which have begotten and upheld our power. The creation of a North African as well as of a South African Empire is no part of my programme. But when I am told that the possibility of such an Empire being established hereafter is a fatal objection to my proposal that we should occupy the Isthmus of Suez, I can only reply that England is far better fitted to rule the valley of the Nile than the valley of the Ganges. If we are to shrink from a step admitted to be essential to the safety of our Empire, because it may possibly lead to an ultimate extension of our Imperial liabilities, then – to borrow a phrase of Mr. Gladstone's in a recent speech to a deputation which waited upon him at Hawarden – we should be 'unworthy of our name, unworthy of our ancestors, unworthy of our country'.

ENGLAND'S MISSION*
William Ewart Gladstone

'Gentlemen, we bring you peace; and peace with honour.' Such are the reputed words, with which Lord Beaconsfield and Lord Salisbury, the two British Plenipotentiaries at Berlin, rewarded the admiring crowds who, on their return to London in July, formed part of the well-organised machinery of an obsequious reception, unexampled, I suppose, in the history of our civilians; and meant, perhaps, to recall the pomp of the triumphs which Rome awarded to her most successful generals.

> Deliis
> Ornatum foliis ducem,
> Quod regum tumidas contuderit minas,
> Ostendet Capitolio.[1]

To whatever criticism it may be open, it was certainly a bold challenge to Fortune thus to blazon deeds which at best were no more than inchoate. Peace and honour are most musical, most attractive words. But as to the first of this 'blest pair of Sirens,' two questions at once occur: what was it that they brought, and in what sense were they the bringers? Those of us who think that for six months they had been hindering peace by wanton obstructions, and frightening away the gentle messenger of heaven by the tramp of armed men, can only regard them as the bringers of peace in the sense in which the approach of a street-rioter, put into duresse, brings to us the fact that the riot is at an end. As to the thing brought, I shall try to be more cautious than the Plenipotentiaries in describing it, for thousands of gallant men have already bit the dust in the attempt to give effect to one of the pacific arrangements: the only one, indeed, which is associated with the initiative of England, for it was a British plenipotentiary

* From *Nineteenth Century*, vol. 4 (September 1878), pp. 560–84.

[1] Hor. *Od.* iv. iii. 6.

who proposed that Austria should become mistress of Bosnia and Herzegovina. In Crete, in the Rhodopè, at Batoum, masses of men remain in arms, as they were before the Peace of Berlin. In Albania, they have rushed to arms since it was concluded. On the Greco-Turkish frontier, it remains as yet a dead letter, and Turkey at present refuses to entertain any negotiation. But let us cherish the hope that these war-clouds will, one and all, melt away. In any case, though they may damage many a rickety reputation, they cannot do away with the liberating work, which, imperfect as it may be, and beset with drawbacks, has gladdened the mind and heart of Christendom, and enlarged the area of human civilisation.[2]

But as to the 'honour' which figures in the Ministerial announcement, no one will question that the Government here may point to something which is unequivocally their own. And what is it? It is not that they prevented war: for they refused to pursue either the policy of constraint upon Turkey, or the policy of inhibition to Russia, by which, and by the last no less than the first of them, as we are now informed[3] upon authority, war might have been prevented. It is not that they have liberated the subjects of Turkey; for they frustrated by their own action the pacific measures taken for their liberation, and as to war for enforcing such measures, they frowned upon it, cavilled at it, and finally hampered it with threats and adverse military preparations. Not that they have saved the integrity and independence of the Sultan: they have not only

---

[2] The public cannot but await with anxiety the Report of the Commission appointed by the Congress in consequence of the complaints which, as we have found within the last few days, fill forty-three pages of 'Papers', No. 45 of 1878. They allege, against Russians as well as Bulgarians, a multitude of cases of cruel and revolting outrage. It would be idle to suppose that the Russian authorities can, under circumstances so terrible, stop every excess. But they are surely bound to make every so-called Christian, be he Russian or Bulgarian, who commits murder or other inhuman crime, pay, and that very promptly, the forfeit with his life. If they fail or falter in this duty, they will cover their Emperor and nation with disgrace: and, unless they can confute some very definite statements of British agents in these papers (pp. 52–5), it would appear that they have already and lamentably failed in it; besides prosecuting against the Mussulmans measures which seem nearly to approach to wholesale confiscation of their lands. On these matters there can in England, as I trust, be no difference of opinion.

[3] Speech of the Earl of Beaconsfield in the City on the 27th of July, 1878.

taken part in a great dismemberment, not only have themselves proposed that Bosnia and Herzegovina should pass into the hands of Austria, but also, that they might not appear before the nation empty-handed, they have similarly clipped off from the truncated Empire the island of Cyprus for themselves. Not that they have maintained the authority of public law; for they have broken European law in the most flagrant manner by settling, in a single-handed convention with the Porte, provisions most gravely affecting its integrity and independence in Asia, which by the treaties of 1856 and 1871, and by the practice under those treaties, were solemnly declared to be the common concern of Europe. These negatives are undeniable. What is then this 'honour', the envelope of their 'peace', which they have flaunted in the face of the nation? Is it a figment, or is it something substantial?

Justice requires the admission that it is very substantial indeed; but whether honour is the right name for it must depend upon what is held to constitute honour. The honour to which the recent British policy is entitled is this: that, from the beginning of the Congress to the end, the representatives of England, instead of taking the side of freedom, emancipation, and national progress, took, in every single point where a practical issue was raised, the side of servitude, of reaction, and of barbarism. With a zeal worthy of a better cause, they laboured to reduce the limits within which the populations of European Turkey are to be masters of their own destinies; to keep as much as they could of direct Turkish rule; and to enfeeble as much as they could the limitations upon that rule. Nor was this only to restrain or counterwork the influence of Russia. For, upon the record, they have done more than any other power to assist Russia in despoiling Roumania of her Bessarabian territory; they have worked energetically against Greece, which represented the only living anti-Russian force in the Levant; and this opposition to her case, considering the promises made to her on the 8th of June[4] of a careful consideration of her territorial pretensions, merits no milder phrase than that of a betrayal. Mr. Waddington, the French Plenipotentiary, in his speech of the 20th, is ominously silent about the English alliance and the Anglo-Turkish Convention,

[4] Papers, No. 39, 1878, p. 3.

but says, in so many words, that France, '*by her persistent intervention*, obtained for the Greeks' what they got from the Congress. The honour, which the Government have earned for us at Berlin, is that of having used the name and influence, and even, by their preparations, the military power of England, to set up the principles of Metternich, and to put down the principles of Canning. We, who have helped Belgium, Spain, and Portugal to be free, we who led the way in the establishment of free Greece, and gave no mean support to the liberation and union of Italy, have at Berlin wrought actively to limit everywhere the area of self-government, and to save from the wreck as much as possible of a domination which has contributed more than any other that ever existed to the misery, the debasement, and the extermination of mankind. After the publication of the protocols and the debates on them in Parliament, this grave impeachment has passed out of the state of mere allegation into that of established fact. The honour which is claimed is, then, a spurious birth, which tarnishes the fame of the England that has been and is, and only can be coveted in an England that has unlearned her best traditions, and that is willing to be known to the world not as the friend of freedom, but as its consistent foe.

But it is plain from the nature of the case that, however true this may be, it cannot be the whole truth. The abandonment of the traditions of British freedom, and the loss of every diplomatic position which had been successively occupied, are not in themselves titles to support, do not of themselves open the mouth of adulation. We have yet to search out, then, an explanation for the strange phenomena, that have been passing before our eyes. How is it that a government, distinguished beyond every other administration for the long list of its disastrous failures in Eastern policy, should be in a condition to assume the airs of triumph without exciting a worldwide laughter, should hold together overwhelming parliamentary majorities, and, in the more significant province of new elections as they occur, should not yet have exhibited conclusive signs of political discomfiture?

It is among the better characteristics of this nation, and of the parties into which it is divided, that failure, as such, does not entail a marked loss of confidence and support. The same spirit prevails among us, which led the Romans to receive with more than equanimity the general who caused and suffered the ruinous defeat of Cannæ, because he had not despaired of the Republic. It has not been indeed by leaning on the higher side of British character, that our Ministers have, on the whole, maintained their position during these last three anxious years. Not peace, not humanity, not reverence for the traditions established by the thought and care of the mighty dead, not anxiety to secure the equal rights of nations, not the golden rule to do to others as we would fain have them do to us, not far-seeing provision for the future, have been the sources from which the present Ministers have drawn their strength. They are the men, and the political heirs of the men, who passed the Six Acts and the Corn Laws; who impoverished the population, who fettered enterprise by legislative restraint, who withheld those franchises that have given voice and vent to the public wishes, whose policy in a word kept the Throne insecure and the Empire weak; and would, unless happily arrested in 1832, and again in 1846; have plunged the country into revolution. But half a century has passed away, since last they had an opportunity of exhibiting their modes of government through a period of time sufficient to admit of their being adequately tested by results. No memory is so short as political memory. The party, which can count upon forgetfulness, need not trouble itself with repentance or conversion. The Government have enjoyed all the advantages of a *tabula rasa*, and have profited by their new start. They abandoned from the first all idea of living, as Sir Robert Peel desired that his Government should live, by great measures of legislation addressed to the national benefit, and they substituted a careful regard to interest and class, from Bishops down to beerhouses. But the tame inglorious existence thus defined, however safe might be its rules for the mere purposes of party, was not such as could bear the concentrated force of criticism, or as could satisfy opinion, or minister to fame. It was only the working dress of the Government, which needed also the bravery of Sunday clothes. These were to be sought in the field of foreign policy; and a vigorous foreign policy was the aim which it proclaimed from birth, with every prospect of impunity and of success. For a vigorous, that is to say, a narrow, restless, blustering, and self-asserting foreign policy, no Ministry has ever been punished in this country. Foreign policy, as a long experience has now shown, does not figure among the causes which bring about the downfall of administrations, unless, indeed, when they are suspected of being too yielding and pacific; as was the case with Sir Robert Walpole in 1741–2, and, yet more notably, with Lord Palmerston and his Conspiracy Bill in 1858. The present Government is, indeed, the only one which has played this game so extravagantly or so ill, as to force a most reluctant Opposition to join issue upon it; and for the first time in our history two-fifths of the House of Commons have, through two successive years, been recorded as dissentients. Yet three-fifths are, it must be owned, stronger than two; and, while safe from actual danger, on its positive side the vigorous foreign policy exhibits all the advantages of a good and available political speculation. First, by forcing upon the public mind a stronger excitement, it produces a comparative indifference to the humdrum detail of legislation, and effectually covers all domestic shortcomings. Hardly any one, for example, ever remembers that the present Minister promised, at the general election, the repeal of the Income Tax, which he has doubled, and which he may possibly yet nurse into still more consider-able proportions. Secondly, instead of asserting what are, or may be called, the views of a party, a vigorous foreign policy asserts what are presumptively claims and interests of the nation, and thus sheds a halo round its acts. Thirdly, in thus appealing to the self-love and pride of the community, it is pretty certain to carry its influence and drawing power for a time beyond the circle of its sworn followers, and to enlist the support of all those good citizens who, from the shilling gallery and elsewhere, enthusiastically applaud the lines –

> Methought upon one pair of English legs
> Did march three Frenchmen.[5]

But last, and best of all, as they are contending, forsooth, on behalf of the greatness of England, it follows that they are enabled at once to place all opponents in the category of contenders for its littleness. All those who will not be put off by their devices, who track out and expose a long series of shifts, and who resolutely denounce the sacrifice of the future to the present, are at once condemned by the large classes I have mentioned, as men who prefer their party to their country, as friends of the foreigner, and as conspirators against the

[5] *Henry V.*, act iii. sc. 6.

greatness of the Empire. From the sources now indicated, a
Government may provide itself, not indeed with a confutation,
but with a counterplea against any charge. 'You failed to maintain peace in the East.' 'But we made the Queen Empress of
India.' 'You failed to uphold the integrity of the Turkish
Empire.' 'But did we not buy shares in the Suez Canal?' 'You
failed to procure the punishment of even one of the miscreants
who did the work of lust, torture, and rapine in Bulgaria.' 'But
we poured in remonstrances as the sand of the sea; and surely
you would not have us compromise, for trifling matters, our
influence with the Porte.' 'You did not prevent Russia from
gaining fresh territory, fresh influence, fresh means of intrigue.'
'But we denounced her as the breaker of the peace, and spent
six millions in preparations; exhibited to her a foretaste of our
Indian army, and, while giving her all she demanded for herself,
we cut down considerably the freedom which she had acquired
for others.' 'You have not saved the Treaties of 1856 and
1871.' 'But, by breaking them ourselves, we have obtained a
protectorate reaching from the Dardanelles to the Persian Gulf,
and have thus covered a great part of the road to India.'
'You have maintained at Berlin the cause of servitude and of
barbarism, and have broken your recorded promises to the
Greeks.' 'But we have increased the "prestige" of England by
the virtual acquisition of Cyprus.' 'You took it by a negotiation
concealed from Europe and from Parliament.' 'Yes: for if all
the world had known what we were about, it is probable[6]
that the Sultan would not have signed, and we should not have
added to the Empire.' Such is the strength of the case of the
Government. At first sight, it is Turkey which is the object of
their affections. To 'concentrate' and (in the English of the
Foreign Office) 'rejuvenate' her withered and withering
tyranny, the old English love of liberty, the old English good
faith to the trusting Hellenes, have been torn up and cast away
like a noxious weed, sacrificed as Agamemnon sacrificed his
daughter, only without a pang.

But this semblance of love for Turkey is only on the surface.
No heavier blow has been inflicted upon that Empire, than the
Protectorate in Asia and the amputation of Cyprus. It is
the Treaty of Kainardji over again; and much more than the

---

[6] Speech of Mr. Bourke on Lord Hartington's motion, July 30, 1878.

Treaty of Kainardji, which did but give indirectly the power of interference that the Anglo-Turkish Convention confers with almost a brutal directness. The link, that connects Cyprus with the Protectorate, is transparently a figment. Cyprus has no more of real connection with the defence of the Armenian, than of the Canadian, frontier. Neither has it any relation at all to a Protectorate of moral suasion, but only to a Protectorate resting upon force. Whether force will be used, no one has yet told, or probably can tell. But a right to use it, in a contingency respecting internal government of which we are to be by treaty independent judges, has been given; and the Porte, horribly maimed at Berlin in its integrity, has now, by our act, not an acre of ground left to it, throughout its vast and once mighty dominion, on which it retains its independence. In Europe and Armenia, all its plans for the government of its subjects are subject to the supervision of all the Powers; in the whole of Asiatic Turkey, by England. It is plain, then, that as freedom, civilisation, and good faith have been sacrificed to Turkey, so Turkey must take her turn, and be immolated to some other and more commanding divinity.

The Anglo-Turkish Convention was extorted, on the 4th of last June, from the poverty and necessity of the Sultan. The time was as remarkable, as the mode of the operation. The unfortunate representative of the Bajazets and Amuraths was about to enter, whether he would or not, into an European Congress, where he could not count upon a single friend. For England to present to him such an instrument at such a moment meant, and could mean, nothing but this. 'We are ready to fight your battle in the Congress against Russia, against the Slavs, against the Greeks; but if we fight it, this must be for a consideration. Home we cannot go with empty hands. You are very dear to us, as we prove to you by waiving so freely, on your behalf, not only the foolish abstractions which ideology calls principles, but also the goodwill of eighty million men in Russia, and the affection we might earn from eighteen millions more, who have been under your yoke in Europe. But you will readily understand, that our own life is dearer to us than yours can be. Our ministerial existence is well known to be required for the welfare of the British Empire; and it is now at stake. Give us Cyprus: it is but a mote in the Mediterranean: but for our people it will seem another Gibraltar or another Malta. It is not money we want; our souls are far above it; we will pay you net all the revenue, which it formerly yielded you for your harems and your ironclads. If you want a *quid pro quo*, we will undertake to defend your Armenian frontier; only you must promise, once again, to govern your subjects properly. Only subscribe to this; we shall be safe at home, and you will be safe, as safe as circumstances will permit, by our aid, at Berlin.' What motives were present to the mind of this man or that, I do not undertake to pronounce. But the only interpretation of the Convention which approaches to coherency is that Cyprus was its Alpha and its Omega: that we did for this island that which Dido did for this island's Queen.

> Te propter eundem
> Extinctus pudor, et quâ solâ sidera adibam
> Fama prior.[7]

It is no wonder that this deed was done in the dark; that it was done also by the Sultan in fear and trembling, and that we should now know it probably could not have been done at all except in the dark. Had the unhappy monarch been allowed to act in the daylight, he might at least have put himself up to auction for the Congress, and might have obtained bids from Russia or elsewhere which would have provided him with an advocate on easier terms.

And what is this Cyprus, which has shown in so singular a manner its possession of the tempter's power, for which we are to pay so heavily in the good name and fame which are 'better than rubies'? It is an island of very limited extent, and of ample natural resources. It has been, like the rest of Turkey, vilely misgoverned and miserably depopulated; and the one white side of a very black business is, that the hundred or two hundred thousand people, whom it contains, will, for the first time since their servitude began, enjoy the elementary blessings of civil government. We shall probably lay out large sums, which will never be reimbursed. We shall make an addition, it may be a great or it may be a small one, to our already excessive and perhaps perilous military responsibilities. It would be worthless as a military post, even had we already spent the heavy sums necessary to invest it with that character.

---

[7] Virg. *Æn.* iv. 322

The harbour of Malta, and its central position, must in all likelihood render it far preferable. The first exhibitions of its sanitary character, carefully kept back as they have been, seem, as they force themselves into view, to be deplorable. But that is probably a matter of money too. It is not, however, in these details that, one way or the other, the heart and root of the matter lie. Cyprus is above and before all things a symbol and a counter: negative and valueless for any purpose of ours in itself, but a sign of the vastness of our Empire, and an effectual sign that, in the opinion of our Government, that Empire is not yet vast enough.

Viewed in this sense, as the earnest of a policy, the acquisition of Cyprus, instead of silly and unmeaning, becomes eloquent enough, even if mischievous. The most devoted adherent of the Ministry must inwardly feel a wish, that it had been acquired with cleaner hands: but, on the other hand, their most resolute opponent must admit that this assumption of new dominion is thoroughly in keeping with their behaviour throughout. At no time have they failed (except in a momentary aberration of Lord Derby's) to maintain both at home, and by the mouths of their Ambassadors Sir Henry Elliot and Sir Austen Layard, that the law of British interests was the supreme law; or said one word inconsistent with the belief that the multiplication of engagements is the secret of imperial strength, and that the further enlargement of the bounds of the Empire is the noblest achievement, to which statesmanship can aspire. These materialistic conceptions of the place and work of England in the world they have propagated with authority. Nor could it be without effect; for there is a side of human nature, to which they are particularly acceptable. Nor, again, have they failed to suit the action to the word. Since their accession to office we have taken to ourselves, by way of proving to the world our equity and moderation, (1) the Fiji Islands; (2) the Transvaal Republic, in the teeth, as it is now alleged, of the wishes of more than four-fifths of the enfranchised population; (3) the island of Cyprus; (4) if recent information be correct, the island of Socotra, lying a little beyond the Straits of Babelmandeb; (5) we have begun to protrude our military garrisons beyond our Indian frontier: in order to warn Russia how justly indignant we shall be, if she should take, at Merv or elsewhere, any corresponding step. I do not speak in condemnation of each one of these proceedings. It may be true that annexations are sometimes necessary, but it ought to be understood that they are, as a rule, new burdens added to the old, and that in augmenting space they diminish power. I look at them, as a whole, in connection with the doctrine of the First Minister that the people do not dislike to see the Empire increased, and of his faithful echo and mirror, the Foreign Secretary, who proclaims that commerce only flourishes with or through territorial dominion. When authority thus appeals to cupidity, when the lips of the State-priest, that should speak wisdom, are given to its opposite, the wonder is not that many are misled by those who pollute the fountain-heads of knowledge, but that many are still found to confute, if they cannot stay, their rulers, and to check the present deviation from those ways of sober, measured, and considerate energy, by which it is that England has grown great. Some seem actually to believe they are increasing strength, when they multiply the points they are to occupy and defend, without adding a single man to the force they can arm, or a pound to the fund by which that force is to be sustained. But it is well to cherish no illusions, and to look the matter in the face. Territorial aggrandisement, backed by military display, is the *cheval de bataille* of the administration. Empire is greatness; leagues of land are empire; your safety is measured by the fear you strike into other nations; trade follows the flag: he that doubts is an enemy to his country. This creed of aggrandisement, made real to the public imagination by the acquisition of a Mediterranean and virtually European island, has operated a relative success: it has covered the miscarriages of the Government, and it enables them to say that they have not been condemned to capital punishment by the country.

It is very disagreeable for an Englishman to hint to Eng-lishmen that the self-love and pride, which all condemn in individuals, have often lured nations to their ruin or their loss; that they are apt to entail a great deal of meanness, as well as a great deal of violence; that they begin with a forfeiture of respect abroad, and end even in the loss of self-respect; that their effect is to destroy all sobriety in the estimation of human affairs, and to generate a temperament of excitability which errs alternately on the side of arrogance, and of womanish and unworthy fears. For the performance of this disagreeable duty, we are entitled to look in the first place to the Queen's Govern-ment; which ought in foreign affairs invariably to play, and which in other times usually has played, the part of moderator; and which thus has supplied much of that correction, which in domestic matters we supply to one another by the free contact, and even conflict, of opinion. It is their duty to act as counsel for the absent. It is bad enough when men without the responsibilities of office condescend to appeal to selfishness and prejudice. When, on the occasion of Mr. Pitt's treaty with France, Mr. Fox made himself the organ of an old antipathy, and described France as our natural enemy, he greatly erred: but had the parts been reversed, and had Mr. Pitt given utterance to such a sentiment, the offence committed, and the mischief done, would each have been multiplied an hundredfold. Substantially it is just that inversion of parts, which has taken place in our controversy on the Eastern Question. The doctrines of national self-restraint, of the equal obligations of States to public law, and of their equal rights to fair construction as to words and deeds, have been left to unofficial persons. The Government, not uniformly nor consistently, but in the main and on the whole, have opened up and relied on an illegitimate source of power, which never wholly fails: they have appealed, under the prostituted name of patriotism, to exaggerated fears, to imaginary interests, and to the acquisitiveness of a race which has surpassed every other known to history in the faculty of appropriating to itself vast spaces of the earth, and establishing its supremacy over men of every race and language. Now I hold that to stimulate these tendencies, to overlook the proportion between our resources and our obligations, and above all to claim anything more than equality of rights in the moral and political intercourse of the world, is not the way to make England great, but to make it both morally and materially little.

The sentiment of empire may be called innate in every Briton. If there are exceptions, they are like those of men born blind or lame among us. It is part of our patrimony: born with our birth, dying only with our death; incorporating itself in the first elements of our knowledge, and interwoven with all our habits of mental action upon public affairs. It is a portion of our national stock, which has never been deficient, but which has more than once run to rank excess, and brought us to mischief accordingly, mischief that for a time we have weakly thought was ruin. In its normal action, it made for us the American colonies, the grandest monument ever erected by a people of modern times, and second only to the Greek colonisation in the whole history of the world. In its domineering excess, always under the name of British interests and British honour, it lost them by obstinacy and pride. Lord Chatham who forbade us to tax, Mr. Burke who forbade us to legislate for them, would have saved them. But they had to argue for a limitation of English power; and to meet the reproach of the political wiseacres, who first blustered on our greatness, and then, when they reaped as they had sown, whined over our calamities. Undoubtedly the peace of 1782–3, with its adjuncts in exasperated feeling, was a terrible dismemberment. But England was England still: and one of the damning signs of the politics of the school is their total blindness to the fact, that the central strength of England lies in England. Their eye travels with satisfaction over the wide space upon the map covered by the huge ice-bound deserts of North America or the unpenetrated wastes of Australasia, but rests with mortification on the narrow bounds of latitude and longitude marked by nature for the United Kingdom. They are the materialists of politics: their faith is in acres and in leagues, in sounding titles and long lists of territories. They forget that the entire fabric of the British Empire was reared and consolidated by the energies of a people, which was (though it is not now) insignificant in numbers, when compared with the leading States of the Continent; and that if by some vast convulsion our transmarine possessions could be all submerged, the very same energies of that very same people would either discover other inhabited or inhabitable spaces of the globe on which to repeat its work, or would without them in other modes assert its undiminished greatness. Of all the opinions disparaging to England, there is not one which can lower her like that which teaches that the source of strength for this almost measureless body lies in its extremities, and not in the heart which has so long propelled the blood through all its regions, and in the brain which has bound and binds them into one.

In the sphere of personal life, most men are misled through the medium of the dominant faculty of their nature. It is round that dominant faculty that folly and flattery are wont to buzz. They play upon vainglory by exaggerating and commending what it does, and by piquing it on what it sees cause to forbear from doing. It is so with nations. For all of them the supreme want really is, to be warned against the indulgence of the dominant passion. The dominant passion of France was military glory. Twice, in this century, it has towered beyond what is allowed to man; and twice has paid the tremendous forfeit of opening to the foe the proudest capital in the world. The dominant passion of England is extended empire. It has heretofore been kept in check by the integrity and sagacity of her statesmen, who have not shrunk from teaching her the lessons of self-denial and self-restraint. But a new race has arisen; and the most essential or the noblest among all the duties of government, the exercise of moral control over ambition and cupidity, have been left to the intermittent and feeble handling of those who do not govern.

Between the two parties in this controversy there is a perfect agreement that England has a mighty mission in the world; but there is a discord as fundamental upon the question what that mission is.

I. With the one party, her first care is held to be the care of her own children within her own shores, the redress of wrongs, the supply of needs, the improvement of laws and institutions. Against this homespun doctrine, the present Government appears to set up territorial aggrandisement, large establishments, and the accumulation of a multitude of fictitious interests abroad, as if our real interests were not enough; and since the available store of national time and attention is a fixed quantity, there ensues that comparative remissness in domestic affairs, which is too conclusively shown by the beggarly returns of our legislation, the aggravation of our burdens, and the fast-growing arrears of business.

II. With the one party, the great duty and honour and charge of our transmarine Colonial Empire is, to rear up free congenital communities. They receive a minority of our emigrants, of whom the larger number go to the United States of America; but, in receiving this minority, they enlarge for our outgoing population the field of choice, and by keeping them within the Empire diminish the shock and severance of change. Commercially our colonies unhappily embrace to a great extent, like the United States, the principles of Protectionism, and they are quietly suffered to carry them even into caricature by enforcing them against the parent country; but they have not within themselves the same scope and variety of production which allow those principles to receive in the United States such large effect; and from many causes, none of them involving coercion or command, the capitative addition made by their population to our commerce is larger than in the case of any foreign country. It is felt at the same time that Great Britain has, against the merely material advantages of these possessions, greatly enlarged her military responsibilities in time of war. Energetic efforts, indeed, have been necessary to relieve the mother country from military charge for the colonies in ordinary years of peace; and these have been largely, but not as yet uniformly, successful. Still, whatever be in these respects the just balance of the account, it is felt that the colonial relation involves far higher elements of consideration; that the founding of these free, growing, and vigorous communities has been a specific part of the work providentially assigned to Britain. The day has gone by, when she would dream of compelling them by force to remain in political connection with her. But, on the other hand, she would never suffer them to be torn away from her; and would no more grudge the cost of defending them against such a consummation, than the father of a family grudges the expense of the food necessary to maintain his children.

> Put the world's whole strength
> Into one giant arm, it shall not force
> This lineal honour from us.[8]

There is then probably little difference among us as to the practical propositions, which bear upon our colonial relations with British North America and the magnificent Australasian group; relations, that may now be stated, on one side at least, to have reached a normal condition.

But here also the frame of mind is different, with which, from the two sides respectively, our colonies are regarded. It is the administrative connection, and the shadow of political subordination, which chiefly give them value in the sight of the party, who at home as well as abroad are striving to cajole or drive us into Imperialism. With their opponents, it is the welfare of these communities which forms the great object of interest and desire; and if the day should ever come, when in their own view that welfare would be best promoted by their administrative emancipation, then and then only the Liberal

---

[8] Shakespeare's *Henry IV. Part II.* act iv. sc. 5.

mind of England would at once say, 'Let them flourish to the uttermost; and, if their highest welfare requires their severance, we prefer their amicable independence to their constrained subordination.' The substance of the relationship lies, not in dispatches from Downing Street, but in the mutual affection, and the moral and social sympathies, which can only flourish between adult communities when they are on both sides free.

The vainglorious boast, which Ministers, aware that there could be no reply, have inserted in the speech of her Majesty on the prorogation of Parliament, as to aid which the Colonies would have given in a war that might have been, can only excite ridicule. No man of sense believes that the Colonies are likely to become, in a serious manner, parties to any great European war. Handfuls of men or even of money may be supplied by individual zeal; but it is hardly to be desired, for their own sake or ours, that they should become real parties to contests, over the inception, conduct, and conclusion of which they can exercise no effective control. Ostentatious proclamation to the world of the military aid they are to give us is much more likely to check, than to develope, any disposition of that kind; and savours strongly of an age of imposture. Here again the material view has eclipsed every other. What we want from the Colonies is something better than 'food for powder'. To give birth and existence to these States, which are to form so large a portion of the New World, is a noble feature in the work and mission of this nation, as it was of old in the mission of Greece. Nor are the economical results of this splendid parentage to be despised. But to suppose that these territories, severed greatly from one another, and uniformly from us, by thousands upon thousands of miles of dissociating ocean, can ever be to the mother country like continuous territories, is a superstition equally gross and mischievous, and, by setting up imaginary sources of strength, tends only to enhance that neglect of domestic interests, which has already become so serious an evil.

Moreover, the prospective multiplication of possessions oversea is, to say the least, far from desirable. It is difficult to regard without anxiety the formidable extension, which has been given to our boundaries at the Cape. During the last forty years, those possessions have cost us probably from twenty to thirty millions sterling in wars and military establishments; and an annexation like that of the Transvaal will entail the heaviest responsibility on the Government, should it be found that our sovereignty has been imposed by force on an unwilling population. We do not want Bosnian submissions. Especially is it inexpedient to acquire possessions which, like Cyprus, never can become truly British, because they have acquired indelibly an ethnical character of their own. In them we remain as masters and as foreigners, and the connection at its best has not the ennobling features which, in cases like America and Australasia, give a high moral purpose to the subsisting relation, and compensate for the serious responsibilities which in given contingencies it may entail.

III. There is another great branch of the mission of England which passes entirely beyond the limits of our local Empire. Many, indeed, there may be who will accept these words and interpret them in a sense full of mischief. These are the men whose minds alternate between visions of unbounded influence and bad dreams of a foe behind every bush, between high pretensions and panic fears; and who have no other key to the duties and sympathies of England, than their artificial and inflated conception of British interests. If we recognise any obligations towards Portugal, it is, according to them, only that we may uphold in the Peninsula a counterpoise to the influence of France. If we have taken a prominent part in the defence of Belgium, it is because Napoleon said England would not be safe if France had possession of Antwerp. The same morbid temper raises up a kindred brood of visionary dangers in the East, and by its bungling uneasiness hastes to make them real. The most extravagant exaggerations do not in the least serve to undeceive its victims: so that they are now delighted with the idea of keeping Russia out of India by defending Armenia, which is much as if we proposed to keep the United States out of Canada by defending Jamaica. As every tract of country, which can by possibility be used as a road to India, becomes thereby a British interest, and therewith a legitimate subject of military care, there is no saying what preposterous guarantees may be proposed for Khiva, or Bokhara, or Badakshan. Nay, China is a possible road to India; why should not China have a guarantee? Now I hold that indulgence in these inflated conceptions is not singly but doubly mischievous. It involves us in engagements and responsibilities which are causeless: and in so doing it disables us for duties which are legitimate, and may be imperative. We have just undertaken new duties in the East: I ask, will they leave us as free as we were before for the performance of old duties in the West?

It is not pleasant, but it seems necessary, to recall to public memory, by way of illustration, the notorious Benedetti project of 1870. Of this plot, the parentage was disputed between the Government of Louis Napoleon and the Government of Prince Bismarck; but with this advantage on the side of the Prince, that the circumstantial evidence was in his favour, and that he was the person who, on the outbreak of the war with France, at once brought it to light. The terrible events and overpowering interest of that war cast a veil of oblivion over the proceeding, which must under other circumstances have been probed to the bottom by public curiosity. It was a plan of partition, under which the free and happy, but small Kingdom of Belgium was to have been absorbed, by force if need be, in a division of spoil between Germany and France. It is needless to enter upon details. Suffice it to say that hardly is there a baser transaction recorded in history.

It excited the strongest defensive emotions in this country, and the Government at once proceeded to propose to each of the belligerents an armed cooperation against the other, should that other violate the Belgian territory with a view to conquest. The German Government accepted instantly, that of the Emperor after a very short interval; and the British Ministers proposed an addition to the estimates and the military force, which were then on a more limited scale than they are now. Here was the vision of a great danger. But it was not (in my view) properly a danger to any immediate British interest. The Napoleonic saying about Antwerp is exaggeration carried to the confines of nonsense. But it was a peril to the public honour and public law of Europe, which is perhaps after all not our meanest interest. England was ready for all contingencies; and the danger to Belgium was averted. Now what has been may be. Other schemes, resembling more or less the Benedetti Treaty, may come into existence. Absorption has been the fashion for some time, and our Propagandists of the great empire, who practise it on every opportunity, and who are at present under the charge of practising it upon the Dutchmen of the Transvaal, in defiance of their will, do not morally occupy the best possible position for denouncing it. But what will be our position materially? Suppose a project of this character again to spring from the brain of a Benedetti; and to be revived, as is perfectly possible, with the connivance of Russia. Should we be as well prepared, as we were in 1870, to negotiate and arm for the defence of Belgium, when we had upon us the responsibility of fighting against Russia in the defiles of Turkish Armenia, to repel an invasion there, which might be on her side no more than a feint, but which would direct a large part of our military force to a distance of four thousand miles? I should be glad to know whether the Belgian Government and people, who naturally lean upon us more than on any other Power, contemplate, with the same satisfaction as our Imperialists, the mode now in fashion of strengthening England by giving her plenty to do all over the world, and no means of doing it. The truth is, that England has had a position in Europe unrivalled alike for its moral elevation and contingently for its material power. Long ago M. Guizot, in describing the attitudes of the several states and their several ambitions, aimed his indictment against England only in her policy *hors d'Europe*, and allowed that in European questions she had clean hands. We have a true superiority, as to moral questions, in European affairs, over the other great Powers of this quarter of the globe. Not perhaps because we are less 'far gone from original righteousness', but because the inestimable boon of our insular position has, ever since the consolidation of France into a kingdom, relieved us from temptation. We would not, because we cannot; what was at first a conclusion of mere necessity has grown by long tract of time into our mental and even our moral habit. Unhappy Turkey apart, we have become tolerably impartial in European questions. The only selfish interest which we had, or believed we had, was in the Ionian Islands; and with that we have parted company. Our own misdeeds, if they exist, are distant; and on the whole we are admirably placed for upholding, by voice and influence, the interests which are so cruelly traversed by the emotions of selfishness, those, namely, of sheer justice and humanity.

There could not be a fairer or a wider field for the discharge of this noble duty, than in Turkey. The Crimean War had not impaired the dignity of our position, for it was made in the name of public law and European concert; not by single-handed action, not in order to maintain a Turkish Empire as a barrier thrown across the 'road to India'. We held it in 1875. But, from that time onwards, the policy of the Government has been avowedly addressed to the purpose of maintaining the Ottoman Empire in spite of its vices, because its destruction would be detrimental to our interest in the maintenance of our Indian rule. The first effect of this superlative egoism is to emasculate all our representations on behalf of humanity in Turkey. In vain we denounce the loathsome crimes, committed in Bulgaria or elsewhere by the Turkish forces, and advisedly covered, or even rewarded, by the Government. For the Pashas have been told all along, especially from the mouths of our Ambassadors, that we are bound by our own interests to maintain their dominion over the subject races while it stands, and to restore it as best we may when it falls. So that our verbal protestations are smitten with impotence from their birth: and it might even be conceived that they form the subject of smiles and winks between the agents of the Porte and those who, under instructions from London, recite the formula of remonstrance. It is not only on the Turk, however, that we have lost our hold. Over the entire field of the Eastern Question, this doctrine, pushed under the auspices of the Ministry into superlative extravagance, has altered our presumptive character of an umpire into that of a partisan. We are at this moment led to anticipate the appearance of a Report to proceed from an international Commission on the conduct of the Bulgarians to their Mohammedan neighbours during the Russian occupation. We are told to expect a tale of horror worthy of the Turks themselves: of outrages tolerated, or even shared in, by the Russian forces. If this terrible anticipation shall be realised, if the name of Christianity has been shamed, and the work of liberation tainted, by deeds loathsome in proportion to what we think the superiority of our creed, who does not at once perceive with what power we might have interposed had we upheld our impartial character intact, and how that power is crippled by the fact that British interests will be alleged, and may be believed, to be at the back of every remonstrance and complaint? Having made it our rule to treat all Turkish questions with reference to their bearing upon British interests, we shall be held bound by the formula we ourselves have framed; and, even if we emancipate ourselves from its domination, we shall not now be believed. So true it is, and in so many ways, that either pretentious orations or ambitious dispatches, which are but 'tales of sound and fury signifying nothing', add nothing to our greatness. Neither an individual nor a state can heap upon itself offices of supererogation, without displacing primary duties: just as every weed that we suffer to grow in our gardens occupies the place, which ought to be filled by some vegetable good for food.

The heroic mood cannot be the standard of ordinary national conduct; and for the Continental nations, separated as they are by slight boundaries or even imaginary lines, it would require nothing less than heroism, to raise themselves above the power and the suspicion of selfish aims in Continental questions. But for us, on whom Providence has conferred that exemption, by making us an island, it does indeed require a perverseness beyond the range of ordinary human infirmity to force our way into conflicts of self-interest, which are none the less fruitful of practical mischief, because the pleas on which we found ourselves are imaginary; such as that, for instance, which uplifted at Berlin into a question of peace and war for England the question whether Bulgaria should or should not include the Valley of the Maritza, inhabited by the southern Bulgarians.

It must, indeed, be admitted that most of the Continental Governments lure us onward into these follies. They have not complained of the Anglo-Turkish Convention, although it is a distinct breach of the Treaty of Paris. Neither, when Russia in 1870 declared she would not be bound by the clause of that Treaty which restrained her from keeping a fleet in the Black Sea, is it probable that they would have complained, if England had not led the way. Temporary causes would account for the present silence of France; Italy is hardly strong enough to venture on a single-handed initiative. But there is a cause more positive and effective, which acts upon most of them in this direction. Almost every one of the Great Powers has, either in the West or in the East, separate views of its own to prosecute, views not associated with the general interest nor with peace, but with a bias to territorial aggrandisement, or, as it is called, revindication. Nothing can be more adverse to those views, nor more distasteful to their promoters, than the presence of a Power in Europe, temperate, impartial, attached to liberty, and strong because disengaged; such a Power, in short, as England was in 1870, when she stamped out in a fortnight the embers of the Benedetti project. To all statesmen so minded, as they cannot heave England into the mid-Atlantic and put her physically out of the way, it is as great an object to see her

laden and overladen with embarrassing engagements, which
morally shift her out of the arena, as it would be to a set of
rioters that all the policemen of the district should be hand-
cuffed. If, for example, it be true that Russia entertains
vindictive designs against us in the heart of Asia, what could
be more convenient or acceptable to her than that we should be
involved, as we are to be involved, in thorny controversies
with the Porte on the government of Asia, should rouse the
jealousy of France by overriding her presumptive claims in
Syria, and should spend funds and forces upon Cyprus? In
pursuance of such motives it has been that for years there has
been a practice, not confined to the Continental newspapers,
of twitting us with an abstention which has never at any period
existed, paying hollow compliments to our resources, which
we know very well without their telling us, and inciting us
through our vanity, alternately mortified and pleased, to what
are called displays of vigour. Every sensible Englishman, when
such remarks meet his eye or ear, should recognise in them the
proofs of the traditional moderation of his Government, and,
reading between the lines, as it is called, should at once perceive
that his interlocutor desires either to bring us on the scene of
action for a purpose of his own, or to see us with our hands
well filled elsewhere, so that at all events he may have nothing
to apprehend from us in the execution of his plans.

The foreign policy of Mr. Canning, though approved by
colleagues like Lord Liverpool and Sir Robert Peel, was always
detested by pure Toryism, because of the boldness with which it
proclaimed the function of England as the advocate of rational
freedom and self-government. It was this policy, and not the
foisting into every question of pretended British interests,
which would have destroyed alike its dignity and its influence,
that Lord Palmerston prosecuted with such energy and skill in
the case of Belgium and of the Peninsula. To say that regard
was always paid to British interests is simply to say that Mr.
Canning and Lord Palmerston were not out of their right
minds.[9] But though that regard be alike just and indispensable,
just as it would be among individuals in private life, the
incessant and ostentatious proclamation of it is a very different

[9] See, for example, the admirable statement of principles by Mr. Canning, in
connection with the Greek Question, republished by Lord Stratford de
Redcliffe in the last number of this *Review*, p. 381.

matter. It is needless; for who has ever heard of a nation which did not sufficiently desire to study its own interests? It is vulgar. It is offensive. It affords a precedent and example, of which every unscrupulous Government may avail itself. It disturbs the relative importance of objects, mistaking small for great and remote for near. It leads us to bear the burden of work, which belongs to others. Finally, it makes us mean, and makes us little, by disabling us for the work which is properly our own.

Thus far I have referred to those branches of the great work assigned to the Imperial State of the United Kingdom: government at home, government in the Colonies, and the exercise of foreign influence as a member of the great community of Christendom.

There remains yet a fourth, the government of India; in some respects the most difficult and critical of all. In all the other three we derive aid from the records of human experience in divers ages and countries. Here we are travelling on a journey to which honour and duty inexorably bind us, but on a route which plainly leads into the unknown. As to the money tribute which, in the shape of interest on capital, or of remuneration for service, we may be said to draw from India, it is but a third-rate factor in a question of overwhelming magnitude. Five or six millions a year are a large sum; yet they can count but for little to a country with an income of a thousand millions. But here is a tutelage, unexampled in history. It embraces from one-fifth to one-sixth of the human race: the latest German reckonings of the population of the globe carrying it beyond fourteen hundred millions. Over this population, and the vast territory it inhabits, we hold a dominion entirely uncontrolled, save by duty and by prudence, measured as we may choose to measure them. This dominion is *de jure* in the hands of a nation, whose numbers, as compared with those of its Indian subjects, are one to seven, and whose seat is at the other end of the world; *de facto*, it is wielded by a handful of their agents, military and civil, who are not as one to three thousand of the peoples spread, as an ocean, in passive obedience around them. Of the seventy thousand Anglo-Indians, not one, except mere waifs and strays, strikes root in the country; and all but a handful have their stay limited to a very brief term of years. At home still less provision is made for the adequate discharge of a gigantic duty. It depends upon a Cabinet, which dreads nothing so much as the mention of an Indian question at its meetings; on a minister, who knows that, the less his colleagues hear of his proceedings, the better they will be pleased; on a Council, which is not allowed to enter into his highest deliberations; and on a Parliament, supreme over them all, which cannot in its two Houses jointly muster one single score of persons, who have either a practical experience in the government of India, or a tolerable knowledge of its people or its history. Thus it is that truth beats fiction, and that fable cannot keep pace with fact, nor design control results. What is most of all singular is that this relation, unparalleled in the history of the world, is not founded upon, or warranted by, a general inferiority in the Indian mind, or a civilisation less matured by time. It is in comparative force of manhood and faculties of action alone that those conditions are found, which not only bring the British supremacy within the limits of the possible, but invest it with a humane and beneficial aspect. In this view, it presents a resemblance to the old sovereignty of Rome over the Hellenic races when their active powers had sunk below the level necessary for their independence; but that sovereignty was exercised in circumstances, which did not present the same character of violent paradox.

This astonishing fabric was in the main built up by a mercantile Company, with secondary aid from the counsels and control of the Government, and under the guidance of the practical good sense which is so remarkable in our countrymen, except when some peculiar Atè bewilders and misleads them. Its military system was proved, in the tremendous trial of 1857, to be more efficient, than that of the Home Government had been found on the outbreak of the Crimean War. The finance was sound; the debt moderate, as, even when swollen after and through the Mutiny of 1857, it did not reach sixty millions; the code enlightened. The deadly error of the Affghan War, which it is to be hoped we are not now to repeat,[10] was the error of the Queen's Government. The Company delivered

---

[10] If it be true that a mission is gone or going to Caubul, three hundred sabres strong, it recalls the saying of Tigranes, that the Romans were too many for an embassy, and too few for an army. But it recalls much more ominously the conduct of the Government in 1859, which sent Lord Elgin with a small naval force to sign a treaty. That small naval force invited the attack at the mouth of the Peiho, and brought on the third China War.

India in 1844 from the flighty genius of Lord Ellenborough, who leant to the ostentatious policy that has lately received, upon more dangerous ground, a more serious development. The toleration they established was one only too wide. They boldly gave education to the people. They established a free press half a century ago. They laid the foundations of the railway system. They discouraged, to the best of their ability, aggression on the native princes, and on neighbouring territories. Their policy was in the best sense conservative; and, at the time when they handed over their high office to the Government, there was not a point in the whole of our case with India at which we could say they had neglected duty or precaution, or had either feigned or courted danger. Since that time also much good has been done; but the course of improvement has been continued, not initiated. Both before and after 1852, our rule, while it rested materially upon military power, was based morally upon its bounteous and beneficent operation, and upon the sense of that operation which had been generated in the native mind. Whether the general rules of prudence have been as well observed, whether the foundations are as safe now as they were then, is another matter. The questionable and precarious revenue from opium has been largely increased. The salt tax has been raised, and it is stated to amount to eighteen times the price of the article in Cheshire.[11] Revenue is nearly stationary.[12] The last quinquennium of trade does not exhibit an increase. The military expenditure reaches nearly twenty millions; and has the melancholy distinction of being probably the highest, except one, in the world. Not only has the debt been raised from 59,000,000*l.* to 130,000,000*l.*, but it is even contended that, if guarantees and indirect charges are included, the total amount now reaches 234,000,000*l.*[13] It is unquestionable that the aspect of Indian finance grows gloomier instead of brighter, and brings back to the minds of those few who care for past or future the declaration of Sir Robert Peel[14] that, in the well-being of Indian finance, British finance had a substantial concern. Under these circumstances

[11] Wilson, *Resources of Nations*, i. p. 71.

[12] *Ibid.* p. 73.

[13] Wilson, *Resources of Nations*, p. 59.

[14] March 11, 1842: Hansard, vol. lxi. p. 428.

it is that we cannot find a day for the discussion of the Indian Budget earlier than August 13, when the House of Commons has already sat for seven months, and when the exigency of an important division on the subject can rally to their places no more than seventy-nine members. And this, too, in the year which has seen opened, without the slightest examination of the grave and manifold consequences certain to ensue, the pretentious scheme for introducing our Indian army into European warfare; and which, at nearly the same date, has witnessed the most deplorable and senseless measure of retrogression that marks our recent annals in the extinction, at a day's notice and with closed doors, of the liberty of the Indian vernacular press.

The truth as to India cannot too soon be understood. There are two policies, fundamentally different; and it is the wrong one that is now in favour. One of them treats India as a child treats a doll, and defends it against other children; the other places all its hopes for the permanence of our Indian rule in our good government of India. Sound finance and moderate establishments, liberal extension of native privileges, and, not least of all, an unfailing regard to the sacredness of the pledge implied in privilege already given, these acts of government will secure the way to prosperity, to contentment, and to confidence in India. Let us only make common cause with her people; let them feel that we are there to give more than we receive; that their interests are not traversed and frustrated by selfish aims of ours; that, if we are defending ourselves upon the line of the Hindoo Coosh, it is them and their interests that we are defending, even more, and far more, than our own. Unless we can produce this conviction in the mind of India, in vain shall we lavish our thoughts and our resources upon a merely material defence. But we have produced it in a good degree already; and, although not by using her as a military tool for purposes not her own, and not by proscribing her free thought and speech, we may do it more, and do it thoroughly. Thus covered and protected in our rear, we shall find it a task well within our means to repel the foreign invader, come he when he will. Between the two methods of procedure there could be no competition, were we as a people free to give to the affairs of India anything like the attention which they demand, and which it may some day cost us many a fruitless pang never to have given.

The truth is that, turn where we will, we are met on every side with proofs that the cares and calls of the British Empire are already beyond the strength of those who govern and have governed it. A protracted experience of public affairs, not unattended with a high estimate of the general diligence, devotion, and ability of the Parliamentary as well as the civil servants of the Crown, has long convinced me that of the more difficult descriptions of the public business, apart from simple routine, it is only a small part that is transacted with the requisite knowledge, care, and thoroughness. We have undertaken, in the matter of government, far more than ever in the history of the world has been previously attempted by the children of men. None of the great continuous Empires of ancient or modern times ever grappled with such a task: the difference of discontinuity, even if it stood alone, is an essential difference. The nearest approach to our case was perhaps that of the Macedonian conqueror, to whose organising power posterity has not always done justice. But he did not rule the vast countries under his sway from Pella, as we do from London. He accepted the change in the centre of gravity, and became, as he could not but become, an Asiatic sovereign: a transformation for which it may be presumed that the line of British monarchs is not by any means prepared. Nor does it appear that our task is likely to be attenuated by the tendencies of the times; for, with the advancing development of civilisation, it seems too plain that they multiply, instead of reducing, the demands legitimately made on the time and care of governors. Our Colonial Empire rests so largely on devolution of legislative power and practical self-government, that of the four great branches of our office or mission, this is the one in which our performances fall least short of its normal standard. And yet here too we have had great and egregious failures. We failed to manage the Ionian Islands; and when we reproached Austria with her arbitrary conduct, she was able to retort by pointing to our own undoubted illegalities and excesses. We did not give to Canada the self-government now found so harmless and beneficial, until we had been warned by two rebellions. The Negro emancipation was a great and noble deed; but the slovenly manner in which it was worked out, and the material retrogression of what were the slave Colonies, if they do not indicate an exhausted patience, show that the rushing mill-stream of our affairs, when once the popular demand had been met, and the excitement had died away, prevented the expenditure of care needful in order to secure the elevating and civilising aims of the emancipation. It was a wretched consummation when, some ten years ago, we handed over Jamaica to arbitrary power. Nor has experience shown that the vices of a despotic system have been neutralised by the very high character and abilities of those who were charged with its administration. If any Englishman will take the pains to read the official Report, dated December 19, 1877, on the condition of the great Reformatory at Stony Hill, in Jamaica, for a series of years, he will see that under the mild sway of the British Government abuses may prevail, such as ought to raise a blush upon the cheek of any despot in the world.

With respect to domestic policy, the accession of energy, imparted to our Parliamentary system by the first great struggle of Reform, appeared to endow it with the faculty of grappling with every public need as it arose. But for the last twenty years, in despite of the exertions of Governments and Parliaments, there has been a great, if not a constant accumulation of arrears, and we have now reached the point at which it may almost be termed hopeless. It is unquestionably a point at which the discovery has been made, that the merest handful of men may, if they have a sufficient stock of personal hardihood and indifference to the opinion of those around them, avail themselves of the impeded state of the political traffic to stop altogether the chief of all the Queen's highways. For the benefit of those who doubt, I add in a note a slight sketch of some of our unredeemed engagements.[15]

It is at such a time as this that, instead of resolutely con-

[15] 1. London Municipal Reform; 2. County Government; 3. County Franchise; 4. Liquor Laws; 5. Irish Borough Franchise; 6. Irish University Question; 7. Opium Revenue; 8. Criminal Law Procedure; 9. Responsibility of Masters for Injuries to Workmen; 10. Reduction of Public Expenditure; 11. Probate Duty; 12. Indian Finance; 13. Working of the Home Government of India; 14. City Companies; 15. Burial Laws; 16. Valuation of Property; 17. Law of the Medical Profession; 18. Law of Entail and Settlement; 19. Corrupt Practices at Elections; 20. Expenses of Elections; 21. Reorganisation of the Revenue Departments; 22. The Currency. In not a few of these cases, the mischief amounts to positive scandal.

I do not add those subjects which are at present only pressed by a section, though often a large section, of the community; such as the redistribution of seats, the Church Establishments, the law of Primary Education, and very many more.

fronting the vast and noble duties which cry out from every quarter against our neglect, we exult in new acquisitions, new engagements, new responsibilities, and refuse to recognise the daily increasing neglect of the old. There is no doubt whatever that such a course is popular with a part, and no small part, of the community. The case was very ably and very truly set forth in a recent number of the *Pall Mall Gazette*, on 'Ministerial Popularity and its Causes'. Truly, that is to say, not as to the facts, but rather as to the impressions about the facts, which impressions constitute the main question at issue. The Liberals, according to that ably written newspaper,[16] have now imbibed as a 'permanent sentiment' a 'distaste for national greatness'. This distaste is now grown into 'matter of principle'. Not only does it teach us to 'mind our own business', and to avoid 'supposing ourselves better than other people', which appear to be rather rational ideas; but generally, to 'leave things alone', 'to keep out of European scrapes, and to put up our shutters when there is a fight in the street'. 'The disgust at these principles of action ever grew in depth and extent', so that in the Danish, the American, and the Franco-German wars, there was 'an increasing portion of the nation ready to engage in the struggle on almost any side', as a protest against the position that it was 'bound not to engage in it at all'! The climax of the whole matter was reached, when the result of the Alabama Treaty displayed to the world an England over-reached, overruled, and apologetic. It certainly requires the astounding suppositions, and the gross ignorance of facts, which the journalist with much truth recites, to explain the manner in which, for some time past, pure rhodomontade has not only done the work of reasoning, but has been accepted as a cover for constant miscarriage and defeat; and doctrines of national self-interest and self-assertion as supreme laws have been set up, which, if unhappily they harden into 'permanent sentiment' and 'matter of principle', will destroy all the rising hopes of a true public law for Christendom, and will substitute for it what is no better than the Communism of Paris enlarged and exalted into a guide of international relations. It is perhaps unreasonable to expect, that minds in the condition of the 'increasing portion' should on any terms accept an appeal to

[16] Aug. 8, 1878.

history. But, for the sake of others, not yet so completely emancipated from the yoke of facts, I simply ask at what date it was that the Liberal Administrations of this country adopted the 'permanent sentiment' and the 'matter of principle' which have been their ruin? Not in 1859–60, when they energetically supported the redemption and union of Italy. Not in 1851, when, on the occurrence of the Trent affair, they at a few days' notice dispatched ten thousand men to Halifax. Not when, in concert with Europe, they compelled the Sultan to cut off the head of his tyrannical Pasha, and to establish a government in the Lebanon not dependent for its vital breath on Constantinople. Not when, in 1863, they invited France to join in an *ultimatum* to the German Powers, and to defend Denmark, with us, against the intrigues which Germany was carrying on under the plea of the Duke of Augustenburg's title to the Duchies; and when they were told by Louis Napoleon in reply that that might be a great British interest, but that it had no significance for France. Not when, in 1870, they formed in a few days their double Treaty for the defence of Belgium. Does, then, the whole indictment rest on this – that, in conformity with the solemn declaration of the European Powers at Paris in 1856,[17] they cured a deep-seated quarrel with America by submitting to the risk of a very unjust award at Geneva; and reconciled a sister nation, and effected a real forward step in the march of civilisation, at about half the cost which the present Administration has recently incurred (but without paying it) in agitating and disturbing Europe? Or is it that during all those years, and many more years before them, while liberty and public law were supported, and British honour vindicated, territorial cupidity was not inflamed by the deeds or words of statesmen, British interests were not set up as 'the first and great commandment', and it was thought better to consolidate a still undeveloped Empire, which might well satisfy every ambition, as it assuredly taxes to the utmost every faculty, than to excite the enmity or suspicion of the world by the greed of an endless aggrandisement?

Of all the Empires whose rise and fall have been recorded in history, there is not one that has owed its ruin or decay to checking the lust of unmeasured territorial acquisition. The

[17] Treaty of Paris, Protocol xxiii.

wisest of the Roman Emperors was also the one, who even recalled the boundaries of his dominions from beyond the Danube. Every one can discern and denounce the private folly of the farmer who covets more and more land, when he has neither capital nor skill to turn to account what he has already got; though he does not commonly proceed by covenants taken in the dark lest his landlord should come to know what sort of deed he is signing. But it requires a steady eye and a firm resolution to maintain the good tradition of all our bygone statesmen at a juncture when all tradition is discarded for new-fangled, or, as Mr. Roebuck calls them, 'original' devices, and the mind of folly finds utterance through the voice of authority. England, which has grown so great, may easily become little; through the effeminate selfishness of luxurious living; through neglecting realities at home to amuse herself everywhere else in stalking phantoms; through putting again on her resources a strain like that of the great French war, which brought her people to misery, and her Throne to peril; through that denial of equal rights to others, which taught us so severe a lesson at the epoch of the Armed Neutrality. But she will never lose by the modesty in thought and language, which most of all beseems the greatest of mankind; never by forwardness to allow, and to assert, the equal rights of all states and nations; never by refusing to be made the tool of foreign cunning, for ends alien to her principles and feelings; never by keeping her engagements in due relation to her means, or by husbanding those means for the day of need, and for the noble duty of defending, as occasion offers, the cause of public right, and of rational freedom, over the broad expanse of Christendom.

IMPERIALISM*
Robert Lowe

The time cannot be remote, it may be very near at hand, when we shall be called upon to elect a new Parliament. The election when it does arrive will, as far as we are permitted to see at present, turn upon questions very different from those which have agitated the public at least during the memory of the present generation. For reasons too obvious to require statement, the election can hardly turn on the merits or character of any existing statesman. We have not, and, we may be permitted to assert, are not likely to have, any proposal for domestic legislation which is calculated very deeply to interest the feelings or stir the energies of the great bulk of the constituencies. And yet this election will in all probability be ranked by posterity among the most momentous that has occurred during the last six hundred years. It may not turn on persons or on measures, but it will decide that on which the fate of persons and the success of measures must henceforth depend. It will lay down the principles on which statesmen must act, and the kind of measures which Parliament will henceforth view with favour. To many keenly disputed principles the present Parliament has already given the seal of its approbation. During the maximum period of two years which may remain to it, Parliament may give its approval to many more. But two things must always be remembered: one, that the innovations to which we allude have hitherto been the work not of those who are usually regarded as the party of innovation – the chartered libertines to whom nothing, however venerable from age or prescription, is sacred – but of the Conservative party, the party of tradition and permanence; the other, that these signal innovations on the ancient traditions and practice of England have never been brought to the notice and have never received the sanction of the electors, in

* From *Fortnightly Review*, vol. 24 ns (October 1878), pp. 453–65.

whose hands the ultimate decision still lies. Many of these questions have been raised from time to time in the form of criticisms on the declarations or actions of the ministers now in power. Others, though not distinctly stated, appear to be necessary corollaries from them. Others seem to point to analogies of very large and sweeping application. It has occurred to the writer of this paper that, perhaps, something might be gained for that clearness and precision which is so essential in a matter of such unspeakable importance, if he were first to endeavour to lay down affirmatively, rather than by way of hostile criticism, what appear to him to be the leading principles in dispute, and the reasons on which he conceives those principles to be based, reserving for after-consideration the criticism of those principles which appear to have been finally adopted by our present Ministry and Parliament.

So deep does the unsettlement of men's minds go, that the first question on which the constituencies will be bound to give an opinion is nothing less than the very elementary problem, What is the object which all those entrusted with political power ought to have in view in conducting the affairs of the country? The only answer that calm reason can give to such a question seems to be that the one duty of those entrusted with the government of mankind is to act purely and solely, as far as the infirmity of human nature will permit, with the single view of obtaining for that country over which they preside the greatest amount of happiness which the condition of its existence admits of. This is the alpha and omega of the duty of a statesman. As far as he does this, he discharges his duty to the people with whose destiny he is entrusted. As far as he allows himself to be drawn aside by any consideration whatever from this first and paramount obligation, be the temptation ever so great and so seducing, he is false to the trust reposed in him and to the office which he has undertaken. All other objects of desire, how glittering and seductive soever – military glory, success in diplomacy, personal distinction, increase of territory, prestige of all kinds – are not to be regarded as things to be desired for their own sake, but only so far as they contribute to the one cardinal and exclusive object, the happiness of those who have either directly or by their authorised agents entrusted their welfare to his care. Yet, true as this undoubtedly is, in the whole course of the recent controversy we never remember to have heard it mentioned. The whole dispute has turned on secondary matters, and the one end, in comparison with which all others sink into absolute insignificance, has been kept out of sight, and replaced by substitutes of infinitely inferior value.

Supposing this primary and all-important proposition to be conceded, another duty is thrown upon Government, for the performance of which they are gravely responsible. They are bound not only to abstain themselves from misleading the less informed and more excitable part of the community by directing their attention to these *idola theatri*, which may be substituted for the pursuit of happiness; they are bound to warn them against these delusions, and to point out to them that upon them and upon their children the effects of what is called a spirited foreign policy, as opposed to the pursuit of happiness, will surely fall. The business of a just and honest administration was, we think, well illustrated in the case of the Alabama award. Every conceivable motive prompted refusal except one, but that one was the happiness of the people of England and America. It was a case where the ministry of the day might have easily gained a temporary popularity by stimulating the popular passion. They preferred saving the people to trafficking on their weaknesses and passions, and when they incurred unpopularity in such a cause they were discharging the highest and clearest duty of their office.

The same considerations which apply to war determine the duty of a really honest and patriotic government with regard to finance. A really honest and patriotic government regards itself as a trustee, in the strictest sense of the word, of the money which is raised from the people. Not only is it bound not to misapply those funds, it is bound to employ them strictly in the manner which Parliament has decided to be most beneficial to the public at large. When the service of the year has been provided for, the surplus, if any, should return to those from whom it came. It was theirs originally, it becomes theirs again when the purpose for which it was raised is answered. This may be done in one of two ways, either by remission of taxation or by payment of debt. It seems right that the people who contribute the taxes should have the surplus returned to them, rather than that the Government should spend it for them. Every man is the best judge of where the shoe pinches. It is not right to divert the balance to lending money to powerful municipal bodies at a lower interest than can be obtained elsewhere, although it is undoubtedly a means of obtaining popularity. The present Government has made many friends by the lending system. The late Government took off twelve millions of taxes, and paid off forty millions of what was or would have become debt, and we are not aware that by doing so they made a single friend or conciliated a single opponent – but most undoubtedly they did their duty.

The happiness of men, as far as money matters are concerned, is best consulted by leaving them as far as possible to spend the money they have earned in their own way. It may be said that this principle would countenance that of which we have recently had a sample, the postponing the duty of raising money for the payment of sums which are due for the service of the present year, for a period more or less remote. The answer is that the Government is a trustee for the happiness of the people not only during the present year, but for all time; and that nothing tends so directly to foster those habits of extravagance, which are fatal alike to the happiness of nations and individuals, as giving any countenance to the idea that it can be either just or wise to teach the lesson that we have discovered the art by which one set of persons may be forced to pay for that which another set of persons have contrived to enjoy. In these, as in all other cases, a rigid adherence to justice will be found not only the guide to what is right, but also to what is sound policy, not necessarily the policy that will secure a prolonged tenure of office, but a policy which is good in itself, and will give to those who practise it the consciousness of having done their duty, and to those who live under it a respect for the institutions under which they live.

When we turn from domestic to foreign relations, we shall find that the same rule obtains. Our foreign relations have been happy and prosperous just in proportion as we have observed the rule of guiding ourselves by our true interests alone. From the first dawn of history mankind have been subject to the delusion that the happiness of a nation consists in the degree of influence that one people can exercise over the destiny of another; happy if they could make their neighbours tributary, happier still if they could reduce them to absolute dependence, happiest of all if they could degrade them to the condition of slaves. The Romans, who regulated their rights between each other with the most scrupulous exactness, had neither mercy nor justice for foreigners. The heroic stoic virtue of Brutus did not prevent him from starving the whole senate of our new and interesting possession of Cyprus to death, in order to extort from them the payment of interest at the rate of forty-eight per cent. The conquered provinces were plundered without mercy by prætors and pro-consuls to defray the expenses of Roman elections; and things reached such a degree of disorder and misery that the conquerors of the world submitted to a single tyrant, and reduced themselves to the condition of those whom they had conquered and trampled upon, rather than submit any longer to the fearful consequences of their own victories, bought by the extermination of the brave and thrifty inhabitants of Italy. This signal and prerogative instance, to which it would be easy to add many others, seems to show that when a nation has attained a certain amount of freedom and self-government, no step can be more fatal than a career of successful conquests. The dilemma forms itself in this way: if you raise your conquered enemy to a level with yourself, the blood and treasure which you have expended in the conquest have been wasted, and all that you have gained by it is a new element of discord and sedition; if you keep them in subjection they will inevitably, as in the case of Rome, drag you down to their own level.

It must also be remembered that the modern conqueror is in two respects worse off than his Roman predecessor: the ancient conqueror could impose a tribute, which the comparative mildness of modern notions will scarcely tolerate; and it was once worth while to conquer poor and savage races for the sake of obtaining slaves, which the civilisation of modern Europe no longer endures. Thus it appears that the principal motives which spurred men on to war in former times no longer exist, and that if it is the duty of statesmen to act solely for the happiness of the people they govern, it is equally their interest to avoid wars from which the mildness of modern manners prevents them from winning even the miserable advantages that war, if successful, could once afford.

But the case against war is still stronger when we consider that we have already obtained, without shedding a drop of blood, all and more than all that the most successful war could possibly give us. We won Canada by a series of bloody battles, but Australia we obtained without any battle at all. We sought in the most imperial way to make our colonies in North America our tributaries, and they separated from us, after inflicting upon us defeat and humiliation unknown to us before. We supposed that we had lost a great and irreplaceable dominion, but we found that for all useful purposes we had lost nothing by the separation; for all pacific uses the United States were still at our service. So long as vacant lands in temperate latitudes exist on the earth we have at our disposal, without shedding a drop of blood, all that the most successful war can give us. Just as we have discovered that any amount of territory may be acquired without war, so we have discovered and clearly proved that wealth beyond the dreams of avarice may be acquired without plunder. The way to grow rich is not to plunder and ruin other people, but to assist them in becoming rich themselves. The Roman empire perished because the subjects were unable to endure the weight of taxation. England flourishes because her peaceful industry can supply the demands of her Government, and yet leave enough in the hands of her people to stand against the competition of the world.

We trust that the observations which we have made will be found an appropriate introduction to the question which must be decided at the next general election. That question is, Shall we adhere to the policy which we have on the whole consistently adopted since the close of the Crimean war, or shall we discard it and substitute for it what in the language of our Secretaries of State is called Imperialism?

Every one of us when he enters upon life has before him two courses of action. He may take for his guide the simple rule of treating others as he would wish to be treated himself; he may consider their feelings, their interests, their prejudices; he may strive to place himself in their position; he may remember how often he has required indulgence himself, and how often he may yet require it; he may reflect upon the uncertainties of the most assured position, and the probability that he may at some time find occasion to ask for that fair consideration which he is now asked to give to his neighbour. Without entering into the moral merit of such conduct, we are in the habit of considering such a man, it may be, as a good but certainly as a prudent and judicious person. Take a person of the contrary cast of character – a man who, bent only on his immediate advantage, pushes every opportunity to the utmost, avows cynically that his own interest is the sole guide of his conduct, and shows by words and actions that he recognises no other limit to the liberty which he allows himself in his dealings with others than the strict law, and not even that, unless there is a strong probability of its being enforced against him. Which course should we, speaking in the abstract and without any special temptation before us, desire those who are adopted as the agents for a nation of which we are members to follow? Surely we should say, we prefer the fair and generous course, more especially when we remember that man is but a transitory being, but that nations are endowed with almost boundless longevity, and have therefore much stronger motives than individuals for establishing a good character. To do the Tories justice, the name of Imperialism and the theory were foreign to their opinions and traditions. But now the party has obtained not only office but power, and this is the contribution which its new position has brought us. We are invited to cast aside what we had fondly conceived to be the universally recognised principles of foreign policy, and to adopt those in their stead which it was hoped and believed we had finally discarded.

Let us examine this new idol to which we are summoned to bow down, as suddenly and as unreasonably as the subjects of Nebuchadnezzar himself. What does Imperialism mean? It means the assertion of absolute force over others. If we can gain some purpose by persuading our adversary that we are right and he is wrong, that is mere logical and rhetorical dexterity. There is nothing imperial in it. If we can, by abating somewhat of our extreme right, or even by larger concessions, avert the calamities of war, that is utterly repugnant to Imperialism. But if by the menace of overbearing force we can coerce a weaker state to bow before our will, or if, better still, we can by a demonstration of actual force attain the same object, or, best of all, if we can conquer our adversary in open fight, and impose our own conditions at the bayonet's point, then, as Dryden sings, 'these are imperial arts and worthy thee'. It does not follow that the strongest party is always in the wrong, but the triumph of Imperialism is most complete when power is most clearly manifested; and of course the victory is doubled when the victory is not only over weakness but over right.

We do not say that in her long and chequered history England has not often abused her power, but we believe that this is the first time that the leading members of her Government in England have descended so low as to teach their party to put forward such a symbol. Let us see what it is, and whither it will lead us. We are told as a matter of reproach that the question is between a great and a little England. Whether there may not also be a choice sometimes between a happy and a great, between an imperial and a just England, we are never desired to consider. Let us then analyse this light, and see whether it is of heaven or of the fogs and swamps of earth.

Imperialism is the apotheosis of violence. From the point of view of Imperialism, the less that there is to say for it beyond brute force the better. Every scintilla of justice that there is in your case is just so much deducted from its imperial quality. If he is thrice armed that has his quarrel just, he that has his quarrel unjust is thrice imperial. This doctrine in a nation like ours is as impolitic as it is iniquitous. We have a great deal more to lose than to gain by the spread of violence and rapine, and should, if it were only out of mere selfishness, adhere to the theory that sanctions existing rights and possessions. These cynical pretensions suit well with the insolence of prosperity, but have a bitter recoil in the days of adversity. Imperialism, so far as it is a leading motive, is the claim to be judges on our own cause – a claim which is neither just nor honourable. The Athenians, in their controversy with the Melians, cynically declare that 'justice is to be applied when the forces on each side are equal; but what the strong shall exact, or the weak shall yield, is a mere question of power'. Was that their opinion when, ten years afterwards, they found themselves at the mercy of the Spartans? There lurks a delusion, a prestige, in the proper sense of the word, in the very notion of Imperialism. One can imagine a single despot exulting in uncontrolled power, but what application has this to some thirty-five millions of people? We call them England by a figure of speech, but how many of them understand the glories of Imperialism, and how many of those on whom her glories descend would be willing to pay for them, if they knew the cost at which they are obtained, and had the question fairly put before them. We have recently had two samples of Imperialism which might, one would think, cool the aspirations of the most ardent Imperialist. The Emperor of the French, having no just title to fall back upon, determined to be ultra-imperial, *i.e.* to maintain by glory what he had gained by fraud and murder, and plunged into a most unjust war, with results which corresponded much more nearly to his deserts than his expectations. And we have a striking example in Prussia how little mere military success contributes to the happiness or content of the victor.

The introduction of this new and most unacceptable addition to our vocabulary calls to memory Swift's comment on the pretentious motto of Chief Justice Whitshed: –

'Libertas et natale solum,
Fine words! I wonder where you stole 'em.'

The real strength of a nation is measured not so much by what it does as by what it is able to do. Our strength in the day of trial, if it should arrive from unavoidable misfortune or be brought about by ministers imperially minded and in search of prestige, will consist mainly in this, that we have not trained away the flower of our youth from innocent and useful employment to spend their lives in barracks and cantonments, that we have not squandered our finances in vain military flourish and bravado, and that by these means we have kept our country in a state which will enable us to put forth considerable power if it should become necessary. How long this will be the case under the notions that are dominant in the most influential quarters, it is impossible to say. We may at any rate point with some pride and satisfaction to what was once the non-imperial policy of this country. Hitherto, as being more anxious for defence than attack, we have availed ourselves to the full of the advantages of our insular position, and safe behind our watery rampart have dispensed ourselves from the duty of vying with continental armies. But now it would seem all this is to be changed, and the principles to which we owe so much are to give way to a ruinous competition with the great continental armies. The Crimean war has taught us, if we did not know it before, how rapidly the wear and tear of war tells upon an English army, and how easily a force which can go anywhere and do anything may be transformed into the body of half-trained boys who were unable to hold the Redan. It is best to look our position boldly in the face, and to admit what is really undeniable, that the necessary concomitant of an imperial army and the first condition of giving effect to our new ideas is to adopt some form of conscription as soon as possible. As long as we were content to trust to our insular position, as long as we could count on being the attacked and not the attacking party, we were well justified in relying on an army of volunteers. But the attitude which we have now

assumed really leaves us no other choice, unless we are prepared to be as ridiculous as we have been presumptuous, than
to place our little army in some degree on an equality with
our inflated pretensions.

We admit that there is one exception to the line of policy
which we have pursued, but that exception only proves the
rule. The conquest of India was not the work of the English
Government but of a mercantile company. At the time when
it passed into the hands of the Crown, as it virtually did about
a hundred years ago, we had a wolf by the ears which it was
as difficult to let go as to hold. We could not go back, we
could not stand still. We had no choice but to advance. We
are committed to this experiment, but the exception, we repeat,
proves the rule. The greatest part of the difficulty in which we
are involved arises from an over-strained and ridiculous anxiety
as to the probability of an attack on India from the west. The
existence of this periodical panic only shows the danger of
such possessions and the rashness of committing ourselves, as
we have just done, to other continental engagements, which,
being less under our control, may very probably be even more
dangerous and burdensome.

The objections which we have taken to the doctrine of
imperialism have turned very much on its immorality. It is
founded on the reckless acceptance of any means which appear
likely to attain the ends in view, on the grossest selfishness and
the most absolute disregard of what all men admit in the
abstract to be their duty towards each other. Its principle, if
anything so utterly unprincipled can deserve the name, resolves
itself to the oppression of the weak by the strong, and the
triumph of power over justice.

The Government seem to be labouring under the impression
that the disorder from which the inhabitants of the British
Islands are at this time suffering is a want of self-appreciation,
and so they proceed logically enough to administer the strongest antidote to this disorder in the form of the grossest appeals
to our national vanity. The effect that 'Violet Crowned' is said
by Aristophanes to have produced on the Athenian populace,
our ministers evidently expect from the administration in large
doses of the term 'imperial'. We are self-governed in England;
we are the governors of others in India; and it is evidently
thought by our guides and instructors that it is a much finer
thing to govern others, than to be able to govern ourselves.

They think that we are deficient in a due share of national vanity, and that it is their duty to raise us to a proper appreciation of our own merits. The only other supposition would be that the Government were playing the odious part of seeking low popularity by the arts of flattery and sycophancy, which, of course, is not to be entertained. But without inquiring too deeply into motives, we should like very much to be told when the Government has succeeded in flattering and fooling the people to the top of their bent, when each of us has come to consider himself as an Alexander or a Sesostris what shall we have gained, and what will the Government have gained by it? We must refer those who are rude enough to ask this question to Falstaff's Catechism of Honour, reminding them that if Imperialism pricks you on, it may also prick you off, and that it has no skill in surgery.

How desirable it is for those who do not share the views of the Government to bestir themselves may be gathered from the following extract from the *Times* correspondent from India of September 11th, who is evidently writing under official inspiration. 'It is necessary', he says, 'to provide for a strong strategic position. It is indispensable that we should possess a commanding influence over the triangle of territory formed on the map by Cabul, Ghuznee, and Jellalabad. War would be an evil of infinitely less gravity than Russian influence in Cabul, which would extend hostility to British power in India.' The only construction that we can put on this passage is that unless the Ameer of Cabul, who is notoriously hostile to us, will enter at once into a treaty of amity, we will at once enter upon a repetition of the invasion of Affghanistan of 1838–9, just to see whether we can re-enact the sanguinary drama of 1841–42. In other words, we will leap into the furnace, in order to save ourselves from the flames. The pretension thus put forward really seems to amount to this. Great Britain and Ireland are only a kingdom after all. India is an empire. But an empire is more worthy than a kingdom, and though it may happen that our whole strength lies in the kingdom, and our weakness mainly in the empire, it is the interest of the empire rather than the interest of the kingdom by which our policy is to be regulated. What is called a far-sighted policy is not always a wise one. A microscopic ingenuity may find for itself more profitable employment than in discovering causes for war. To search for a cause of offence, to find it, and by a sudden attack to convert an unpleasant possibility into a still more unpleasant certainty, is not one of the highest achievements of statesmanship. It is well to remember that the impact which we receive will be exactly in proportion to the violence of the attack, and that it is often wiser to watch and wait for mischiefs that may never happen, than by headlong precipitation to convert them into certainties. When every day brought a fresh challenge to Russia, it was only reasonable that she should seek what appeared to her the readiest mode of retaliation. Had we not better wait and see whether, the cause being removed, the effect may not also cease.

But we have still to consider Imperialism in another aspect in which it is even more odious. We know not of what materials an imperial conscience is made, but we think there must be very few English gentlemen on either side of the House who can have witnessed without some feelings of indignation and shame our treatment of the assembled powers of Europe at the Congress of Berlin. For reasons which we will not now enter into or dispute, the English Government had come to the conclusion that it was expedient to form the state of Eastern Roumelia, to cede Batoum to Russia, to guarantee the integrity of the Turkish empire against Russia, and to obtain a decisive influence over the domestic administration of Turkey. They also desired to obtain possession of the island of Cyprus. We are not dealing with the wisdom or expediency of these desires, but simply with the fact of their existence. There was but one fair and honourable way of attaining them. The European Conference was about to meet. These were all matters intimately connected with the questions which the Conference was summoned to discuss. If they were to be insisted on, to state them to the Conference was an absolute duty of ordinary honesty and good faith.

The meeting of Berlin was the Areopagus of Europe. It was acting in a judicial as well as an executive capacity, and no duty can be clearer than that of every member of the Congress to abstain from any secret arrangement which might limit its jurisdiction or mislead its judgment. But England had a point to carry, and that point was most easily if not most honourably attained by underhand negotiations and secret conventions. The moral principle once broken down, the choice lay between force or fraud, each founded on the maxim that the means justify the ends – both alike imperial and alike disgraceful. The powers of Europe who were not tainted by these transactions understood their dignity too well to waste time in fruitless reclamations; but Europe will not forget that England just before entering into a conference of a judicial nature on the affairs of Turkey, which bound her to the utmost purity and impartiality, stooped to receive a bribe from the country on whose destiny she was about to arbitrate, and forestalled the decision of the Congress by clandestine negotiations.

We have hitherto considered the spirit of Imperialism only as it relates to our dealings with foreign nations. But unhappily this does not exhaust the subject. We have yet to say a word on the influence of this pernicious innovation on our own constitution. Belial is a divinity who will not be served by halves, and no nation ever cast away the principles of just and fair dealing in its relations with others, without speedily feeling the recoil in its domestic affairs. Of all countries in the world England is the one which affords the readiest opportunity for unscrupulous persons to practise the arts of Imperialism as we have explained the term. The history of the English constitution is a record of liberties wrung and extorted bit by bit from arbitrary power. The shell of absolute power has been allowed to remain, so much of substance being removed as the emergencies of a particular crisis rendered necessary. When the prerogatives of the sovereign have been grossly abused, they have been restricted, but, owing to a certain moderation and phlegm in the character of the people, they have been more studious to guard against the mischiefs that have actually arisen, than to reduce the constitution to a clear and logical consistency. Thus most of the prerogatives of the Crown remain untouched, the country having been content with the assurance that they can only be exercised under the advice of responsible ministers.

It is the happy discovery of the present Parliament that responsibility has no terrors for a Government possessed of a large and manageable majority. Our institutions are framed in a spirit of generous but, as it now appears, mistaken confidence. The power of entering into treaties without the consent of Parliament has been only retained, because it was believed that it would not be abused. That by the abuse of this power the members of the Cabinet, without consulting Parliament, should be able to pledge the country to the most formidable engagements, to the clandestine acquisition of new territory peculiarly calculated to wound the susceptibilities of powers with whom it is alike our desire and interest to be on the most amicable terms, and to a treaty under which we may be called upon at a moment's notice to engage under every conceivable disadvantage in a war in a desolate and remote country with one of the greatest military powers in the world, as near to his resources as we are distant from our own, can only be believed possible because it has just been actually done. It is thus that the poisoned chalice of Imperialism which we have held out to our allies and rivals is now commended to our own lips. We have been learning under our present guides and leaders the doctrines of despotic and arbitrary power, and we must not repine if we experience in our own persons that which we are taught by these our new schoolmasters to be the proper treatment of our friends and allies. Thus it has ever been. The laws of good faith and fair dealing are violated towards strangers, in the vain hope that those virtues may flourish at home which are cynically cast aside abroad.

But this can never be. The Spirit which teaches that the means are justified if the end be obtained, will not suffer its sphere of action to be limited to dealings with our adversaries or our allies. If all is held to be fair in war or diplomacy, it is but a slight step in advance to hold that political opponents within our own borders are entitled to no greater consideration. The House of Commons was called together three weeks earlier than usual that the Government might have the advantage of its advice and assistance. We will not weary our readers by recapitulating a history with which every one is well acquainted; but we put it to any candid person whether the treatment which the House has received from the first day of the session to the last of the Conference of Berlin, has not been on the part of Government one long course of deception and mystification. The House was deceived as to the movements of the fleet, kept in the dark as to the transportation of troops from India, and committed without knowing it to a new and most hazardous policy in Asia Minor. It would almost seem that the Commons of England were summoned and kept together mainly to show to the rest of Europe how vain was the notion that this great assembly is the ruling power in the State, and to prove that its functions are practically limited to voting money for expenditure on which it has never been consulted, and ratifying new and most hazardous schemes of policy of which it never heard till they were beyond recall. Just as a bold speculator in cosmogony is said to have declared that it was the duty of the architect of the universe to create it and then to commit suicide, so it seems to be assumed that the duty of a House of Commons is to create a Government, and, having accomplished this feat, to sink into a state of political coma till a new election heralds the advent of a new or the continuance of an old ministry. The result of what we have said seems to be that we are in no little danger of undergoing a very real revolution, however it may be veiled under apparent observance of the forms of the constitution. The House has become a machine for electing, and seems disposed to abdicate its functions of controlling and instructing ministers. The business of the Government is to find it occupation in the hunting of rats and mice and such small deer, while weightier matters are sedulously concealed from it till any practical interference, even were the House disposed to attempt it, has become impossible.

These things call aloud for a remedy if the House of Commons is to be something more, to discharge some higher duties, than the persons whose duty is limited to the election of the President of the United States. The remedy is in the constituencies or nowhere. The time which may elapse before the dissolution of Parliament cannot be better employed than in pointing out to those with whom the decision ultimately rests the great issues that are raised by a condition of affairs like the present. The people should be put on their guard against the flimsy but dangerous delusions to which they are exposed. They should be reminded of the principles by the observance of which this country has hitherto grown and prospered to an extent to which history affords no parallel. These may be summarised in industry and freedom at home, and peace, fair dealing, and moderation abroad. They should be warned against the stupid worship of mere size and bulk; they should be taught that the question is not, as our blind guides tell us, between a great and a little, but between an honest and happy and a disgraced unhappy England. They should be guarded against those odious sophisms which, under the vulgar mask of Imperialism, conceal the substitution of might for right, and seek to establish the dominion of one set of human beings on the degradation and misery of another. And above all, the public ought to be warned against that abuse of the prerogative of making treaties, by which, in defiance of constitutional practice and theory, we have been entangled in the most tremendous liabilities without the previous consent of the Parliament that should have sanctioned, or the people who must bear them.

VALUE OF INDIA TO ENGLAND[*]
George Chesney

In the *Fortnightly Review* for last November Mr. Lowe propounds the thesis that the foreign dominions of the Crown are
more of a burden to Great Britain than a blessing. Putting aside
the Crown colonies which are held as military posts, Mr. Lowe
divides our colonies into three categories – those which are
fitted for the residence of English Labour; the tropical colonies,
in which the European cannot work out of doors; and India;
and he states the case against each separately. As regards the
colonies in the first class, of which Australia and the Dominion
of Canada are the most important, inasmuch as it seems to be
generally agreed that England will retain her connection with
them only for so long as the colonies may themselves desire
its continuance, and that under no conceivable circumstances
would the use of force be resorted to, to keep them if they
wanted to leave us, the question has at most but a speculative
value, while it may certainly be difficult to discover a better
reason for retaining the West Indies than the one suggested by
Mr. Lowe, that it would be disgraceful to allow these beautiful
islands to relapse into barbarism. Passing by these two cases, it
will be the object of this paper to examine how far the argument is a valid one which seeks to establish that England loses
more than she gains by the possession of India.

First admitting that the opinion which he advances on this
point is opposed to the convictions of ordinary Englishmen,
who are accustomed to attach extreme value to the possession
of India, Mr. Lowe proceeds to state the various disadvantages
involved in the connection. And last, but not least, among
these he places what he calls the drain of men involved in
keeping up 'an army of some 70,000 British troops' in that
country. The actual number of these troops, it may be
remarked, is barely 60,000; but this correction does not affect

[*] From *Nineteenth Century*, vol. 3 (February 1878), pp. 227–38.

the principle contended for, and it will be useful to ascertain clearly what is really involved in the condition. 'The pay and maintenance of these English troops', says Mr. Lowe, 'are reimbursed to the English Government from Indian funds, but this does not stop the drain to which we are exposed. The money which we spend can be repaid to us, but who shall give us back our men?' As a matter of fact England does not even advance the money in the first instance, which – or at any rate the greater part of it – is disbursed directly by the Indian Government; but, passing that by, we have still to consider what is meant by a drain of men in such a case, and whether it really constitutes an appreciable burden upon England. Now, in the first place, it is plain that the term can only be used at all in a very strained sense. To supply 60,000 men to India does not involve sending 60,000 men every year, nor are they withdrawn permanently; for to Mr. Lowe's question – 'Who shall give us back our men?' – we may reply that India gives them back. The soldiers who go to India are sent out to take the place of others who come back on the expiry of their service, and to replace those who die during their stay in that country. The real drain of men involved, therefore, after the withdrawal of the 60,000 men in the first instance, is limited to the waste involved by reason of the higher rate of mortality of Englishmen living in India. Now the death-rate of the British soldier in India may be taken at twenty per thousand, while that of the adult male in England of the same age is only about ten per thousand, so that the occupation of India involves the permanent reduction of the population of these isles by 60,000 able-bodied men, and that 600 more able-bodied Englishmen die yearly in consequence than would die otherwise. It is only to the replacement of these casualties that the term 'a drain of men' can be applied; and when we consider that almost pre-cisely the same number of deaths occurs every year in England of males between the ages of twenty and forty from railway accidents alone, we are in a position to appreciate the extreme insignificance, in its effect on the population of the United Kingdom, of what has had so alarming a name given to it.

It must be obvious, moreover, that so far as our connection with India is an evil by withdrawing a certain part of our manhood, its effect must be perfectly inappreciable compared with the effect of emigration. We may assume that during the last ten years about 6,000 Englishmen have died, who otherwise would many of them be still alive, in consequence of having been sent to India. But during the same time more than 1,000,000 persons have emigrated from these islands (over and above those who have returned to them), and so have become lost to the country for ever, and of these about one-half would appear to have been adult males. In view of these figures the drain involved in garrisoning India becomes practically inappreciable. But further it may surely be affirmed that this extra mortality, trifling though it be, and still more this permanent withdrawal of 60,000 working men from the country, so far from being a loss, is, on the contrary, an absolute benefit to all those who stay behind. I am not of course arguing with those who measure the prosperity of the country by the competition for employment as serving to keep down wages, or who regard a mere increase of the population with complacency, as a matter for satisfaction in itself, without considering whether the field of employment is extending in a corresponding degree. But those who regard high wages, especially among the agricultural working classes, as a thing to be greatly desired; who recognise in the emigration from Ireland the one effective cause which was able to rescue that country from the depression and poverty into which it had been brought by over-population; who have noted with satisfaction the gradual improvement in the condition of the peasantry in the west of England, since a part of the surplus population has been taken off by emigration, or by change of residence to other districts – those who take this view of the matter will probably admit that the reduction of the English labour market to the extent of even 60,000 able-bodied men is a distinct, if only a small, benefit to the remainder; and also that, except in so far as every premature death is an evil by adding to the sum of suffering endured by humanity, the increased rate of mortality due to residence in India affords a relief, although it may be very slight in degree, to the labour market in an over-populated country.

It may be replied, however, that, granting all this, it fails to refute the case put, which is not based on a consideration of the whole population of the country, but that limited section of it which is found in practice to be willing to accept military service, and which alone should be taken into account when estimating the military resources of the country. These particular 60,000 men, it will be argued, form a large deduction from those resources, and the necessity of keeping so large a body of troops in India involves an addition to the strain, already sufficiently severe, of keeping up an army by voluntary enlistment. In peace time, however, this strain does not arise, except in so far as that possibly a higher rate of pay has to be given to the soldier than would be found necessary if the whole establishment were smaller than it is. The strength of the home army is not regulated by the supply of recruits, but by the supposed needs of the country. The required establishment is now quite full, and if the Indian garrison were withdrawn to-morrow, the result would not be to give us an increased army at home, but that 60,000 soldiers would be discharged. Nor is it at all certain that the recruiting for Indian service enters into effective competition with that for the home service. With a large class service in India has special attractions, and they will be ready to go there when they would not care to do soldiering at home. Further, under the new system, by which all soldiers are to be transferred to the army reserve for the latter period of their service, England will get the benefit of the reserves supplied from these 60,000 men, the cost of whose training has been paid for by India. In this sense the European garrison of India, far from being a drain upon them, forms a substantial addition to the military resources of the country.

On the whole, therefore, and as regards peace time, it would appear that the European garrison of India is a burden on England, only in the same sense that emigration is a burden, by tending to keep up prices and to limit the labour market. It probably makes the home army somewhat more costly than it otherwise would be; against this the reserves which it furnishes may be regarded as a set-off. There still remains to consider the effect of this obligation in case of war. Mr. Lowe draws a vivid picture of the danger that would have fallen on England if the Mutiny had happened during instead of after the Crimean war, and the resources of England had been distracted between the needs for recruiting our wasted forces before Seba-stopol and the call for succour to the handful of Englishmen who were defending themselves against desperate odds in India. The difficulty may be admitted, but the extent of it may readily be exaggerated. There is, says Mr. Lowe, 'but one weak point in our cuirass', the difficulty of raising a large army; 'and of this we have no cause to be ashamed, for it is caused by the mildness and freedom of our institutions. But it exists nevertheless, and this is entirely owing to the demands of India on our military resources.' That is to say, England could not furnish 60,000 soldiers for India, and carry on an European war at home. Now, judging from the precedents of the past, it by no means follows that even if there were not this Indian drain, and supposing – what, however, is not necessarily a consequence – that the 60,000 men thus set free would not have emigrated, and would be all ready to serve elsewhere – it by no means follows that they would be turned to useful account. During the great war with France the Government had usually more soldiers at its command than it knew what to do with, and was perpetually frittering away its resources on profitless expeditions, as those to the Plate River and Walcheren, the troops employed on which might as well have been serving in India for any useful influence they exerted on the real fortunes of the war. It may be said that we should be wiser now, and that if we ever go to war again, we shall apply all our strength at the critical point of action. Let us hope so. But in that case would the demand for keeping up our Indian garrison cause such stress as to deserve the name of a drain on our resources? If we have India, has not Russia her Poland, and all the Continental nations their different frontier lines to be left guarded, absorbing a far larger number of effective soldiers than India requires? Yes, but then, it will be replied, the Indian army is a much larger proportion of our available force; we have a small army, the Continental nations have large ones; they can afford these detachments, we cannot. The assumption implied in this argument is, however, the perfectly untenable one that we have a small army because we cannot help it, whereas all that can really be said is that we have never tried to help it. All the little devices which have so far been adopted, of an extra penny a day here, and twopence a day there, are very good as far as they go, and are perfectly adapted to supply what is needed for a state of peace. But no one yet has seriously proposed any plan for giving us a large army in time of war. Yet there is nothing insuperable in the thing; a conscription is not the only alternative. There are now four and a half millions of able-bodied men in the United Kingdom of an age fit to bear arms, and the question is how, while preserving our free institutions, to obtain the services of a sufficient number of them for any great emergency. To do this might possibly involve a radical change of our military system, but there appears nothing insuperable in the way of procuring, for time of war or great emergency, a volunteer army of numbers sufficient to represent adequately the power of England. Nor, when we bear in mind how small a proportion of the total war expenses of a country is represented by the mere pay of the troops, should such a force be inordinately expensive. England, more frugal during peace of the wealth embodied in her manhood than those countries which employ the conscription, can afford, when war does come, a liberal outlay from the savings she has thereby accumulated. In fact, provided we are ready with a plan for rapid increase of our army on emergency, it is true wisdom to husband our resources at other times by maintaining it on a reduced scale. Unfortunately we have so far only got as far as the second part of the scheme; we have the small peace army, but have not perfected, indeed can hardly be said to have made a beginning of, the arrangements for its expansion when necessary. But the point here contended for is that if we are ever called upon to go to war again, the thing above all others to be avoided is the extravagance of going to war with a small army; and that, if we employ a large one, the absence of a small fraction of our manhood in India ought not to be seriously felt. We may remember, too, that our greatest wars in India were waged and the most important conquests made in that country during the extremest crisis of England's struggle with Napoleon.

Moreover, if India draws troops from England, it is able to furnish them in return. That country affords a practically unlimited recruiting ground, and the Indian Government is the only one in the world which finds no difficulty about keeping up an army of any strength required by voluntary enlistment. There is not a native regiment in India without its followers, the brothers and cousins of the men in the ranks, hanging on to the camp, looking out to be enlisted whenever vacancies occur. The Indian army is now on a very reduced establishment, made up of a large number of skeleton battalions, but the Indian Government has only to give the signal to draw recruits to its colours to any extent necessary, from the perfectly inexhaustible supply available both within and without its borders, of manly races possessing the qualities for making a splendid soldiery. In this way the military resources of India are capable of immediate and indefinite extension without an additional soldier being sent from Europe. The proportion of Europeans to native troops is at present far in excess of what has been found necessary in all former wars, the native army being kept in peace time on the lowest practicable scale for political as well as economical reasons; but a native army is dangerous only in peace time, without excitement and occupation, and if military operations had to be undertaken on a large scale in the East, the Indian army could be expanded with safety and certainty to any degree thought necessary. England is in fact, through her Indian Empire, a first-class military power, and could bring into the field an army quite as large as those with which recent history has made us familiar, and containing material which for sobriety, power of endurance, and contempt of death, would be found quite equal to the men whose gallantry has been lately the admiration of Europe.

It may perhaps be replied to this that the statement merely proves that India is able to defend itself. Granted that India may be able to furnish means for opposing invasion, it would be still better not to be called upon to defend it at all. Even supposing that the employment of the Indian army were not restricted to the East, but that Indian troops were brought, say to Egypt or the eastern parts of Europe, still they would be brought there to defend interests arising out of our possession of India. We should not need to maintain the right of way to that country if we were not more deeply concerned to get there than other nations. So that, it may be objected, this argument at best amounts to this, that the disease contains its own remedy.

The validity of this objection depends, of course, on whether or not India is worth defending – that is, whether the possession of India is a benefit to England or the reverse. And this brings us to the real point at issue. Hitherto we have been considering the drawbacks entailed by the connection, and I have endeavoured to show that these have been over-estimated; it now remains to consider what are the advantages which it confers.

The chief, indeed almost the only, benefit which Mr. Lowe is disposed to admit is the great stimulus which has been given to education, and the brilliant prize which is held out to industry and ability, by throwing open the Indian Civil Service to competition. I should venture to assert on the other hand that the stimulus which this competition has given to education is surprisingly small. A great result was undoubtedly expected by the original framers of the scheme, but these expectations have not been realised. If it had been found that the great centres of English education had been sensibly affected by the establishment of this competition, and had modified their systems to adapt them to the new state of things, then we should be entitled to say that this stimulus had been given; but nothing of the sort is to be detected. It was expected by the framers of the scheme that the Indian Civil Service, when thrown open in this way, would attract to these competitions a large part of the ablest of our young men from the different universities, and that the latter would lay themselves out to prepare their students to take advantage of this new career for talent. As a matter of fact the universities have, until quite lately, done nothing whatever in the matter, and the only result, so far, in the way of stimulus to education, has been the establishment of two or three private establishments, at one or other of which all but a very few of the successful get their training, and the managers of which deserve all the remarkable success which their energy and intelligence have enabled them to secure. But this result, as curious as it was unexpected, is not a necessary condition of competition, but of what appears to be the defective arrangements of this particular competition; although it may certainly be expected that whatever might be the changes or reforms introduced into the system, the establishments in question would still more than hold their own, because there the art of teaching and the value of industry are both thoroughly understood. As to the merits of competition itself, however, I would take leave to say that a prodigious quantity of nonsense has been talked about the supposed disadvantages of the system. The prophecy that it would bring the wrong men to the front, and furnish a set of effeminate and prematurely worn-out bookworms for the public service, has been entirely contradicted by the event, equally with the prediction that it would alter the whole course of English education. There has been ample time now to judge of the result and the experience gained of the successful candidates furnished to the Royal Engineers and Royal Artillery, which services have now been open to competition for twenty years, as well as in other branches of the public service, shows that, while the intellectual standard has been raised, there has been no falling off in physical qualifications. In fact the material which open competition supplies to these, to the civil services, to the Indian engineer service, and to other lines now entered in the same way, is quite up to the standard that could be desired; and all the authorities who are concerned with these competitions, rationally conducted, and with the successful candidates afterwards, are perfectly satisfied with the result. The objection that may be taken to the Indian civil service competition, is not to competition *per se*, but to the faulty method under which that particular one has hitherto been conducted. It would be impossible in the limited space here available to substantiate this at length, but it may be just stated that the test appears to be defective in two ways. First, it attempted far too much, considering the age of the candidates. To expect young men of nineteen and twenty to master such a subject as moral science, for example, or the language and literature of Greece or Rome, or of France or Italy, as one among several subjects to be taken up, was, on the face of it, unreasonable. The result of this vagueness of the test has been to encourage vagueness in reading, and to render it very much a matter of chance whether the candidate will be examined in any of the particular portions he has attempted to cover of the wide field of knowledge. There has also been a want of unity in the mode of valuing the work done, so that the relative value of the different subjects in the examination has been left to depend on the idiosyncrasy of the examiner for the time being. One year moral science, for example, is marked lightly, and so it pays to take up moral science; next year the candidates in moral science get no marks to speak of, and the classical scholars or the mathematicians draw the prizes in the lottery. In the next place, the test, being determined by the aggregate proficiency of the candidates in a number of different subjects which have no sort of connection with each other, is diametrically opposed to the system in force at all the educational institutions of the country, where honours and preferments are determined by the proficiency exhibited in separate and distinct branches of knowledge. There are honour lists at the universities in mathematics, or classics, or philosophy, or natural science; the principle kept in view being to encourage accuracy and thoroughness in one particular field of knowledge as a better test of mental power than a superficial knowledge of many things: it has been reserved for the framers of this scheme to devise an examination at which a senior wrangler or a senior classic going up straight from the university after taking his degree would have absolutely no chance of success. Happily some of the gravest defects in this competition are now about to be removed, but speaking of the past it would appear that so far from deserving Mr. Lowe's eulogium, the system was good only so far as it was a competition at all, and that little or no advantage has been taken of this important opportunity to influence English education generally for good or evil. And when Mr. Lowe goes on to say that 'this experiment has created for us the best civil service in the world', it is obvious to remark that the Indian civil service was not created by competition, but that it was already the best civil service in the world before competition was established, although it may have been still further improved by the change.

But, after all, important though the influence of competitive examinations may be, many people will possibly think that it is estimated even too highly when put foremost among the advantages conferred on us by the possession of India, and will prefer to pass on to the consideration of what we gain by our trade with that country. This is usually deemed to be the greatest advantage drawn from the connection, but Mr. Lowe disposes of it in a single paragraph. The argument advanced on this head will be best done justice to in the writer's own words.

> Among the advantages which we reap, not exactly from the possession of India, but from the peace and order which we have established there, and which, undoubtedly, would not exist without us, may fairly be included the large trade which we have with her. The interest of England as a manufacturing and trading nation is that every country should be at peace, industrious, and thriving. But that interest rests entirely on the further assumption that we are able to provide them with something better and cheaper than they can find elsewhere. It is also very possible, in the opinion of very competent persons, that we may be raising up a very effective competition against ourselves. The Hindoo, by his fine touch, his exquisite taste, and above all by the extreme cheapness of his labours, is a formidable antagonist. This is no reason for keeping India in barbarism, but it is, as far as it goes, an answer to the argument drawn from the trade which we derive by means of the peace which we enforce.

That is to say, trade is of no value to a country if there is any danger of losing it. With what country, then, it may be asked, is England carrying on a trade that has any value? If the

Hindoo is likely to undersell us eventually in his own markets, is not the same thing to be feared of the Americans in regard to most of the commodities in producing which the English have hitherto excelled? Is not Belgium underselling us in the manufacture of iron, and are not Prussian guns more in demand than English? England, in fact, has been for long educating the rest of the world in the art of manufacture, and must expect that some of her pupils will learn in time to do without their teacher. But that is hardly a complete view of our trade relations with India, which considers only the smaller part – our export trade – and leaves out of sight the much larger trade in the commodities which we import from that country. Some idea of the magnitude of that trade, and of the interests involved in it, may be gathered from a cursory glance at the daily newspaper, where whole columns of advertisements appear of steamers and ships sailing to India. Consider, too, the number of mercantile houses and banks engaged in the India trade, and the multitude of people in various capacities who gain their livelihood, indirectly as well as directly, in connection with these fleets and these great establishments. And this, after all, would be a very inadequate view of the matter. For, as the late Mr. Cairnes observed in one of his essays, one might as well measure the advantages of learning by the salaries paid to the teachers, as measure the benefit which foreign trade confers on a country by the profits of the agents who carry it on. The real benefit of foreign trade to a country is surely that it is supplied in this way with things at a cheaper price than that at which they can be produced within the country, or with things which it cannot produce at all. The great difference in the nature of the products of India and England has hitherto constituted the special value of the trade between the two countries. It is unnecessary even to mention the commodities in the production of which India has almost a monopoly, but in addition she is now becoming able to supply various articles of home production on equal terms. This branch of Indian trade, indeed, is advancing with such rapid strides as to even threaten to affect seriously the conditions of English agriculture; and although there may still be some people who regard the competition of the foreign producer as an evil, probably most persons in these days are satisfied that the real interests of the population of this country are best advanced when all their wants are supplied from the cheapest markets. Mr. Lowe says that whereas 'the Romans would have drawn thirty millions per annum from India, the English Government does not draw a single penny'. The English Government does not, but the English people does, draw a great deal more than thirty millions a year from India, yet this increase to their wealth is not obtained at the expense of India, which is enriched by an intercourse mutually profitable to both sides.

A word must be added about the field of employment offered to Englishmen by the Indian public service. The state of the case in this respect is familiar to every one. There is hardly a middle-class English family which has not a relative employed in some official capacity in India, which thus comes to our aid in a practical difficulty, by drawing off a portion of that supply of English youth which seems to be always tending to exceed the demand for it. We may, if we please, imagine a different state of things, under which the trade and population of this country should both become stationary, and no more people be born than there are places for them to fill; but so long as the view obtains of our duties and obligations on this point which is commonly held at present, when, so far from it being considered immoral to contribute towards the evils of over-population, even the ministers of religion set the example of bringing more people into the world than they have the means of providing for, so long the outlet afforded by India is a very real benefit to the class in question. In this case at least, India cannot be said to cause any drain on this country; whatever may be the difficulty of getting soldiers, there is certainly none in filling up the gaps occurring in the market for educated labour; and those who get out of the way of their crowded fellow-countrymen at home by taking themselves off to India, not only thus afford direct relief, they also benefit England by spending a large part of their savings here, and for their numbers they are directly and indirectly large employers of English labour. This is one form of the tribute paid by India to England, and when we bear in mind how small is the proportion of Englishmen living in India to the total population of these islands, the amount of business in London alone which meets the eye, arising in this way from the occupation of that country, is surprisingly large.

Considering then the array of interests involved, of the army of officials, of the merchants, distributors, producers, and consumers, who gain a livelihood from, or whose convenience and prosperity are bound up with, our connection with India, it may be said that the effect on them, and by consequence on the people of this country generally of whom they form so considerable a part, of the loss of India, which Mr. Lowe regards as a matter of trifling importance, would really amount to a tremendous calamity affecting every class of English society. For all this trade and all this field of employment would be sacrificed if we surrendered our possession of that country. The loss of India would involve consequences quite different from those likely to result from the loss of any of our colonies. Canada or Australia might separate from us without any change in our commercial relations with them, and still affording the same outlet as before for the energies of our redundant population. But the loss of India means the destruction of our Indian trade, for the maintenance of it is entirely dependent on our occupation of that country. What its fate would be if we were from any cause to withdraw from it no man can indeed foresee. The state of anarchy which followed upon the decay and destruction of the Mogul empire, which explain the early and easy successes of the English, and to a certain extent excuse their high-handed and often unscrupulous proceedings; the overthrow of ancient dynasties by robber hordes and upstart adventurers, and the substitution of the rule of might and violence for all legal sanctions; the chaotic state of Indian politics with its attendant desolation of the country until succeeded by the strong and equable rule of the British, forbid the framing of sober speculations on the probable condition of India at the present time if the English had not taken possession of it, and equally as to what its condition would become if they were now to leave it. But one thing may be predicted with certainty. In the event of such a catastrophe the rule would not pass into the hands of the class which the English public is accustomed to associate with their notions of the Indian people. The educated Indians, the product of our State schools and Presidency universities, are still an extremely small minority, although their numbers are stimulated by the system of gratuitous education in force, and they are the very last class likely to succeed to our power. Yet these are the men who make themselves most heard of; who, in default of getting places under government, take to editing seditious newspapers, the existence of which the Government tolerates with scornful yet lazy indifference. Wisely perhaps, for in truth there is no more reality about the treasonable aspirations of the youthful Bengalee than in the education which he has acquired. The invocations to the shades of Brutus and Demosthenes, and appeals to their countrymen to emulate the part of Hampden, which come so glibly from Bengalee pens, are a not unnatural corollary from the system of education which trains lads who have never seen a mound as high as Primrose Hill, or a bigger stone than the broken granite on the Calcutta streets, and who are living in a tropical climate, to write analytic essays on Wordsworth's *Ode to Helvellyn*, or Cowper's *Winter's Walk at Noon*, or from their experience of life gained in the cluster of mud hovels which makes up a Bengalee village to paraphrase Johnson's *London* or Pope's *Dunciad*. In neither one case nor the other has the essayist any real conception of what he is writing about; the images he uses so glibly convey no sort of notion to his mind. Let us not therefore suppose that we are educating a governing class to take our place; a Government of India, or even of Bengal, by educated Bengalees, is not among the possibilities of the future. What does seem probable, in the event of our withdrawal from the country, is that India would again become a prey, as it has so often been before, to the warlike and barbarous races beyond the frontier. What seems certain in any case is that the rule, if such a name could be given to the state of things resulting, would everywhere fall to the more manly and unsophisticated but unscrupulous classes, whether within or without the frontier, whose impulse would be to protest against the evidence of civilisation in any form, and whose uprising would be followed by the destruction or decay of the roads and railways and telegraphs, and all marks of English occupation, with the total cessation of foreign trade. But let us charitably hope that before the desolation occurs, which would otherwise follow when the English retire from India, Russia or some other Power may step in to take our place, and avert some part of the consequences which must otherwise fall on the unfortunate people of that country. Yet in pursuing the subject so far we are passing the bounds of sober speculation; for of all wild political fancies, that of the occupation of India by Russia, always supposing she has not the command of the sea, but must approach it through the steppes of Central Asia, is surely among the wildest. It is almost as extravagant as the

conception of an independent government of Bengal by Bengalees. And if Russia has the command of the sea England must
have lost it, and with it of course the possession of India.

The considerations which have been here put forward will,
it may be hoped, assist the reader towards forming a just
estimate of the relative advantages and drawbacks involved in
our possession of India. I have endeavoured to show that the
supposed drain of men which that possession entails is in
peace time quite inappreciable as compared with the effect of
emigration. In time of war the case is different; the absence
from Europe of 60,000 soldiers is an apparent loss, but
apparent only, because there is no certainty that, if not wanted
for India, they would not have emigrated, while it is small in
comparison with the effective power of England if the English
choose to make use of it. Admitting however the drawback,
and also the contingent responsibility of being called on to
defend a distant dependency, the question remains whether the
enormous benefit resulting to England from its Indian trade –
a trade the existence of which is wholly dependent on our
occupation of the country – is worth the contingent risks
involved. Considering that peace has happily been for many
years our normal condition, and that our Indian trade has,
during this long period, added enormously to the wealth and
prosperity of the country, and therefore to its capacity for
bearing the stress of war whenever it may come upon us: – if
we weigh the good against the evil, and bear in mind moreover
that this contingent risk is much smaller than that which we
actually ran in the great struggle at the beginning of the century,
when with less than half our present population we managed
to defy Napoleon, and to win a great part of India at the same
time; then, apart from all sentiments of pride, or honour, or
patriotism, but looking at the matter simply as one of self-
interest and prudent investment, there would seem to be no
room for reasonable doubt on which side of the account the
balance should be struck. To defend India might conceivably
demand a great effort; to lose it must involve a shock that
would vibrate through every section of English society, and
would go far to work a calamitous revolution in the material
condition of the English people.

[FROM] IMPERIAL ADMINISTRATION*
Henry Howard Molyneux Herbert,
Lord Carnarvon

We have been of late much perplexed by a new word, 'Imperialism', which has crept in among us. The late Chancellor of the Exchequer has written an extremely able and interesting article on the subject,[1] and the present Chancellor of the Exchequer, when recently travelling through some of the Midland Counties, could not confine himself to his political subjects, but was led by the attraction of the subject into a disquisition on the meaning and value of the word Imperialism. Under the shadow, therefore, of two such great names we may very well give a few minutes' consideration to the meaning of the term. It is not free from perplexity. I have heard of Imperial policy, and Imperial interests, but Imperialism, as such, is a newly coined word to me. In one sense the English Constitution knows nothing of Imperialism. It would be unfair, however, to deny that the English Constitution recognises much that partakes of an imperial character. The constitution has often seemed to oscillate between the two extremes in a manner which, though perplexing to a careless or ignorant bystander, has been I doubt not extremely advantageous to our liberties and our national life. On the one side, Sir Robert Walpole used to say that the government of England was a republic in everything except the name; and, on the other, the great Statute of Appeals, in the reign of Henry VIII. Speaks of the realm of England as 'Imperial'. Personally, I have little predilection for the name, for the obvious reason that it suggests uncomfortable Continental associations. But I cannot forget that Mr. Burke has used the word, and Shakspeare has consecrated it; and so we, too, may be prepared to accept it, though with an understanding of its true meaning. Do not let us, as it was said

* From *Fortnightly Review*, vol. 24 ns (December 1878), pp. 760–64.

[1] *Fortnightly Review* for October, 1878 [pp. 261ff. of this volume].

of the Greeks at Troy, fight for the mere shadow of Helen. I believe that there is a true and a false Imperialism. But, what is the true and what the false? We can, perhaps, best tell what Imperialism is by ascertaining what it is not. It is certainly not Cæsarism. It is not that base secondhand copy of Continental despotism – that bastard monarchy begotten in the slime of political and financial corruption. It has nothing in common with that. Despotisms do not easily die. As Mr. Burke has said, they change their furniture and their fashions, but the evil principle prevails and reappears in successive generations. They dazzle, indeed, by enlisting false teachers, by arraying themselves in false colours, by professing false arts; but they are hateful from top to bottom. They are utterly false; the benefits that they confer are short-lived, and they poison the very fount from which their own waters spring. Nor, again, has Imperialism in the true sense of the word any connection with what has been called 'personal government'. Our Constitution is clear on this point. We know that the Crown has certain prerogatives, and that Parliament has certain rights and duties, but that neither Parliament nor the Crown may act alone. They cannot be relegated to independent spheres of political action, any more than the confines of day and night can be parted by a hard and visible line of demarcation. They must act in concert, and in reference to each other; and their combined action is that which the Constitution contemplates and desires. Nor is Imperialism, again, mere bulk of territory and multiplication of subjects. We hear sometimes the words, 'A great England and a little England', but we do not measure nations by their size or numbers, any more than we measure men by their inches. If we did, China would be the model of our admiration; and the hosts of Xerxes, and not the handful of Athenian citizens, would be the people we should reverence in the past history of the world. No! What we look for is not the bulk of territory, but the men that are bred up, and the qualities which those men have; and setting aside the highest of all, we may say this – that steadfastness of purpose, simplicity of character, truth, and the preference of that which is solid and substantial for that which is merely glittering and deceptive, are the qualities by which nations truly live and kings rule; and that these qualities have been the characteristics of Englishmen in past generations.

But if Imperialism is none of these, what is it, if indeed it has a meaning? Clearly its first duty, all will admit, is to recognise, as the Chancellor of the Exchequer very fairly said the other day, that there are obligations which we owe beyond the limits of the four seas; but secondly – what he omitted to say – its duty is to breathe into the whole of that mighty mass I have described, a common unity; to find for it that animating and binding principle which is the nearest approach to the spirit of patriotism that you look for in an individual. But it may be said, What is patriotism? Like Imperialism, it has varied greatly; like the word liberty, it has often been abused. There is a true and a false patriotism. Horace Walpole says that at one time there was no declaration a public man could make that was more popular on the hustings than that he neither was nor had been nor would be a patriot; and we all know Mr. Canning's definition of a patriot, in the man who was the friend of every country but his own. But a true patriot will be included in neither of these descriptions. Nor is patriotism to be recognised in the nation which, so to speak, swaggers down the High Street of the world with its hat cocked, and on the look-out for some fancied insult or affront. For such public characters we occasionally find a counterpart in private life; but all would agree that such a man is an eminently disputatious, quarrelsome, disagreeable companion. No, both patriotism and imperialism, if they are to be true, must rest upon the one sole foundation on which all true things can rest. We cannot with impunity divorce our system of politics from our system of morals. There are not two sides to that shield; or two codes to be observed as convenience may dictate. But this is an unfashionable doctrine: it is even occasionally denied: and I have lately read with amazement in a periodical of high repute the proposition laid down with regard to one of the most unspotted characters of the Italian fourteenth century, that he failed as a statesman because in his political conduct he paid obedience to the laws of morality. But such a doctrine contains all that is detestable and abhorrent to public virtue: and though it may find a sanction in Machiavelli, it will find no echo in the great body of the English people, until at least they depart much further than they have yet gone from the political faith and practice of their fathers.

One word more as to foreign Imperialism. Thank God we have nothing to copy there. Foreign Imperialism means vast standing armies; and at this moment we have before our eyes the nations of Europe divided into hostile and suspicious camps. The 350,000 men who in the earlier period of the Roman Empire were sufficient to guarantee the peace of the world, have now grown into something like six millions of armed men. It is the day of great empires casting their colossal shadow over the smaller States; and through the gloom of that shadow those small States look up and, as they may well do, tremble. It is the day of restless intrigue and of reckless expenditure. It is the day of violence, and, we may depend upon it, it is a day to be followed by a certain reaction. So we have heard the hollow moaning of the wind, or seen the sullen break of the wave upon the shore, presaging the great tempest which is to come; and so, when we look round the horizon of Europe, and see how heavily the thunder-clouds are piling up, who can resist a feeling of deep apprehension for the future, or the earnest hope that this country at least will not be tempted by anything, short of the clearest and most paramount duty, to join in this mad race of waste and bloodshed? But if we turn our eyes from that gloomy spectacle to the great Empire of England, we see, at all events for the present, a brighter and a more peaceful picture in the self-government of the great Anglo-Saxon Colonies. Here lies the true strength of our Imperialism. Mistakes they doubtless have made, are making, and will make; but the manner in which they govern themselves is splendid. No other type of government has tempted them away; they are content to follow in the track of English traditions and belief, and they remain to the backbone Englishmen. 'These are Imperial Arts, and worthy Thee,' it may be truly said; – and though at this moment the future prospects of the world may seem to some to be overclouded, we may cherish the hope that as time goes on the common instincts of language, faith, laws, institutions, of allegiance to a common sovereign, may draw the bonds between them and us yet closer. We should be indeed closely wedded to the dull prose of daily life if we banished wholly from our imagination that noble dream, which may yet in the fulness of time be realised, of a great English-speaking community, united together in a peaceful confederation, too powerful to be molested by any nation, and too powerful and too generous, I hope, to molest any weaker State.

Or, again, if we turn to that far larger empire over our native fellow-subjects of which I have spoken, the limits expand and the proportions rise, till there forms itself a picture so vast and noble that the mind loses itself in the contemplation of what might be under the beneficent rule of England if faction could be still and selfish ambition be held back, and rest from war and war's exhausting burdens could be given. There we have races struggling to emerge into civilisation, to whom emancipation from servitude is but the foretaste of the far higher law of liberty and progress to which they may yet attain, and vast populations like those of India sitting like children in the shadow of doubt and poverty and sorrow, yet looking up to us for guidance and for help. To them it is our part to give wise laws, good government, and a well-ordered finance, which is the foundation of good things in human communities; it is ours to provide them with a system where the humblest may enjoy freedom from oppression and wrong equally with the greatest; where the light of morality and religion can penetrate into the darkest dwelling-places. This is the real fulfilment of our duties; this, again I say, is the true strength and meaning of Imperialism. And lastly, while we speak of an imperial spirit abroad, let us never forget how much depends upon maintaining a free and a generous spirit at home. Here in England – and, thank God, in the word England is included Scotland; for dull indeed of apprehension, and ill-read in the history of their country, ill-read too in the events of our own age, would they be who do not recognise that without Scotland England would be shorn of half her true strength – here in England is the true centre of imperial life and power, the spring of influence, the fount of all inspiration; here are born and bred up the men who are to maintain and defend, and still more, to govern this great empire. England is the heart of the Empire. If that heart be overtaxed and feeble, then the whole body politic is sick and faint – faint to weakness, faint it may be to death: but if the heart be sound and vigorous, then in a right cause, and under the blessing of God, there is no duty which our country need ever decline, there is no burden, however great, which it ever need be afraid to bear.

IMPERIALISM AND SOCIALISM*
Frederic Seebohm

The present crisis in English politics is intimately connected with a still greater crisis in European history.

The distinctive and alarming feature of this crisis is the terrible strain put upon Europe by the fact that her great empires are armed to the teeth, living in constant dread of one another, and almost in equal dread of their own people. Modern Imperialism, wherever tried, has produced *Socialism*. Imperialism in France produced the Commune. Before the first German Emperor had become used to his Imperial crown, he was startled by the presence of Socialist representatives in his Parliament and attempts upon his own life. In Russia Nihilism haunts the air like an omnipresent spectre, and undermines the very palace of the Czar. These great military empires all have their skeleton in the cupboard. They are followed by a shadow – *Socialism*.

There is obviously a relation of cause and effect in this terrible coincidence. De Tocqueville described the great tidal wave of Democracy sweeping over the western world. He likened its overwhelming force, and the certainty of its onward movement, to the great geological changes which have taken place on the surface of the earth. But Socialism is not Democracy, though, under Imperial guidance, Democracy seems always to end in Socialism. Democracy is the claim of a self-reliant people for equal rights and fair play for every man, standing on his own feet, to guide his own life unfettered by needless interference on the part of the State. Socialism is the sad opposite of this. It is the cry of a helpless and enfeebled residuum unable to run alone, calling for a State which, instead of oppressing it and making its life hard, shall do everything for it – feed, clothe, and amuse it. Nihilism is another form of the same social disease, another outcome of political despair.

* From *Nineteenth Century*, vol. 7 (April 1880), pp. 726–36.

How is it that, under Imperial guidance, Democracy, instead of being developed into a healthy and self-reliant manhood, is debased into the second childhood and helpless moral deformity of Socialism?

This terrible result seems to be the logical consequence of a necessary course of action on the part of modern Imperialism – viz, the subordination of internal development to external military ascendency. It would seem that the two ends cannot both be attained. Step by step the pursuance of the one cripples and confines the other. A policy of military ascendency needs for its success more and more of personal rule. This must of necessity depreciate representative institutions. The more Napoleon poses as himself France, the less can senates and parliaments be France. The more Prince Bismarck claims to be the German Empire, the less often will the German Parliament be consulted, and the less needful will it be for it even to meet annually.

The depreciation of Parliamentary institutions hits at the root of the habit of self-government. The rulers take the reins into their own hands, and the nation expects everything from them and less and less from itself. There may be a semblance of rule by popular will, but when the popular will is asked to act, it is to surrender the reins into the ruler's hands. This results in an alliance of the monarch and the mob. The popular will is invoked by appeals to popular passions rather than by argument addressed to the best mind of the nation. The reins are tightly grasped in Imperial hands. Imperial interests rule the roast. The working of the inevitable circle of mischief proceeds. Imperial interests make everything bend to the needs of foreign policy. Home questions are more and more neglected. Popular wrongs go unredressed. The burdens of taxation to support an ever increasing army grow in inverse ratio to the power to bear them. Compulsory military service interferes vexatiously with individual life, commercial education, and the increase of wealth. Life becomes hard to the working classes, and discontent arises with the institutions of the country.

In former times suffering was silent, and the crushed worm did not turn. But since the revolutions of 1848 discontent has found a voice in Europe. It is no longer silent as of old. It even tries to act. It uses constitutional methods first. It sends its Socialists to Parliament. And when Parliamentary influence wanes and it finds no efficient safety-valve there, it takes a lesson from its rulers, who deify force rather than reason: it no longer speaks; it resorts to diabolical attempts to assassinate monarchs and blow up palaces.

There is a tightly-tied logical sequence in this sad process and result. Step by step, by inexorable logic, Democracy is guided and turned by Imperial policy into the curse which undoubtedly Socialism is.

Let us not be too hard upon the great Continental empires. A policy of military Imperialism may at the moment be a hard necessity to Russia, to Germany, and even as an Imperial legacy to now republican France. One fatal step leads to another. The futile attempt of the Second Empire to reproduce Cæsarism in the modern world led to Sedan, and made Germany into an empire whose existence between France and Russia rests upon the sword. It is a hard necessity, from which these empires would gladly be freed.

But there was one nation free from this necessity, which seemed to be committed to a policy the reverse of Imperial. Its government was not a union of the monarch and the mob, but a free Parliamentary government under a Queen, whose special glory it was that, aided by the wisdom of the late Prince Consort, she had read the signs of the times and proved how representative government may best flourish under a constitutional crown. Through a long reign of this enlightened policy it had grown in freedom and respect for law, as well as in population, commerce, and wealth. It was a nation of whom alone among the nations it could be said that her army supplied entirely by voluntary enlistment, and that the masses of her people, if they chose to abstain from a few common luxuries, need hardly know that they were taxed at all; a nation in whose experience democracy had been trained and guided into peaceful paths, until the people, habituated to self-reliance and self-control, had altogether abandoned the old cry of Chartism, the product of former oppressive taxation and unequal laws; a nation in which it might be said without exaggeration that there was no Socialism.

And yet this moment, when Continental Imperialism is everywhere confronted by Socialism, is chosen by the ruling party of the English nation – the party calling itself conservative – to let itself be drawn by its leader into a policy which he himself has cynically and theatrically recommended to the nation under the ill-fated name of 'Imperialism'!

The new-fangled policy of Lord Beaconsfield may be only a *mock* Imperialism, and be intended to stop far short of a real one; but it certainly already has to a most ingenious extent succeeded in adopting, and even ostentatiously displaying, the distinctive marks and notes of its Continental prototype. It is not only that the Queen was made to make herself an Empress, and that the Prime Minister has adopted Imperial terms and used Imperial phrases. With almost incredible cunning he has succeeded in producing some of the first fruits of Imperialism with even hothouse haste. No sooner was English Imperial policy commenced than it promptly proceeded to neglect home questions for the sake of the spirited foreign policy avowedly aimed at from its first advent on the political stage. In the Prime Minister's latest manifesto the same neglect is continued; whilst, in parading his foreign policy before the electors, he cannot keep the word 'ascendency' out of his lips. Again and again the tendency to personal rule and the consequent depreciation of Parliamentary institutions has been already witnessed. The Prime Minister has deliberately used his great Parliamentary majority, not to increase, but to lessen, the influence of Parliament in the councils of the State. No recent Prime Minister has ever taken such pains as he apparently has done to elude Parliamentary discussion. His great strokes of policy have all been achieved in secret behind the scenes, concealed till the appointed time – even, it would seem, sometimes from his colleagues – and sanctioned by Parliament only after they were done.

It is true that this mock Imperialism lacks the courage which the real thing requires. Ostentatious warlike preparations have not gone further than threats. Actual wars have been rather 'shabby' than heroic, and have earned for the armies of England but small glory. A real Imperial policy, on the other hand, would require doubled armaments and not a mere transfer of Indian soldiers into Europe. The present Government have shown even a gingerly fear lest the English taxpayer should feel the pressure of increased burdens. All this may be conceded. But an Imperial game must have its risks, and a single accident at any moment might have drawn the nation into a real war. Were such a war to come about, not with Zulus and Afghans, but with a Continental Imperial rival, the scale and the cost of the armaments would be fixed by the Continental standard, and the hazard may be measured by the enormous cost to both winner and loser of recent Continental struggles. Such a war commenced would require the English army to be doubled and enforced conscription to begin at once. Though, therefore, the present Government may have neither the will nor the courage to pursue a real Imperial policy, still, in assuming its name and aping its methods at a grave crisis of European history, they at least have been playing with fire.

It remains to be seen whether the other great English party can guide democracy to a better goal and pursue a foreign policy more consistent with the greater aim. On the solution of this problem of democracy by England a great deal depends; for England at the present moment seems to be the only great European nation where it has a fair prospect of an early and steady solution. And the position of England in another respect is altogether unique.

We have heard much of late of English ascendency in Asia and English ascendency in the councils of Europe. We have been taught that ascendency comes with Imperial policy, and Imperial policy is obviously based on military power. But military power rests ultimately on population. The size of armies has become the chief factor in modern land warfare. And an Imperial policy in Asia seems bent on giving to England an extended land boundary between Constantinople and the Himalayas. This sort of ascendency, then, will require land forces. And a nation in these days can hardly be a first-rate military power on land without counting its soldiers almost by millions. But the population of England is, and always must be, limited. And to trust to Indian Sepoys would be doubtful policy. To arm provinces is to follow the example which ruined Rome. The hundreds of millions of China also can arm. Another generation may see her armies provided with European rifles and ordnance, and under European drill. This is the future of a race for ascendency in Asia. And the foundation on which it must be built is at present the apex of an inverted pyramid – *the handful of Englishmen in India*. About as many English emigrants have left our shores every year for the West as the whole number of Englishmen in India, soldiers and civilians taken together.

Yes, let us turn to the West before we estimate the true

nature of our duties, and incur these perils in the East. Let us turn from the lesser problem of military ascendency in Asia to the greater problem of the internal development and true guidance of our own democracy, and see whether in the true solution of that great problem new light may not be thrown upon English relations to other European States and to India.

The unique peculiarity of the English nation is this, that she is peopling the New World – the new Englands beyond the oceans in the West and the South, the temperate zones of the world, where her people can live.

Do we realise sufficiently what this great fact means? The English-speaking people in a very few years will number 100,000,000. Our children may well live to see the numbers swell to hundreds of millions. The present rate of increase in the United States – by far the largest factor in the question – is said to be 2½ per cent. per annum. The question whether at the end of the next century the English-speaking peoples will number more or less than 1,000,000,000 is dependent, of course, upon other causes than the mere ratio of increase, but as a question of possible figures it depends simply upon whether the rate of increase in the future slightly exceeds or falls short of what it has been in our own times. And if by a vast free-trade system such a population can be fed, there is room in the territory of English speaking America for 1,000,000,000 of population, without coming up to the limit of density which prevails at the present moment in the old country. Does England, the mother of these future nations, realise what this vast possibility means?

Is it too much to say that the future of civilisation depends upon whether the great problem of democracy, which it seems to be the chosen destiny of England and her children to grapple with, can be fairly solved? Are we to neglect our part in the problem of the internal development of this vast people for the sake of some Imperial phantom of ascendency in Asia? Is a mind impregnated with Eastern mystery to lead us away, by trailing a red herring in our path, from the great realities which plainly lie before us in the West? With this tremendous stake in the problem of the guidance of our own democracy, are we to ape the methods, the style, and false glitter of Continental Imperialism, which has succeeded before our own eyes in turning Democracy into Socialism, and which everywhere trembles before its own progeny, like Milton's Sin in the presence of her offspring?

Nothing would guide the English voter at the present juncture with a surer logic and to a clearer choice than an adequate conception of the magnitude and importance of the political problem which lies before the English nation. Its solution involves a foreign policy consistent with it; for the home and foreign policy of a nation with so unique a destiny must be consistent. This fact alone excludes Imperialism. Imperialism, too, seems to fail altogether in its perception of what democracy is. It poses as the saviour of society from it. It distrusts democracy, whilst plunging into universal suffrage in order to use it as its tool. It distrusts democracy, because it confounds it with Socialism. It praises and imitates Cæsar, because it thinks he saved society from Roman democracy and founded the Roman Empire. It ends in itself producing, not a stable Empire, but the 'Commune'.

Probably the confusion in thought between democracy and Socialism comes from a superficial appreciation of the fact that the democracy of Greece and Rome *was* Socialism. It was not a true democracy, in the modern sense of the word. It was, in fact, a democratic Imperialism, which grew logically into an Imperial-Socialism. The vice of Imperialism which pervaded the false democracies of Greece and Rome was exactly what forced them into Socialism, just as it forces democracy into Socialism now.

For the classical democracy was a democracy of citizens ruling an empire. The Demos was the despotic and tyrannical ruler of dependent provinces. Itself composed of thousands of citizens, it governed hundreds of thousands or millions of enslaved people. The trading and farming and working classes were, speaking roughly, excluded from citizenship and from the franchise. Even in the governing city, Athens or Rome, society was based on slavery. The trade, the work, was done by slaves. The citizen cared not to soil his fingers with such servile labours. There was a democracy among the citizens, but the curse of it was that it was an Imperial democracy, which ruled its empire to enrich its own privileged, and therefore demoralised and enervated, class. The upper ten thousand were nursed in luxurious ease. No wonder they excelled in taste, in art, in education and refinement of manners. The world has never ceased to admire the results of the genius of cultured and refined Athens. But even in the select democracy of citizens there grew up a proletariate. Refined and polished citizens are selfish as other men. Wealth gravitates into the hands of the few. Ambition and greed seize the rich like a disease. Then arose, therefore, the inevitable contrast between rich and poor. Enormous fortunes grew up in the hands of the few. The mass of citizens, proud and poor, enervated and helpless (like the mean whites in the slave States of America), looked to the State to provide them with food and to keep them amused. The mob followed the leader who most lavishly fostered and fed their appetites. This was Socialism. The true idea of democracy did not exist in reality, nor even in the brain of the classical world. Even the dream of Plato's Republic is a dream, not of a true democracy, but of a Socialistic State.

Therefore, perhaps, it is not surprising that those who are so destitute of political originality as to imitate Cæsar in the nineteenth century are also so destitute of political insight as to confound modern democracy with the Socialism which follows Imperialism like a shadow.

The true democracy has another origin, and runs along entirely different lines. Its origin was not classical. One finds here and there a stray glimpse of the true spirit which underlies it – *e.g.* in the remarkable flash of thought which Xenophon puts into the mouth of Cyrus in his romance, the *Cyropædeia*, when he makes the dying monarch charge his sons, next to respect for the gods, to have regard to the good of the whole human race. But Greek thought was neither mastered itself by this nascent regard for the human race, nor did it impress it on mankind.

The real effective power of modern democracy had its well-head in a soul whose humility instinctively claimed brotherhood with the poor and the heavily burdened, whose refinement of feeling and tenderness for human nature surpassed that even of modern womanhood. It was no mere sentimental feeling, but a deep and lasting power, able as a matter of fact in history to enforce itself on others, and thus, by sowing a seed in the human heart the growth of which not even empires could stop, to turn the civilisation of the leading races of the next 2,000 years into a new channel. It is not in the history of dogmas, or in the history of rival Churches with their rival theologies, but in the history of the Christian spirit, that the secret will be found of the reason why modern civilisation is called Christian, or why Christian civilisation is identified with the true development of modern democracy. At this very moment when the hold of rival theologies on men's minds is most loosened, the Christian spirit is achieving its highest political victory.

At this crisis, when there lies before the English-speaking race that vast and startling combination of expansive power and room all ready prepared wherein to expand, so that it might almost be said that a new world of opportunity is opened to its view, this victory of the Christian spirit over the political mind of England gives a new possibility that the English people may be able to solve in this vast field and under new conditions the problem which Continental Imperialism cannot solve – that of guiding democracy into something better than the Socialism which is the shadow and curse of empires.

For the first time in the history of mankind has such a vast future been opened to the conscious vision of any people: and, with such a prospect before it, for the first time in the history of mankind has a people consciously set about so absolutely noble a political task. I say 'consciously', because it *is* consciously that the best of modern English statesmen, of whatever political party, set about the solution of the problem with the principle acknowledged as settled beforehand, that the State is henceforth to exist for the good, not of a privileged class, but of the whole community, not on the basis of the old classical Socialism under which the State was to feed and clothe and amuse its citizens, but on the truer basis of individual freedom and responsibility, each man standing on his own feet, sowing his own seed and reaping himself the crop, whether sweet or bitter; every man respecting every other's rights and working under the cover of just laws which serve all alike and meddle needlessly with none. This is the avowed ideal of statesmen for the first time in history.

The mass of the hundreds of millions of English-speaking people that our children may live to see will dwell no doubt in the other Englands across the Atlantic. It needs not much political foresight to see that most of them will be citizens of English-speaking America, in whose vast territory, as already said, there is room for the whole thousand millions without its being more thickly peopled than England is now. The Australian colonies will have their share. A small portion only of the English people can possibly live in the old island; and new destinies will arise for England out of these new relations to her children. She cannot cut up her land at home among peasant proprietors contrary to economic laws, and if she could, only about, one million of them – whatever her population – could be so disposed of. Her peasant proprietors, nevertheless, exist across the ocean on larger farms and under better circumstances than they could have done here. They have helped us to feed our own millions at home with cheap bread, notwithstanding the failure of home crops of corn. We cannot any more establish again in our Yorkshire and Lancashire dales peasant looms and spinning-wheels in cottages and at cottage doors. That idyllic stage of manufacturing enterprise has vanished for ever. We cannot for a moment, whatever may have been our manufacturing ascendency in the past, dream that we shall be able to spin all the cotton and weave all the cloth that the hundreds of millions of Englishmen across the ocean will require to clothe them. The time may come when we may have to import even coals from America to feed our furnaces. But the commercial prosperity of the older England, if she wisely acts her part, can hardly be other than vastly increased by the presence of fresh hundreds of millions of English customers in the New World for whatever in her own special line she may excel in making. England, moreover, ought to be able to make herself in some sense the centre of this extended English life. She ought to be able to make herself the Athens of the English-speaking world – their classical land – the home of the highest English culture without the Imperial vice which confined it to the few and ruined Athens. Life ought always to be worth living for Englishmen in England, if she can solve wisely her social problems and convert her proletariate into sober and educated citizens with a stake and interest in their country. Some of her children self-dependent, others still choosing to remain as colonies, all bound together by ties of common kindred and mutual interest, the more prosperous they are the more will they be likely to add to the prosperity and dignity of the mother-country; provided that England and her children can hold firmly together as one great kindred of peoples, keeping their hands from Imperial policy, and guiding their own vast democracy into peaceful and orderly channels.

This brings us back to the old question. The same great common domestic problem lies before England and the new Englands to be solved for their own sake and the sake of the world. They are alike in the absence of Socialism from their midst now. They are alike in practical freedom from the excessive burden of Imperial armaments on the modern scale. But if England allows the attraction of Continental Imperialism to draw her away from a true liberal policy and her possibly noble future into the trap of a race for ascendency in Asia; if little by little she lets herself be drawn still further into that Eastern policy which the Liberal party honestly and solemnly condemns, and asks the voters at the present election to condemn; then a single false step may any day lead to a war – the first, it may be, in a series of wars – which may strangle and cripple her future, whilst (yes, let us even then hope that it may be so) England's children may be wiser than herself, refuse from the first to listen to the siren's voice, and preserve for us at least new Englands where the great problem of the future may yet be peaceably solved.

In that case – we bearing the burdens of enormous armaments, enforced enlistment, and consequent taxation, whilst they are free from them – the competition would indeed be hard and ruinous to us. But it would be our own fault. The curse would be brought upon ourselves with our eyes open. It would be the defeat of a destiny at which wise men to the end of the world might well grieve.

There is no possible need why England should court so adverse a fate.

The possession of India is the only argument ever used to enforce the claims of an Imperial policy for England. It was in India that the Queen was made to make herself Empress.

And yet as regards the defence of India, was there ever a country better defended from foreign foes? With the mountains to the north, and the sea to the south; with the English fleet mistress of the seas, with this fleet in the Mediterranean, and a station at the Indian end of the Suez Canal, from which it would be but a few hours' work for a couple of ironclads to stop the canal against all comers at our own free will; with the ocean route round the Cape of Good Hope, and the Cape itself in our hands – what more could we ask? By the confession of the present Government, all that was wanted was a scientific frontier and a friendly neighbour in Afghanistan. They have given us what they call a scientific frontier. But it is, unfortunately, no frontier at all. It is merely two roads with a military post at the end of each road. They have stretched out two

vulnerable points like the two sensitive horns of a snail, and
call it a frontier. And their Afghanistan is no friendly neighbour
as yet. They have spoiled the simplicity of the defences of the
old India, and the logical end of the beginning they have made
of the new Imperial policy in India seems to be to absorb or
defend all the countries between India and the Levant. If we
let ourselves be led on this path, when can we stop?

There is surely a wiser foreign policy that a Liberal Government might well pursue consistently with proper attention to
home problems and England's duties to her colonies and
kindred nations.

Its cardinal point must doubtless be for England not to
isolate herself from European politics, but to seek to re-estab-
lish the broken concert of European nations; to abandon the
Imperial project of ascendency as a bad dream, and base her
policy on that real equality in right of nations which from
Grotius downwards has been the established maxim of international law. The concert – the international law – of Europe
is the only firm guarantee, whether it be of Belgium, the Turkish
principalities, or the future of Constantinople. Go back to
the policy of 1856. Substitute a European treaty for separate
conventions. Again revert to the clause of 1856 abandoned at
Berlin, interposing the mediation of all the contracting nations
between a quarrel and war. The hope may at least be indulged
that when new difficulties arise and fresh Conferences meet,
like that at Constantinople under the treaty of 1856, there may
not happen to be at the head of the English Government a
voice encouraging the defaulting nation to reject the counsels
of united Europe.

The concert of Europe cannot be expected to be recon-
structed by those who aim at ascendency instead of equality
and justice. But a Liberal Government would have different
instincts, and probably with patient labour secure that result
in the course of time, as well as a fair working arrangement
with Russia in Asia.

But the real danger of India, as of other empires, is not so
much external as internal. The handful of Englishmen who
hold India can only hold it by the just government of a contented people. In India as well as in Europe, Imperial policy is
apt to subordinate internal development to outside conquests
– *e.g.*, to use funds set aside for famines to pay for wars!

It is the Imperial character of the Indian Empire which is its great danger and its great snare. It is not a colony but an empire. It is at best an anomalous thing for a free nation to govern despotically, in a country where her people cannot permanently live, six times as many Asiatics as she possesses citizens herself. It raises an ominous resemblance, and makes a parallel dangerously true, between the British and the old Roman Empire. But India, nevertheless, is the foster-child of England. It was not conquered by an English democracy. *It is that corner of the English Empire which has not yet been subdued to democracy.* The duty of England, herself converted to democracy in its true sense, is to keep India and to govern India, not, like the Romans, to fill the coffers of the State, but for the good of India. The success of England's rule will be measured by whether or not some generations hence – when perhaps there are 1,000,000,000 of Englishmen in the New World – the population of India is contented and happy and able to govern itself.

The strength of both England and India depends, therefore, upon the Liberal policy of steadily fostering internal development. Nothing is more likely to weaken both England and India than the subordination of this internal development to the necessities of a false Imperial policy. If ever a struggle should come for the life or freedom of either, the better prepared will both be to bear the strain and to conquer in the struggle the further advanced they may be in the solution of the internal problems which Imperialism everywhere fails to solve, and the less encumbered and fettered their free strength may be by the accumulated burdens of past wars and needless Imperial projects.

Finally, even for the sake of the future of the great Continental nations themselves, upon whom the burdens of Imperialism weigh with so heavy a weight, can there be a better service done by a neighbouring nation than England could do by the refusal to follow their example, by firmly adhering herself to a steady policy of peace on the basis, not of ascendency, but of international equality and concert? No other method seems to lie before them of reducing their tremendous armaments than joining with England and other nations in a course so sound and reasonable. Their interest, like that of England and the English-speaking nations and India, lies clearly in a return to the long-neglected task of internal development. If by this means they cannot convert their Socialism into the true type of a healthy and self-reliant and contented freedom, Socialism may not far hence become their master and end the useless race in armaments by a terrible European revolution.